THE COURAGE TO LEAD

RESILIENCE & COMPASSION IN POLICE COMMAND

ALLAN SICARD

First published by Busybird Publishing 2023

ISBN:
Paperback: 978-1-922954-24-4
Ebook: 978-1-922954-25-1

Cover image: NP1397479 - By Braden Fastier, 05 January, 2015 - CHP_ Export_104363461.jpg

Cover design: Busybird Publishing

Layout and typesetting: Busybird Publishing

Editor: Busybird Publishing

Busybird Publishing
2/118 Para Road
Montmorency, Victoria
Australia 3094
www.busybird.com.au

I would like to respectfully acknowledge the First Nation people of Country throughout Australia, especially the traditional owners of the land where I live and wrote this book, the Dharug people.

I acknowledge the cultural and spiritual connection that Aboriginal and Torres Strait Islander peoples have with the land and sea. I remain committed to listening, learning, growing, and being together on what was, and always will be, Aboriginal land that has never been ceded.

Testimonials

All I can say is "Wow. What a read." Each chapter really is a story to identify a leadership learning. *The Courage to Lead* is a deeply personal reflection on leadership as an officer in the NSW Police. Allan's book charts not only his own leadership journey but how leadership must adapt to change driven from within institutions and in response to broader societal change.

> **Rebecca Pinkstone,** CEO of Bridge Housing, winner of Best Workplace Award 5 years running

Allan Sicard's rise from police cadet to commander provides a rich tapestry for reflection. He shares his setbacks and challenges, connecting these to the caring, committed and courageous leader he became through perseverance and personal growth. He reminds us of what can be achieved through committed teamwork, especially in the face of suffocating situational scrutiny. Allan refused to settle for life's more comfortable paths – demonstrating time and time again the courage to act, to share, to lead and to empower. Consequently, *The Courage to Lead* provides universal life lessons; learning from failure, adapting to succeed, and forging engaged and respectful relationships. Most of all, it is a compelling celebration of the human spirit.

> **Mark Berridge,** multiple award -winning author of *A Fraction Stronger*

I don't believe that resilience itself is a goal to aspire to. There is no glory in hanging around for a long time. The objectives should be: do your best but learn from your mistakes. When you are down, pick yourself up, continue and build experience. Act with integrity. Care for the people you lead and the community you serve. If you do these things, I believe you will be resilient. This is Allan Sicard's story.

> **Former Assistant Commissioner Alan Clarke, NSWPF**

A truly thought provoking read. At times exposing a leader who is not afraid to show his vulnerability. We all need to see these vulnerabilities to enable us to grow and reach our potential.

A very raw and soul-searching account of a leader's highs and lows and lessons learnt.

A leader that clearly cares for his people and is not afraid to create a culture of wellbeing for those that he leads despite the consequences of a negative senior management culture.

Allan is a leader of influence and his values and care for others has made life so much more enjoyable and rewarding for so many. Well done Allan

Kind Regards

Stephen Van Zwieten CPP
Managing Director
EXACT SECURITY

Allan's story lays bare the realities faced everyday by law enforcement and other frontline emergency services, from the uncertainty to the fears and the impact it has on the lives of those who serve the community. Allan's role as a leader and as a mentor to those around him is an example to all, not just the challenges but the professional rewards of having the courage to lead."

"A fascinating and insightful read that peels back the curtain on a lifetime in uniform protecting the community"

David Knoff
Author of Best selling book *537 Days of Winter*

This next testimonial is from my wife, Kerrie. I know it is unusual to have a relative write a testimonial but please indulge me. Kerrie and I spent nearly our entire adult lives as police officers. Her writing skills always exceeded mine. I regularly ask Kerrie to review my writing masterpieces and it would always be returned with a litany of corrections.

Just before this memoir was due for its final edit, I found Kerrie had almost read the whole book in one day. Then she wrote the following review for her friends. I thought that I should share the one instance in 40 years when one of my writing projects received praise.

I sat down this afternoon to read what he has sent through to the editor and it was riveting! This man I have known for nearly 39 years, married 35 years ago … the way he told it was simply fascinating! Such a surprise, because we have conversations and he drives me mad!

I've always known he was very different from me, the way he thinks has always kept me on the hop, but seeing his full thought processes and intentions is simply astounding. Well done to my gorgeous husband, I am very, very proud and can truly recommend his book. We need more leaders like him. I certainly didn't experience enough of them, resulting in my early retirement from the NSW Police. Congratulations, my love

Kerrie Sicard.

Your decisions, words and actions will directly impact not only on yourself, but your people, your command, and your navy, for better or for worse.

Commodore P.M.J. Scott, CSC, RAN,
Command Papers – Submarine Command:
A Retrospective for Submariners (1/2016)

Author of Best selling book - *Running Deep - An Australian Submarine Life.*

Never doubt that a small group of thoughtful, committed citizens can change the world; indeed, it's the only thing that ever has.

Margaret Mead

Contents

Part 3 - Learning from the Past and Paying It Forward

Foreword

Being a leader is not a job title it is a continuing journey, with ups and downs, mistakes and triumphs. Allan Sicard's memoir, The Courage to Lead, is a captivating portrayal of his 40-year journey in law enforcement, demonstrating how he navigated the challenges of a highly scrutinized organisation and built a culture of support and inclusion for his team.

As a reader, I am struck by Allan's bravery, sound judgement, and unwavering dedication to promoting gender equality and innovative responses to homelessness within NSW Police.

His inspiring leadership and drive to empower others to lead is beyond commendable, and deeply rooted in his strong values and unwavering commitment to serve the community.

Through his accounts of personal and professional experiences, Allan demonstrates that courage is more than just running towards danger, but also about empowering others to lead and creating a workplace that supports, respects and values diversity.

Allan's book is an honest and compelling read, peeling back the curtain on a lifetime of service protecting the community.

I have personally known Allan and seen firsthand, his leadership and unwavering commitment to serve the community and learn from others. His legacy, and this book, is sure to inspire generations to come

Alex Greenwich MP
Member for Sydney.

About the Author

Allan Sicard is husband to Kerrie, father to Kirk and Madeleine, and grandfather to Liam, Sylvia, Noah and Luca. Since retiring, he spends his time enjoying life with his family, including all the joy that being a grandparent brings. He has also taken up beekeeping using the flow hive system and is reputed in unbiased reviews to have the best-tasting honey ever.

Allan is the producer of the podcast "The Courage to Lead Interview Series" in which he interviews a suite of leaders who epitomise the skills and attributes to empower others to create supportive and inclusive workplaces, environments and communities.

Allan is the Executive Director of 3R Consulting, the three *R*s representing Resilience, Relationships and Reputation. Allan is a speaker and a specialist in leadership, specifically in empowering others to lead to create supportive and inclusive workplaces, environments and communities so that everyone can do their absolute best. Allan lives in Sydney. *The Courage to Lead* is his first book.

He has worked in the NSW Police Force for 40 years from 1980 to 2020, with the last 15 years of that career as a police commander.

Allan has successfully led several planned and unplanned major events in the Sydney Metropolitan Region. These events and incidents included the Mosman Collar Bomb in 2011 as a police commander and the Lindt Cafe Siege in 2015 as a forward police commander during the first two hours.

Allan led, coordinated and facilitated a multi-agency response to homelessness, housing hundreds of people across central Sydney and the northern districts of Sydney between 2013 and 2020.

Formal Recognition of Allan Sicard's Policing Career

Not long after retiring, I received a letter in my personal email from the Lord Mayor of the City of Sydney, Clover Moore. I treasure that letter above any medals or awards I have ever received.

I firmly believe police officers are there to serve their community. If we do not have the support of our community to fulfil our roles as police officers, we no longer have a purpose. To receive a letter from one of the most recognised and influential mayors in Australia was an unexpected and humbling experience.

Below is a copy of that letter:

5 May 2020

Superintendent Allan Sicard
Police Area Commander North Shore
By email   sica1all@police.nsw.gov.au

THE LORD MAYOR OF SYDNEY
CLOVER MOORE

Dear Allan

40 years of service

I refer to your retirement from the NSW Police Force after 40 years of extraordinary service.

I congratulate you on your outstanding career and positive impact on Sydney. Through your police command roles, you have contributed significant expertise to a wide range of public events and celebrations.

I will not forget your bravery and sound judgement during the Lindt Cafe siege when you were acting Sydney City Local Area Commander. The citizens of Sydney will remember your command on that day with respect and gratitude.

I commend your unwavering dedication to promoting gender equality within NSW Police, for which you were recognised with a Champion of Change Award in 2018. Your commitment to demonstrating and fostering leadership in your team and those around you is widely recognised and appreciated.

I wish also to acknowledge your significant contribution to developing the innovative responses to homelessness that are in place today in the City of Sydney. Many homeless people will continue to benefit from your compassionate and generous policing.

I wish you every success with your new ventures.

Yours sincerely

Clover Moore
Lord Mayor of Sydney

Sydney Town Hall 483 George Street Sydney NSW 2000
Phone 02 9265 9229 Fax 02 9265 9328 cmoore@cityofsydney.nsw.gov.au

O OLM2020 001604 SICARD

Introduction

Below is an anonymous email I received not long after my last day in the New South Wales Police in 2020, thirteen years after I was transferred from my first command.

> *You mention your first command. We cast you out of there like the incompetent man you are. You gave us no support and lacked a spine. Watching you leave was the most satisfying thing. You failed us and we won. Glad to hear you're gone from the job. Gives me the confidence to re-join.*

After my last day in the NSW Police Force on 2 November 2020, I was treated to a beautiful farewell after joining forty years earlier, in March 1980. A lot of friends, family and staff were there to celebrate that day. My parents were at my joining parade in 1980 so it was a touching moment to have my mother there in 2020 to witness my final day, a very proud day for her. My dad passed away in 2017 so to have one parent there was something that not all retiring police officers get to experience after 40 years of service.

I had a wonderful farewell with a Formal March down a street lined with police on either side, to a Police Band Bagpiper belting out "Ole Lang Sine". The video still brings a tear to my eye every time. The organisers closed a busy Chatswood Street where I marched down the centre acknowledging those who were there saluting my farewell.

The police do a great job of this type of farewell. The start of the march is lined with the junior ranks and as you approach your final saluting farewell location, the ranks increase to commissioned officers. Along that street that day were friends, colleagues and staff who had made a difference in my life.

Before I marched down the street the Police Radio operator broadcasted to all who were listening that today was my last day and they wished me well, thanking me for my service.

My acknowledgment was "North Shore 1, signing off for the last time."

A truly throat-croaking, emotional moment.

The end of the procession had Deputy Commissioner Jeff Loy standing at full attention saluting me when I approached him. I saluted him back and with that Mr Loy opened the door of a waiting highway patrol car, a new BMW 5 Series, and put me in next to the driver who drove me away from my final duty as a police officer.

The volume of positive tributes, cards, emails and comments I received from staff, community members and partner agencies I had made a positive impact on was humbling and satisfying. Amongst the volume of positive comments were two negative ones. One was just nasty comments about my family, which I chose not to put in this book as it says more about the author of the comments, that they had to make comments about my family and not me. The other comment was the one quoted at the start of the introduction chapter, and it is a good starting point as to why I wanted to write this book.

I wanted to write a memoir to help other leaders create a workplace that has at its core a culture of support and inclusion, entrust others with the courage to lead.

The title of this book highlights the word "courage".

There is the traditional meaning of courage in which the hero runs towards danger and saves the day. Policing does do that; a police officer's job is all about the skills to run toward danger when everyone else is running away. But I believe courage is more than that.

I have spent 40 years in a policing organisation that is steeped in tradition, rank, authority, rules and regulations.

Everything a police officer does is scrutinised at all levels, either within the organisation or by the wider community. This scrutiny paralyses some people to never make decisions, whilst others use that environment to hone their craft.

My story is about how I navigated this autocracy. I learnt that amazing things happen for people and communities when you have the courage to empower others to lead.

The story is not about being in the spotlight, the story is about empowering others to do their best every day and through those skills lead and influence others, creating a workplace that is safe, kind and inclusive.

Not everyone wants an inclusive workplace, so it takes courage to take on those who thrive on the imbalance of power and who do not want things to change. Courage is also about having an understanding that everything you do as a leader will have an impact on others, good or bad.

There are times as a leader when you must act, and when you do act, you need to predict the fallout, resistance and outcomes.

Those outcomes can affect your standing as a leader.

Are you ready for that?

My story will provide personal examples of the pain and the joy of making courageous decisions.

I cherish the satisfaction of making those decisions, good and bad, rather than sitting on the sidelines and never having the courage to act.

I never failed to act because I was frightened my decisions might impact my ability to be promoted in the future. You must back yourself.

Courage is when the rules do not provide a solution, resulting in others being harmed, either physically or at a wellbeing level, and you decide to do something about changing how things are done.

I will provide examples of how to use initiative outside the norm to obtain positive outcomes in investigations, create other leaders, provide better support for people who are homeless, address exclusion in the workplace and remove the cause in the most confronting of times.

These lessons and experiences transcend a policing workspace.

They apply to any white- or blue-collar workplace that is experiencing challenges, or any family that has challenging situations. Are you going to accept the status quo or do all you can to improve the outcome?

The more I learnt what was possible, after events like the Mosman Collar Bomb and the Lindt Café Siege, I saw that with the right preparation and support, a group of people working together can achieve anything. As a leader, you must create the environment and the culture to make that success possible.

I hope this book demonstrates to you that a leader can focus on empowering others, to step into their full potential, especially in high-risk environments or stressful situations, and that leadership is not about hogging the limelight.

There is so much joy and satisfaction that comes with seeing others shine, going on to lead and creating other leaders, but it does take courage to let others lead.

This book is largely about how I went from failure, several times, to being a successful leader.

The key to my success as a leader came down to the fact that even though I worked in an autocratic organisation, where rank and power were used to get things done, I had the courage to give that power away.

I chose to empower and develop other leaders. I did this by trusting others to lead and creating workplaces where people felt safe, supported and included.

This leadership journey involves some of the most notable incidents in recent Australian history such as the Art Gallery incident, the Mosman Collar Bomb and the first two hours of the Lindt Café Siege.

What I learnt from all these failures and then successes was that a group of people working together – without egos, genuinely working together and not for personal reward – can change the world, it's really the only thing that ever has.

I went on to use this ethos to bring about positive change in the homelessness sector which saw agencies work together to house hundreds of people where they previously worked in silos against each other, making it nearly impossible for individuals to navigate their way out of homelessness.

This same ethos saw large groups of stakeholders brought together under my leadership to create safe, family-friendly, large-scale events including New Year's Eve on the north side of Sydney Harbour from 2011 to 2019, The Sydney Running Festival for 7 years, Vivid Sydney and Sydney Mardi Gras for 4 years and the City to Surf in 2015.

The primary outcome of each of these large-scale events was that everyone worked together, and collectively working as one achieved far more than would ever be achieved individually.

I tested this same ethos to create resilience in a workplace, across stakeholders and a community several times to prepare communities for the next Lindt Cafe Siege. Working with peers in ambulance and fire, I created large-scale emergency training exercises that built trust and understanding of each other's capabilities. These exercises created a realistic environment for people to learn and prepare for the next big thing, like a large bushfire, unprecedented flooding, an earthquake or a tsunami. With the right preparation, anything is possible.

If we prepare our people and our partners for the next big thing, whatever that is, then when that next big thing happens, our people and our partners are prepared. They have a plan, they understand what they need to do, and they also understand what their partners may do.

Everyone brings baggage with them to work each day and brings that baggage back home.

A large part of my story and this book is about support.

I have found if we feel supported, then most of us will make it through any challenge. If we don't feel supported, then we feel despair and everything that comes with despair which impacts the individual, their family and friends and the workplace.

Part 1

New and Naive

1

The First Year (1980)

Why does someone want to be a police officer?

I have asked a lot of brand-new police officers this question over the last 20 years of my career. The most common answer is to make a difference in people's lives. Just before I retired one of my staff set up a new constable to play a prank on me, to tell me why he wanted to join the police. This brand-new officer said the following to the question.

"Because I want to shoot people and win medals."

This answer was given in front of a room full of police at one of our command briefings. Everyone lost it. It was quickly declared this was decidedly a joke and the poor young constable had been set up by his sergeant who was and still is a good friend of mine. We had never heard that answer before. Thankfully, it is not a reason we want to be police. Most of us want to give something back to help people.

My dad's brother had been a police officer from the 1960s to 1970s before dying young from cancer. I think dad always hoped that one of his children would be a police officer.

My dad had been a butcher all his life. His father and grandfather had all been butchers running the family butcher shop in Geurie, New South Wales, about 20 kilometres east of Dubbo. It's one of those blink-and-you-miss-it little towns, but it is a beautiful place.

My mum and dad spent most of their lives around butcher shops, either with Dad owning the shop or managing the shop for other owners. My memory of Mum is that she was always the bookkeeper and delivery person for the butcher shop. It is a hard life with long hours for very little money. The only "holidays" Mum and Dad ever took were from Good Friday to Easter Tuesday, and Christmas Eve to the day after Boxing Day. Those were their "holidays" every year.

To make ends meet and to put my sister and I through Catholic school education, Mum and Dad did extra jobs, Mum as a dressmaker and cleaner, and Dad as the starter for Golf Club competitions over the weekends. Before that, there were countless trips to the orchards around Orange to pick Dad up after a day of fruit-picking on top of his long hours in the butcher shop. Hard and long hours of low-paying work.

Dad's attraction to golf ended up with me learning to play the game at 9 years old, and spending most of my formative years hanging around adults playing golf with them every Saturday and Sunday. I became reasonably good at the game playing off single figures in my mid- to late-teens, all thanks to my mum and dad pouring their hard-earned money into my golf tuition, membership and competition fees.

Golf has always been an expensive game to play so I owe a lot to my parents for working so hard to let me play a game that helped me a lot later in my adult life.

Golf is all about discipline, repetition, and essentially dealing with your own emotions. If you behave like a spoiled brat, no one wants to play with you and normally your game and score fall apart.

Alternatively, if you behave with maturity and fight tooth and nail with all your skills to get a good score, no matter how much bad luck you have, you can end up with a very respectable score. If you are seen to shake off a bad shot or a bad hole, or a bad round, people respect that approach and are happy to play with you any time.

I wish I could say that I was always the mature and well-natured teenager on the golf course, but I wasn't. There were a couple of months when I had a terrible temper. I would swear, walk off on my own, throw a golf club and one day I even broke a golf club. That's an absolute NO on a golf course, especially if you are playing with adults.

One of the adults pulled me aside and gave me a mature talk about choices, about controlling my temper, or not. The choice was mine, I just had to decide.

I never really thought much about joining the police until I was 16. Mum handed me an advertisement out of The Daily Telegraph, advertising for prison warders. Mum did not want me to be a prison warder but suggested I should explore joining the NSW Police Force, like Dad's brother, John had.

I knew the NSW Police had a cadet system that would let high school certificate leavers join the police force in a trainee role before being old enough to join at 19 years of age. I thought this sounded like a good idea, an adventure to start my working life with.

We lived in Orange at the time and after finishing my Higher School Certificate I needed to fill in a few months before I could go to Sydney for the next recruiting opportunity.

My dad ran the local butcher shop and offered to train me in butchering for those few months and to work in the shop with him and his crew.

I thought Why not? and learnt how to break up beef and lamb carcasses so that they could be sold in their correct descriptions and cuts.

I also learnt how to make sausages but mostly I learnt how to spend over half the day bending over a large tub full of very hot soapy water washing some parts of the mincer, the sausage maker, the band saw or the day's stainless steel meat trays.

Everything had to be spotlessly clean, so that meant everything got washed in the hottest water possible with me being the person washing it.

I didn't mind, it is always fun to learn new things. And I did learn how to bone out every bone for beef and lamb which comes in handy when preparing food for large gatherings.

I soon settled into working life as a tradesperson. Tradies always have ways of dealing with the new person in training and the butcher shop was nothing different, especially for the boss's son. Their favourite trick was to come up quietly behind me, and with a quick flick of the sharpening steel that hangs off a butcher's belt hit me in the balls.

My reaction would be guaranteed: a moan, a shriek and most definitely a jump. The thing about this little game was that it would continue until I did not react to the treatment being given. It took me awhile, but I did get there, after a couple of months. I knew I was accepted when the butchers who worked for my dad asked me to play golf with them.

There is always a break in the butcher shop for morning tea and lunch.

I quickly became accustomed to a cream bun for morning tea with a bottle of coke and then a couple of meat pies and maybe another cream bun and a coke for lunch.

With this type of eating regime, I quickly became a larger version of myself. I had a round puffy face and a round puffy body in no time. Football training hadn't started then so I wasn't doing much in the way of exercise.

I was clueless as to how overweight I was getting and how quickly this was happening.

At the same time, since school had finished, I would spend most Friday nights at a local pub with some good mates.

We had this drinking system in that we would play the pub pinball machine that let four people play at any one time, with whoever lost in fourth place paying for everyone else that round of drinks.

We all became pinball wizards quickly so the paying for drinks was shared around evenly, but drinking that much beer, that regularly, also helped stack on a few more pounds.

I was about to get a reality check.

I went down to my dream job recruiting process.

I did the early sessions with the doctor which included eye tests, including colour blindness, and an appointment with the scales and tape measure.

I was a couple of hours into the process when this not-happy sergeant pointed at me amongst the other recruiting hopefuls and beckoned me to him.

I had no clue what this was about, so I went up to him none the wiser.

This sergeant just looked at me, then looked at his paperwork and said to me, "You're kidding aren't you, you're too fat. Go home, we don't want you. You are 88 kilograms, you must lose 10 kilos before we will even look at you. See you next year."

My world just disintegrated in front of me. Just like that, my dream career was over, or at least over for the time being.

My mum was waiting for me in a nearby hotel, so I walked back to where she was. She was surprised to see me so soon and was shattered when I told her that I had been sent home after two hours because I was overweight.

We drove home to Orange. I had to tell everyone what happened which was embarrassing, but I had no one to blame but myself.

I knew what the problem was, eating and drinking too much rubbish with no exercise.

I stopped having cream buns, beer, meat pies and coke and changed to salad rolls and water. Mixed with that when you are 18 years old, it is easy to step up to running 10 kilometres most days, and football training had started as well. I do recall a couple of runs that included a black plastic garbage bag as a t-shirt, but I wouldn't recommend doing that too often. It was 1980, I didn't know any better.

One month later, I was back in the Police Recruiting Office in Sydney. The doctor weighed me, and I was 78 kilograms.

I walked into the waiting area again and the first person I saw was the sergeant who sent me home a month earlier.

He looked at me, pondered at the ceiling and said, "I remember you. What are you doing back here? I told you to come back in a year."

I said, "Sergeant, the doctor just weighed me in at 78 kilograms, that was what you told me I had to be. I went back home and trained my heart out."

The sergeant looked at me again and said, "Go on then, see how you go with everything else."

I can't remember what everything else was that we had to do in the recruiting process, but my main issue had been my weight, so I passed.

I was eligible to enter what they called the Junior Trainee Program and spent my first year working at Maroubra Police Station as a trainee.

A trainee doesn't have a uniform. I answered phones and took over-the-counter enquiries from the public. I also spent a lot of time inputting data onto manual Intelligence Cards about local criminals, learning what they looked like, what their histories were, who they associated with and what type of crime they liked to commit.

These were all good skills to have as I went into my Initial Training when I turned 19 years old. It made everything easier because I had been around the police and what they do for 12 months.

Junior trainees don't earn much money and I remember living in the back veranda of my aunt's place in Chifley, opposite Long Bay Gaol.

All I had was a single bed, a wardrobe and a chest of drawers, with a curtain to make my bed semi-private on the back veranda. My routine would include taking my aunt's lunatic sheep dog for a long run past the Malabar oil refinery every afternoon, so I kept my fitness up.

I also bought a push bike and rode from Chifley to Maroubra and back every day. As a young and impressionable police recruit, my favourite t-shirt to wear on those bike rides was one that had the monogram "PIG" with the words "Pride", "Integrity" and "Guts" underneath.

It wasn't all bad, being a young teenager left to my own devices in Sydney was exciting.

One of the things I had to get better at was typing. Typing was a massive component of being a police officer. The quality, accuracy and speed of your typing showcased your work and opened opportunities because people wanted a good typist on their team.

In those days there was no computer and no electric typewriters, everything was a manual typewriter. To improve my typing skills, I enrolled myself in a typing course at Randwick TAFE College. They were night-time classes. On the first night of the course, I was a bit late. I pushed open the door to the classroom. There were 20 young brilliant women in the class with an equally young brilliant woman teaching the class. In my young immature male brain, I had the misogynistic thought that I must be in the wrong room so I apologised and backed out.

After checking my enrolment and re-checked the room number on the door of the classroom I was in the right place. The teacher and the rest of the class were waving at me to come in. Who knew that typing could be so much fun being the only male in a group of twenty brilliant women? I had a couple of nice nights out with my classmates and slowly started to train my young male brain not to be so sexist.

Initial training as a police officer started for me as part of Class 170 of the NSW Police Academy at Redfern in 1981. I and 120 other recruits started our policing careers together.

Initial training meant going to the Police Academy for three months, Monday to Friday, learning everything about law, first aid, police work and typing, mixed with days of marching and physical exercises.

The trainers' favourite place for physical exercise was called Breakfast Hill at a nearby recreational park called Moore Park. That same hill is used today as a grass version of downhill skiing, such is the level of incline.

Whatever nastiness the trainers could think up for Breakfast Hill, they did it. Their favourite routine was for everyone to join arms and run up the hill in long lines, emphasising teamwork. These sessions continued for as long as necessary until a prescribed number of police recruits had lost their breakfasts on that horrible hill. Once this number had been reached, we ran back to the Police Academy, showered and put back into classes, tired and sweating without any air-conditioning, and maybe not feeling all that well if we had just lost our breakfast on Breakfast Hill.

I passed without any issues, retaining my new level of fitness weighing in for my first police identification badge at 78 kilograms.

Your police badge has your date of birth, registered number, weight, blood group and picture with the signature of the Police Commissioner, who at that time was Cecil Abbott.

I was never 78 kilograms again until just before my retirement in March 2020, forty years later. I retired physically fit, probably the fittest I had been for most of my life with my mental health intact.

Reflections

It is an interesting process to look back on the decisions a younger version of myself had made and what flowed from those decisions. At the end of every chapter is a reflections section.

A large part of successful leadership is about self-reflection, analysing what you could have done better, how you impacted poor performance and what you need to work on to improve. This process is relentless and becomes an ingrained thing done daily.

When I look back on myself as that young police recruit who travelled to Sydney to become a police officer, I am left wondering how I could have been so clueless as to how much weight I had put on and the impact that excess weight would have on the recruiting process. It was such a rookie mistake.

As an 18-year-old, I was only just learning about how the world works. I had enjoyed a charmed life up until that moment of rejection when I was too overweight to become a cadet. As a student at school, I was voted in as school captain in Year 6 and Year 10, with prefect selection in Year 11 and Year 12. I had done nothing to earn these titles, people who I did not know had recommended that I do those roles. It had just happened. My parents had worked hard to provide for my sister and I, and things just happened around me.

I was living a life of privilege, some may say that I was a privileged white male, clueless as to what hardships could occur and did occur to others around me. The only thing I had that challenged me during my younger life prior to joining the police was the choice to control my temper on the golf course. Thankfully, a well-intentioned adult gave me a wise talk about choices. Was I going to be a spoiled brat that lost my temper all the time or was I going to be mature and navigate calmly to get the best outcome?

The obvious lesson of this chapter is if you are going to go for a job and you are serious about it, then know the essential criteria and ensure you meet them before you apply. The second lesson is that we can choose each day the attitude we bring to our day. Traditionally, people enjoy being around people who have a calm manner and stay away from people who have terrible tempers.

At the same time, I am prepared to give 18-year-old me a break. We only know what we know. In those days, having a set of weight scales in the bathroom was not a reality. I did not know that I had become a larger version of myself. As soon as I did, I knew it was no one's fault but my own, and the only way that I could reverse the situation I found myself in was to eat better, train regularly and give myself the best chance to reverse the outcome.

One of the best things I learnt about leadership through my failures is that we must lead people who have failed. If we have experienced failure, and from that failure we picked ourselves up and kept on moving forward, then we are in a good position to coach and mentor people who have failed to have another go.

2
Who's Next? (1981–1982)

My first year of service as a confirmed probationary constable was at Maroubra. It was known as 15 Division with the main station at Maroubra and a substation at Randwick.

A police officer has a 12-month Probationary Constable period before deciding on whether you should be confirmed as a Constable.

The first six weeks of a probationary constable's life are spent with their buddy. Your buddy teaches you all they know and instills in you lifelong practices in your career. It can be a lucky dip who you get as a buddy, depending on the work ethic of the Training Sergeant at each station.

I won the lucky dip. I was given a high-performing sergeant as a buddy. His name was Kevin "Chips" Rafferty. Some might recognise his name as a first-grade Rugby League referee in NSW. Some of my peers were partnered with drunks and lazy officers, and that was how they approached their profession. Chips was a family man, devoted to his wife and children, with enough time to show me how to do the job right, and enough patience to watch me make a few messes.

The Sydney Royal Easter Show used to be held at the Sydney Showground, behind the Sydney Cricket Ground. Anyone who knows that area knows that it is a parking nightmare. What senior police loved to do to junior police like me was to put them on traffic duty at one of the major intersections outside the Royal Easter Show. It was the intersection of Cleveland Street and Anzac Parade, with bus lanes and six lanes of traffic going everywhere.

I will paint the picture for you.

My training officer (not Sergeant Rafferty) donned the white traffic gloves with extended sleeves that go up past the elbows, all white. He then went to the centre of the intersection after the traffic lights have been turned off and started directing traffic, to stop flows and allow right turns. It was magical to watch, it was like choreographed dancing with the traffic.

Then things got interesting.

I was summonsed out into the middle of the intersection with my training officer, wearing my own white traffic gloves. He gave me one more example of what to do, then stopped all lines of traffic, pointed to me with his white gloves and ran off chuckling very loudly.

I am the first to admit that I normally don't grasp how to do a new task first thing, no matter how hard I try. So what happens next was predictable.

I flapped my arms around with my white gloves on, with everything going ok, until I started to incorporate traffic doing right turns. The trick is you beckon the cars wanting to turn right to come near to you and then when the time is right you create the situation where they can turn right safely.

I obviously didn't grasp how to do this part as all lanes of traffic were stopped in the middle of the intersection completely within a couple of minutes. I was in the middle with everything stuck, and my training officer came back laughing loudly. It was like an episode of *Mr Bean*, it was chaos and I was the centre show.

I promise I did improve but it took me awhile. More importantly, I did not give up.

After your first six weeks, you work with anyone senior to you. This was 1980, forty years ago, well before any royal commission corruption reforms. I worked with some great people and some not-so-great people, seeing things, and working with people who I did not want to be like.

The substation of Randwick had a good reputation for good leadership and good productive outcomes where police learnt to be police because they were out on the roads every shift, pulling up cars, identifying suspicious behaviour, arresting offenders, and putting them before the courts.

At that time if you arrested someone you went to court with them the very next day and read out your Facts Sheet about what they had done. I learnt very quickly what was professional and what was not. It would literally be me arresting someone at 2 am for a traffic- or crime-related offence and then I would be at Redfern Court at 10 am that same morning and then back to work at 11 pm that same night. It was so much fun, and I learnt so much so quickly.

I learnt from this first year that if a police officer never spoke to anyone and never arrested anyone, then they never really learnt how to do their job. In my first year as a probationary constable, whilst I did get some exposure to what a police officer was supposed to do, I knew I needed to do more if I wanted to become proficient.

An opportunity came up for a permanent placement at Randwick Police Station. I said that I was interested, and after a bit of homework from the station, I was assigned to duty there. It was a great place to work, and I quickly increased my workload, learning how to identify suspicious behaviour, back my own judgement and put criminals before the court, improving each time with wins and losses in court.

Court was interesting. I won a lot in court, but I also lost a lot, largely because I always had a go and tested the law. A lot of my colleagues would not go to court unless they were one hundred percent sure they would win, letting offenders go if the evidence was a bit shaky. I found this difficult to do as I learnt a lot with each court loss I had. It was normally some bit of the law I had never heard before or did not know and, as a second-year constable, I still had a lot to learn.

In those days as already mentioned, all the paperwork had to be done on a manual typewriter. If you are doing a lot of court work, then you are doing a lot of paperwork on typewriters. I remember I became careless of what the paperwork looked like after awhile, as the exciting thing about police work was and still is being on the road, identifying suspicious behaviour and doing something about it. The last thing I wanted to do was spend time behind a typewriter, so I did that part of the job as quickly as I could. Until something happened to change my poor attitude.

That something went like this.

"Sicard, get in here now," bellowed the first-class sergeant that ran Randwick Police Station.

I went into the sergeant's office, standing at attention because he was a scary man. He told me to sit down. I didn't really want to sit down with this scary man, but I did. What happened next formed a work ethic that stayed with me for the next 39 years as a police officer.

He said, "Allan, you are doing a really good job, we like what you are doing on the street, people like working with you, but something is letting you down. Your paperwork has a lot of mistakes in it and it looks like you don't care. I know that is not the message you are intending. If I can give you one piece of advice, when you sign your name to something, anything, be proud to do so. When people see your name signed on something, they will know it is something good."

I am forever grateful to that sergeant for this message as it is something I treasure for my whole working life.

I have recounted this story, or the message of this story many times over the years to young police, particularly young police that liked putting criminals before the courts.

It is such a common trait to love locking up criminals, but not being bothered to do the paperwork as the street stuff is so much more exciting than the paperwork stuff.

My message to young police who found themselves in this dilemma was simple: what you want the solicitor to say to their client when they see your name as the arresting officer for their case is, "Oh my God, if this officer has locked you up, you are done for. They are good at what they do." You don't want them to say, "This officer is always making mistakes, let's give this one a run and plea not guilty, I reckon we will win."

That same sergeant taught me something else about leadership not too long after.

Some police are out patrolling all the time, looking for that something that is not right and doing something about it. Some police sit in the station all day and all night, and only go out if they must. These police officers do not enhance their skills, the more they sit in the station, the more they lose their skills, eventually becoming too scared to go out because they know they do not know what to do.

This particularly applied at night-time with licenced premises like pubs or hotels. This was still the 1980s so there was no such thing as Responsible Service of Alcohol, exactly the opposite applied, bar staff would pour as much alcohol into people until they couldn't stand up anymore.

There was an unwritten rule in policing in the 1980s. Do not rush to any brawl at a hotel or pub, just let them punch it out and hurt themselves.

One night, there was a brawl at the Coogee Bay Hotel just opposite Coogee Beach. A couple of calls came over the police radio and it sounded bad. People needed help.

I was working with a young policewoman and that would become very relevant, very soon. I was the senior officer in the car, a big Ford F-100 paddy wagon with a big loud V8 engine and a big prisoner cage on the back. You could always hear us coming from a mile away with the roar of the engine. We drove that big F-100 into the courtyard of Coogee Bay. There was a massive fight going on. Chairs and tables were flying, bodies were thrown everywhere. I had let police radio know we were there, and what we could see and there were other car crews on the way to help.

When I got out of the passenger seat of the F-100 paddy wagon, I stepped into a melee that just started in front of me. The main offender causing all the grief was a big outlaw bikie wearing the colours of his gang, swinging a big chain at the people in front of him and intimidating them. That was when he saw me. I wish he hadn't.

At that time, I was thinking of getting back in the passenger seat, and reversing time for five minutes might be a good idea. That's not an option when you are in the middle of things, but these thoughts can and do come to mind.

There was still about five metres of distance between us when my partner came to stand beside me. We faced this guy together. The presence of a young policewoman in the middle of all this mayhem made the guy swinging the chain pause.

Policewomen in the 1980s were a small percentage of frontline staff. The pause felt like time had stopped. The chain stopped swinging and we looked at each other. Then the best part of being a police officer in the city occurred. About five other police cars turned up with more than ten other police officers rushing to the situation.

The guy with the chain melted into the crowd and we never saw him again.

Over the next 15 minutes, we started to clear people out of the hotel to settle things down, the majority were happy to go home peacefully, but a small group wanted to stay and fight the police.

That's when my boss, the first-class sergeant, turned up and I had a lesson in what it means to lead police on the street.

We had already put one offender in the back of the paddy wagon for their behaviour and were in the process of putting another. My first-class sergeant stood at the back of the paddy wagon, facing the remaining offenders. He stood as tall as he could, stared them all down, and yelled, "Who's next?"

And just like that, everyone went home. No police were injured. We took the two people in the back of the paddy wagon and charged them with violence-related offences and went about our work.

***

The next couple of years were a lot of fun. As a young, single guy in the eastern suburbs of Sydney, I partied, did my best at work, and partied again. I played a lot of golf at Bonnie Doon Golf Club in Pagewood and was loving life.

On one of my partying nights at a place called Colonnades at Kensington, I met my first wife. She was an Arthur Murrays Dance School instructor in the city and when she got on the dancefloor at Colonnades, she drew attention. Not long after, as a very young man, I proposed to her. We married and lived a very short married life. We transferred to Bega down the south coast of NSW, and I worked there as a general duties officer for 18 months. Our marriage didn't last. I was too young and wasn't the husband I should have been. I was never unfaithful, but I really wasn't ready to be a lifelong husband.

When my first marriage failed, I was very short of money and needed a place to live. I relied on friends from the Bega Golf Club to put me up for awhile but that was not a long-term thing, so I looked for new opportunities and a way forward.

At that time, highway patrol had a big recruitment drive and they were looking for new officers in several places including Goulburn. My mum and dad owned a Butcher Shop in Goulburn and were working towards their retirement.

Whilst highway patrol wasn't necessarily something I wanted to do, I saw it as an opportunity to learn new skills. The highway patrol has a lot of technical expertise and came with the bonus of doing the high-speed course, which at that time meant learning to drive V8 manual Commodores at their maximum speeds. Whilst I have never been a race fan or a "petrol head", who wouldn't love the chance to learn to drive a car at its maximum capacity and get paid to do it?

I applied to do the Highway Patrol Course and was accepted. I will never forget the first day of the Highway Patrol Course.

Their central location and training rooms were in the old warehouses on the northern approaches under the Sydney Harbour Bridge. It was a cold dark, wet place to go to every day, but everyone was excited, and we were happy to be there.

As we were introduced to our highway patrol instructors all the niceties went out the door when the lead instructor got up to talk to us. He said, "We know some of you shitheads have come here just to get a transfer, we know who you are, we are gonna ride you and weed you out. We don't want you in the highway patrol."

I didn't move a muscle. I thought, *How did they know?* I kept my head down for the next few weeks and passed everything they threw at us. I then transferred from Bega to Goulburn Highway Patrol, working out of Goulburn Police Station in 1984.

Early on in my time at Goulburn I met my wife, my best friend, my life-long partner and the best mum and grandmother you will ever meet. I didn't know it at the time as it took us three years to get married, but from the first time I saw her at the pedestrian crossing in the main street of Goulburn, in active-wear tracksuit and singlet with short pink hair as she had just come back from a holiday in Asia, I was done. She had a spark about her that was infectious and still has that same spark today 39 years later.

Goulburn proved to be a good lesson for me in moving forward when things didn't work out. Getting a divorce from my first wife and setting up a new life was not a fun thing to do. It was full of challenges but because I chose to move forward and not dwell on the failures of the past, some amazing opportunities opened for me in the police.

Goulburn Police Station had a part-time Police Rescue Squad. We rescued people in all sorts of situations: car crashes, industrial accidents, caving and cliff accidents, and being lost in the bush. Some of my fondest memories go back to being in the rescue squad. The Goulburn Police Rescue Squad members did so much training and then transformed that training into the real thing almost every week. You couldn't imagine where you would end up.

One very cold and dark, stormy night when the rain was torrential, I was chosen to go into a swollen river and extricate a drowned grandmother who we could see was tenuously being held in place by a gnarly tree despite the force of the river. I knew what the job was going out, so I brought my windsurfing wetsuit with me.

My partner tied a long length of rope around my chest, wrapped it around another tree further upstream and in I went to retrieve this drowned grandmother so her family could say goodbye. Looking back on this job, it was a risky thing to do but good planning outweighed the risk, and the outcome was worth it.

Goulburn also had a part-time Special Weapons Squad. The Special Weapons Squad was a team of police within the police station who received extra training on shotguns, sniper rifles and automatic AR-15 rifles like the type used in the army. We trained all the time, doing building entries and bush searches for armed offenders. We generally had a great time increasing our skills, practising all the time on the shooting range with pistols and a whole range of weapons.

As highway patrol officers, we were always deployed within a 200-kilometre radius of the main station at Goulburn. We were in quick-response vehicles. We were ideal officers to be part of the Rescue Squad and the Special Weapons Squad if we wanted to be involved. I quickly signed up for the training for both part-time squads and learnt lifelong skills in rescue and high-risk armed offender situations. I loved it.

Reflections

I have never forgotten what that first-class sergeant showed me that night outside the Coogee Bay Hotel, 39 years ago.

All any police officer wants, all any staff member wants, is for their leaders to turn up and support them. We were already doing our jobs, arresting those who were causing harm, and our boss turned up and supported our actions by the stance he took towards those that would do us harm, leading from the front.

A leader by their actions can influence the lives of others forever.

This leader, the first-class sergeant, left me with two major lifelong lessons.

Firstly, if your name is on something be proud of it and make it reflect the reputation you are creating.

Secondly, if you are leading people, show that you support what they do. Just showing up and being with them can make all the difference. Just by being there, your people know you care.

That period also highlights the brashness and impatience of my youth.

I met my soon-to-be first wife and married her too soon. My first wife did nothing wrong, except marry a man who was not ready to get married. This led to us separating and getting a divorce. We still both cared about each other at a human level but not at a marriage level, so it was not a fun time.

There are countless sayings that people offer you when going through hard times but the most relevant concept I have held on to is "keep moving forward". Acknowledge where you have come from, learn from it, and keep moving forward and improving who you are and what you do.

A low point of my life, a divorce, led to some new opportunities, new skills and ultimately my forever life partner and friend. None of this would have happened if I had stayed living in that low point feeling sorry for myself. You must move forward. Some have a saying: "If you are going to fail, fail forwards, not backwards."

3

Rescue Squad (1985–1986)

My wife Kerrie and I stayed in Goulburn from 1984 to 1992. We married in 1987.

As she was in general duties as a first-response officer in the same police station, we went to all kinds of jobs together, some of them scary, some sad, and some scary and funny.

These jobs included suicides and fatal accidents where we could support each other because we had been to the same or similar jobs in the past.

One job that Kerrie and I went to together, with a few more police who also happened to be couples, was riddled with danger but also humour.

It was on a very starry night when shots were allegedly fired near Goulburn Gaol. When we turned up, all was quiet and we thought it was just a hoax. This same night was supposed to be a night to see Halley's Comet so when all was quiet, we all gazed at the night sky.

Then things changed in a couple of seconds and we were reminded that our situational awareness should have been a whole lot better. Shots were fired from a nearby house, not towards us, but away from the house in another direction, and we all hit the ground.

When we deployed as the Special Weapons Operations Squad (SWOS), we wore all-black clothing, including a black balaclava when needed. This type of clothing was ideal for camouflage in any type of shaded environment and at night. During siege-related exercises, I had laid inches away from police commanders in bushes, right next to their boots and they never knew I was there until I had told them after the exercise.

On this night near the Goulburn Goal, after hearing shots fired, I got myself to what I thought was a very secure location hidden in a garden bed by some bushes. I wasn't that concerned when I heard footsteps approaching as I knew if I remained still I would not be discovered.

Then the footsteps got closer and closer ... and then I was nudged in the neck. I thought I was done for. Then a hot stream of air snorted down my neck. I nearly died in fright. For a moment, I didn't know what was going on until I realised, to my relief, that it was just a horse. He was very curious about what I was doing on the ground in his paddock.

This job turned out to be just two drunken mates letting off shots from their front verandah but we didn't know that going in. Everything feels like a real job until it's not. We waited till all was quiet in the house, then forced entry, arrested the two men without incident and later charged them with firearms offences.

The one job I remember most was an accident out on the Federal Highway about 20 kilometres out of Goulburn.

It was one night in the mid-1980s at around 8 pm, a single-car accident where the driver, a young woman, was trapped in the car by her foot after running off the road. I went to this job as a member of the Police Rescue Squad with my rescue partner.

Before I go into the story of this young woman, this phase of my career illustrates the opportunities that are there in our lives to learn new skills that ultimately can help us, but also help others.

To become a police rescue operator and a roping expert there were a lot of different skills I had to learn, both book-based and experienced-based. I can't remember all of it but there were some standout memories in the physical domain.

Much like a soldier learning about every piece of their firearm, taking them apart and putting them back together again, we had to learn how to do the same with a chainsaw. A chainsaw and other cutting accessories were part of our kit. We had to learn to pull a chainsaw apart and then put it back together again in a ridiculous time, something like 60 seconds. Once you do it enough, it is relatively easy. But in the first few weeks, if you have never even touched a chainsaw before, it was almost like an impossible task.

Chainsaw training brings back memories that make me laugh now as the trainers did things to us trainees that would never be allowed now. Someone like me had never used a chainsaw in their lives so the trainers thought it important that we learn. Our trainers took us to some random street in the inner western suburbs of Sydney. They informed us that the local council had asked Police Rescue to come in and prune all the trees in this street.

From memory, the trees were paperbark gums, most at about 5 metres tall. Our job was to climb up the trees and trim the highest branches so they didn't impact any powerlines or other infrastructure.

Imagine this scene in which I had never used a chainsaw before. I was sent up the tree, climbing the tree, with the chainsaw and without any safety harness or ropes to restrain me if I happen to fall. My job was to start the chainsaw in the tree and then go to work. I did all this well, mostly without incident, until the chainsaw started to get heavy. Nowadays, chainsaws contain a lot of plastic parts making them relatively light. In the mid-1980s, chainsaws were a lot heavier being almost all metal.

There I was up the tree, I had eye goggles on, earmuffs, heavy work gloves and a chainsaw. It was also raining. If you have ever used a chainsaw, it doesn't take long for the goggles to fog up and you can't see much at all. I was using the chainsaw above my head to cut down most of the branches that needed to go, and I decided to have a little rest.

I had just finished cutting a branch and then rested the chainsaw on my thigh for a little break. The only problem was the chain was still running. Thankfully, I was wearing heavy-duty work overalls and the chain cuts through the overalls and leaves a slight graze on my leg, not breaking the skin. It could have been a lot worse. Our trainer nearly lost it with fright – an "oh shit" moment – and yelled at me to get out of the tree immediately. I did get down; I think the trainers re-assessed what chainsaw training looked like after that moment. OH&S in the workplace was not really a big thing back in the 1980s.

One other thing that sticks out in the police rescue training was map reading. One of the final components of becoming a rescue operator was the ability to map read. The trainers took us out to the Sutherland National Park in a small minibus and divided us into pairs. We were given something like four hours to find several map grid points in the depths of the wild bush, each one highlighting where the next grid point would be with the final one being returning to the bus within the time limit.

My partner and I were doing ok, until we weren't. We got to our last grid point before the bus a little late and then we started running and crashing our way through the bush until we hit the road where our bus should be. I think we came out onto the road about a kilometre from where the bus was. Even though we were exhausted, we had less than 10 minutes to run along a rough inclined dirt road, in police rescue overalls and boots, to make it back to the bus. We had already been at it in the bush for over three and a half hours, so we were already knackered but somehow, we made it.

If we didn't make it in time, we would have failed the whole course, no matter how well we had performed in every other competency. We were the last pair back and we were exhausted. We sat on the ground, sucking the air in, just relieved to pass this final test. Thank God we were in pairs that day as if I was on my own, I would be still lost out there in the Sutherland National Park.

Another amazing part of rescue training was the additional roping qualifications you can acquire. Goulburn is an area that has the Bungonia Gorge and Caves, both of which require professional knowledge of how to abseil and rescue others who had misfortune when doing their own abseiling.

The Roping Course and Advanced Roping Course were like nothing else I have ever done in policing. To get ready for the course I was doing chin-ups off the Metal Hills Hoist Clothesline in our backyard and running long distances every day. The course required us to spend most of our time on ropes, with most of that time spent lifting our own body weight higher on the rope so we could rescue someone else. Much like the chainsaw experience, I feared heights and had never really been exposed to roping or abseiling except for a couple of sessions with fellow operators in the rescue squad at Goulburn.

In the roping course, the trainers challenged us every day to abseil in different environments until we were confident with our kit and where and what we could abseil from. We went from the cliffs of the North Head of Sydney Harbour, the ceiling of the old Entertainment Centre in Sydney, and out the floor of a container crane in Port Botany, 150 metres in the air. There is nothing quite like getting onto a rope from a container crane when the wind is blowing the rope almost at right angles to the ground.

One of the highlights of this training was abseiling down high waterfalls in the Blue Mountains as part of canyoning training. That training day took over eight hours. We had to hike to a location where other climbers did the sport of canyoning. They abseil down various parts of the canyon system, including several waterfalls, and then hike back out again. The water is freezing, you take a lot of gear to do what you need to do, including a wetsuit.

The reality of this type of training is that when things go wrong in canyoning or caving, people die or get injured, and someone must go get them. I can remember spending several hours inside a cave in Bungonia, in a section known as the "rib breaker" because if you breathe out in the wrong spot you could break your ribs. Because I am not a big person, my job that night was to spend a long time at the rib breaker point of the cave, ferrying gear belonging to a group of cavers who had become exhausted back up to others above me so we could get the cavers back to safety.

This takes us back to that night when the young woman was trapped in the car on the Federal Highway. My wife Kerrie went to the job as a Goulburn general duties car crew and was the first car off at the job. At that time, I was a part-time police rescue operator, so I turned up with my rescue partner in the old F-350 V8 rescue truck, a true beast to drive because of all the equipment we had in it. By that time, I had been doing rescue long enough to be a proficient member of the team.

As I was normally the smallest person in the rescue crew it was normally my job to go in first, into the vehicle, and suss out what was happening. I climbed into the front of the car with the young woman. The woman was in her mid-20s and looked scared but relieved that the rescue squad had arrived. All she knew was that she was stuck and that she could not get out of the car.

I was immediately taken aback by her courage.

She had a level of determination that saw her listen to everything I told her, and not once did she scream or moan in pain despite the extensive ordeal she was going through. When I climbed into the car and got down into the footwell of the driver's seat to see how the woman was trapped, I saw quickly she wasn't trapped at all. The problem was her shin had completely fractured and torn through her calf muscle and the only thing keeping her leg attached was the back flap of skin on her calf.

We planned how we were going to get her out with the ambulance crew and then I spoke to the young woman about it. My job was to be in the car with her and when the ambos and my rescue partner lifted her, I was to lift her fractured and severed calf with her at the same time so that it did not become completely detached.

Again, the courage of the woman blew me away. She did not scream or cry and just let us get her out of the car and onto a stretcher. The ambulance took her to the emergency ward at Goulburn Base Hospital about 30 minutes away. As a rescue operator that's normally the last time you see people that you have rescued.

The next day I was working the day shift at Goulburn Police Station in the highway patrol. I wanted to go to Goulburn Base Hospital to see how the young woman was going. It wasn't something I had done before and something I don't think I ever did again, but I wanted to acknowledge her courage the night before and make sure she was ok. I turned up at the hospital in uniform, and the nurses let me into her ward. She was no longer in emergency but back in the normal recovery wards so that was good news.

When I approached her, she was not exactly pleased to see me.

Her hair was a hornet's nest, she was brushing her teeth in her bed and spitting into a small tray with toothpaste dribbling down her chin, and she was in one of those not-so-elegant hospital gowns that never do up properly. The visit didn't last all that long but I got a chance to tell her how impressed all the emergency crews had been that night with her courage and bravery.

I never really thought anything more about this young woman again other than maybe don't visit people who you don't know the day after they have been admitted to hospital.

About six months later, I got the shock of my life in the office at Goulburn Highway Patrol. A young woman dressed in business clothes ambled into our office and said that she was there to see me. She looked vaguely familiar, but I had no clue who she was.

She then proceeded to tell me that she was that same young woman in the car on the Federal Highway several months before. She came in to thank me and my partner for looking after her that night and to show me that she had made a full recovery because of our efforts and that of the medical staff at Goulburn Base Hospital.

I have done a lot of amazing things as a police officer, but nothing really tops this moment and experience.

A group of people working together, focused on one outcome, removing this young woman from a horrible situation, and getting her to medical attention in as best a condition as possible, then with the beautiful bonus of seeing her happy and healthy several months later. An amazing outcome.

There are so many stories in each of those facets of my policing and personal life, but I will end this chapter with two of the best excuses I ever heard as a highway patrol officer which led me to let the drivers go without a traffic ticket or fine.

The first driver I let go was on the Federal Highway between Goulburn and Collector.

I stopped this little white car going too quickly but not stupidly so. When I walked up to the driver's door, the driver was a young woman in her mid-20s. She was inconsolable, weeping, sobbing, real tears coming down her face. I really didn't care about the traffic ticket at that time, I wanted to find out what was wrong.

In between her sobbing and gulping to get air into her lungs, she pointed to this beautifully laid-out white dress in the backseat. That dress was her wedding dress. She was getting married on that day in Canberra, and through a series of misadventures on the way out of Sydney she was now cutting it very fine to get to Canberra for her own wedding.

I'm a sucker for a good story, I hadn't heard that one before so I asked her to promise me she would drive safely the rest of the way, and my present for her wedding day was no traffic ticket and all the fines and demerit points that come with that. I watched her drive away, not speeding or anything dangerous, with tears still flowing down her face, but not too badly. There were no accidents on the Federal Highway that afternoon, so I hope she made her wedding safely.

The second driver was a guy. He was the tenth driver I had stopped on this Sunday morning to give a speeding fine. The first nine drivers had all argued excessively and nastily when I stopped them and whilst I was writing out their traffic fine. This was an unusual day for me. People did not normally get upset with me, even when I was giving them a traffic fine. I always had a good demeanour in most situations and more often than not, people would say "thank you" to me after I gave them a speeding fine.

I was feeling a bit frazzled as I approached this tenth driver on this Sunday morning getting ready for another tirade.

What happened next just made my day, and I think I made his day shortly after. When I stood beside the driver's car window, the tenth driver's first words to me were, "I am so sorry, Officer, yes, I was speeding, I deserve the ticket you are going to give me. I have no excuses."

There was a long pause, I just looked at Driver Number 10.

I said, "Sir, you are the first driver today to admit you were speeding with no excuses. You have a good day, I am going to walk away without issuing you a speeding fine. Drive safely."

Driver Number 10 just sat there; I think he didn't know what to do. I got into my highway patrol car, and drove off leaving him there wondering what had just happened.

Reflections

Sometimes a change in the workplace or a change in life circumstances can be a good thing. It's all about the attitude you take with you to that new opportunity.

Goulburn was a wonderful workplace to learn new skills. I had gone there after a massive failure in my life, having to admit that my first marriage was over.

Despite that low point in my life, what happened next was confirmation of the adage "we write our own story". Keep learning, learn as much as we possibly can, be open to change and keep moving forward.

In my eight years in that workplace at Goulburn, I was a:

» Highway Patrol Officer

» Police Rescue Operator

» Special Weapons Operator

» General Duties Officer where I had the privilege to train new police officers just as my buddy Chips Rafferty had trained me

» Licensing Officer

» Education Training Officer

» Designated Detective.

My personal life was wonderful. I had married that beautiful and intelligent woman I saw walking on the pedestrian crossing on one of my first days in Goulburn, and we then had a son to add to our family. At a social level, we made some lifelong friends becoming very proficient in sailboarding and horse riding.

I had completed some tertiary management courses at the local technical college and was building the platform to do further university-level studies in leadership.

4

Ego (1994)

In January 1992, my wife and I decided we would leave Goulburn after eight years to pursue developing our careers in Sydney. When we came back to Sydney to live, I worked at a few interesting places. I found not every work move I made was a great experience. Each move taught me a little bit more about myself, how I acted and what I needed to learn.

This was never more relevant than when I worked in the Cabramatta area. I had just transferred from Task Force Oak – Organised Asian Crime to work as one of two detectives in a team of Proactive Police who worked from Wetherill Park Police Station.

We predominantly targeted drug dealers in Cabramatta at a street level and property offenders in the southwest of Sydney. By this stage, I had been a detective for six years and had a good reputation of what my skills were. I was now a detective senior constable, and I had a level of confidence in what I could do. As it turned out I had too much confidence.

The officer in charge of the proactive team was a detective sergeant. He had built up a good team of young officers who had good all-round skills. One of the regular strategies this detective sergeant adopted was to check the quality of every court matter that his officers submitted. This meant reading through each statement and the evidence contained in the brief of evidence to make sure they had the greatest chance of success. I had been a detective for 6 years up to this point. I had never seen a detective sergeant do this level of supervision or checking.

In the NSW Police, there is this idiosyncrasy that dictates each rank writes with a different coloured pen. A constable uses a black pen, a sergeant uses a blue pen, an inspector uses a red pen, and a superintendent uses a green pen.

When I got one of my briefs of evidence back from our detective sergeant, I found my statement was full of blue pen corrections, and as I went through the rest of the brief of evidence, I found that there were masses of corrections all the way through it. I was shocked, I was confident in my abilities and here I was getting my work back covered in corrections like I was back in school. I was not happy. None of us like to have the quality of our work questioned and it took me awhile to calm down over the corrections in my work.

I have learnt that the "24-hour rule" is a good thing to employ if I find myself triggered emotionally to anger, especially in the workplace. The 24-hour rule is if you find yourself emotionally triggered where you want to tell someone that they are an idiot, do not act on that impulse immediately.

Wait for 24 hours, think about what is triggering you, and then after 24 hours if you still want to act, go ahead, but at least you have thought about it. I would like to say that I do this all the time, but I am human so sometimes I don't. I am pleased to say on this occasion, I did employ the 24-hour rule.

When I reviewed what the detective sergeant had done with a clear and impartial mind, I could see that he had done me a favour and his actions came from a good place.

He wanted me to improve my work.

For the last six years, no one bothered to do that for me. Instead of me acting emotionally and reacting in anger towards the detective sergeant and causing myself more embarrassment, I amended all the corrections and kept the corrections made by the detective sergeant as a guide for myself for future statements.

Reflections

When I look back on that moment and the actions of that detective sergeant, it was a defining moment for me as a leader, at whatever rank I held.

The actions of the detective sergeant in taking the time to review my work and to list the necessary corrections to get my work to an exceptional standard was a gift.

The gift was that the detective sergeant was showing me that he cared about me by improving the quality of my work.

I paid this act of caring forward for the rest of my career.

As a sergeant, I would review every brief of evidence that my staff submitted. Rather than return the statement to the constable without explanation, I would sit with them and talk it through.

I learnt to take this one step further. Every constable has several investigations or cases to work through, whether a uniformed constable or detective. As a sergeant, I normally had up to eight constables to supervise. Once a month I would sit down with each constable and go through their cases with them, to review their work and help them with strategies. Above all, I used this time to spend one-on-one with them, so they knew that they mattered and that I cared.

As an inspector, I would do the same process with the sergeants who reported to me, and as a superintendent, I would repeat the process with inspectors.

As you read this book you will see that sometimes I overreached and did reviews on issues that were outside of my sphere of responsibility, raising the ire of some by creating an impression that I was micro-managing.

I learnt that if I was critical in my reviews of someone's work, the only way to communicate that critique for improvement was to have a face-to-face conversation. On occasion, I did fail to have that face-to-face conversation, and without fail, it always ended badly. I only did it once, and I would never do it again.

The gift a leader can give their people is the knowledge and the feeling that the leader does care.

The simple act of spending one-on-one time with the people you are directly responsible for on a regular basis is a simple and honest strategy that is easy to do.

The detective sergeant who gave me back my statement covered in blue pen corrections, once I got over my own ego, gave me the greatest gift a leader can give. He showed me that he cared. The title of this book is all about courage. It would have been easy for the detective sergeant described in this chapter to not provide the level of critique that he did about my work. His day would have been the same, his pay would not change. Instead, he took the risk and he backed himself, knowing what quality he wanted his whole team to have, including me.

The final gift I took away from that experience was the detective sergeant had shown me firsthand how to do the job of a supervisor to a standard where I not only had my own work performance improved but I learnt what a good supervisor should do and how they should act.

Leadership is about empowering others to lead and showing people what leadership is. Someone is always watching what the leader does, they will either learn from you what to do or what not to do.

5

Executions (1998–2000)

After becoming a criminal investigator at Goulburn, I went on to have 14 years as a detective. I had a great time in this role from constable to sergeant as a detective. I worked in Goulburn and then in the city in places like Blacktown, in Task Force Oak which targeted Organised Asian Crime as part of the then Crime Agencies and the Region Special Operations Group targeting drug supply in Cabramatta, then Riverstone before getting promoted to detective sergeant at Bankstown.

There are countless stories as a detective but one of the jobs was Strike Force Helvetia.

A strike force or a task force is created in the NSW Police when something, normally a major crime or emergency has occurred, and that event needs a coordinated and structured response. For example, Task Force Oak was first formed when heart surgeon Victor Chang was murdered in the northern suburbs of Sydney.

Strike Force Helvetia was created in April 1998, to which I was appointed leader, after two men were executed in an organised crime hit in Allum Street, Bankstown. Seven men had lured two other men to a house on Allum Street and once there executed them. Five guns and a knife were used to kill two men. As a result of the mayhem, there were three blood trails leading away from the house. One man, the occupant of the house, remained there with a gunshot wound to the hip. His story was that he had killed one of the men in self-defence after he had been shot.

The occupant of the house, who claimed self-defence, was a giant of a man. He was of Albanian descent and was well known to law enforcement as a member of organised crime. He had previously been shot in the hip when he killed another man in the toilets at Sweethearts in Kings Cross, in a drug deal gone wrong. He also claimed self-defence for that incident and escaped conviction. This previous crime occurred prior to the royal commission into corruption in the NSW Police Force in the mid-1990s.

One of the investigators of the Sweethearts Toilets crime was well known to the Police Royal Commission. When I researched this crime, I found that the crucial photographs that demonstrated what had occurred in the toilets at Sweethearts that day were never shown to the jury, and the man claiming self-defence walked away free. Here he was again, with two dead men in his house, claiming the same self-defence story, with almost the same self-defence wound to the fleshy part of his hip, the inference being that this man shot himself to the hip both times to maximise his self-defence claims.

The two victims were lured to the home on Allum Street, and once inside were confronted by seven other men. One victim, the larger protector of the smaller man, was taken out first with a gunshot to his neck that paralysed and killed him almost instantly.

The smaller victim unknowingly came to a gunfight with a knife. He must have put up a real fight as he slashed one of his attackers severely opening his forearm with a serious laceration that required a weeklong stay at Liverpool Hospital. His associates dumped him at the front door of Liverpool Hospital as he was in such a bad way. The smaller victim was shot several times, and in the melee some of the other attackers were shot by their mates so they also required the medical attention.

At the time, I had never come across a crime quite like this one.

The crime scene was extensive, and all the names potentially linked to the crime were all high-level organised crime targets with no one talking about what really happened.

I oversaw a rather daunting crime that had significant law enforcement and media attention. I sat on the gutter outside the crime scene and took advice from a highly experienced detective sergeant in the homicide squad, who was a previous workmate of mine in the Randwick days, on what steps I would have to take. I filled quite a few pages of my official police notebook, in dot points, about what our team would have to do. Not something you see on any of the crime shows on television. You never see the lead detective sitting in the gutter, unless he is drunk.

I recall there was a flavour of "who cares" as the offenders and the victims involved were organised crime and they were only hurting each other. I looked at the situation through a different lens and saw an opportunity.

With some good detective work by a team of young and keen detectives from Bankstown, we had the opportunity to take out of commission a level of organised crime that had never really happened before. The names involved in this crime had always avoided serious convictions, and appeared to be untouchable. Key witnesses linked to these offenders in previous crimes either went missing, forgot their evidence or ended up dead somewhere, allegedly through their own misadventure.

I had the pleasure of working with one of the best detective sergeants there ever was: Lindsay McGillicuddy. Lindsay was one of the most methodical, energetic investigators that I had ever worked with. He had the ability to get the best out of young investigators because he invested his time into them and helped them excel in their chosen endeavours.

We chipped away for several months at this high-level organised crime execution. The irony was not lost on me. This crime occurred not long after the royal commission for corruption in the NSW Police Force was over. Before the royal commission, such a crime would have been done by the most experienced of teams, normally heavy drinkers with their own clique. Our up-and-coming investigators, made up of young men and women, did not fit the mould of "big city detectives" and would not get a look-in. They would be relegated to doing menial tasks like getting lunches.

Our young team did chip away despite the constant oversight and pressure to close down the strike force due to budgetary concerns. As the leader, I prepared a weekly one-page summary and budget statement that showed what we achieved, what the costs involved were and why we had to keep going. Thankfully, these one-page summaries did show what we were achieving, and we were allowed to keep on going. This had never been a requirement in investigations previously so this was a new challenge, but also an opportunity to highlight good work and why the investigation should continue.

As the investigation progressed, we identified that seven men had met up in a shop close to Scruffy Murphy's Hotel on Goulburn Street in the centre of Sydney, just off George Street, down from the Hoyts Cinema complex. This shop was owned by organised crime and was viewed as a secure location to meet. Through phone records we were able to track the progress of these seven men from the centre of Sydney to Canterbury, then Bankstown, then Liverpool near the hospital and back to the centre of Sydney. It took months to track down and speak to all the leads that flowed from the telephone records, but about seven months into the investigation we had the story of what had transpired.

The two victims had overstepped their entitlements around drug supply, and as such offended the wrong people and were arranged to be dealt with. At the house on Allum Street was a trailer, a roll of carpet and some lengths of rope. The purpose was to dispose of two people. We had intelligence that indicated our homeowner in Allum Street, the self-defence expert, was possibly an executioner who had taken other bodies to the National Park in Sydney and disposed of them.

When the two victims entered the house, after being lured there by the owner, they were set upon, and killed in an extremely violent way, not without real efforts to survive.

As a result of the efforts of the second smaller victim, one of the assailants was severely injured with a knife wound to his forearm. He was assisted from the Allum Street address with a blood trail leading away to a nearby street. This injured offender was taken to a unit block in Liverpool, but his injuries were too serious to be cared for by non-medical people so he was unceremoniously dumped at the front door of Liverpool Hospital not long after. Our investigation found out about this injured offender quickly. The linking of associates to those who had visited him in the hospital turned out to be very useful.

Another offender was shot in the bicep during the melee. It was a serious and incapacitating injury, but he never went into the hospital system. He was cared for by members of the outlaw motorcycle gang fraternity until he was well enough to get back into circulation. Once offenders started to recuperate, they nearly all ended up back at the shop near Scruffy Murphy's on Goulburn Street. Surveillance photos helped put names to telephone records and within a short time, we knew the seven men who were present to execute the two victims. DNA evidence helped place some of these offenders at the Allum Street crime scene.

When we started to investigate the intelligence around some of these offenders, their level of reach and influence at an international level was mind-blowing. We had pictures of two of our offenders meeting with the family members of Southeast Asian political leaders. What would two well-known Australian organised crime figures be meeting with political leaders' families for? We had intelligence of these two offenders having high-level organised and violent crime associations along with a high-end drug supply. The inference was scary but the opportunity our investigation offered was exciting.

As the investigation progressed and the opportunities presented themselves to make a serious dent in organised crime, the Commander of Organised Crime for Crime Agencies – of the Kalajzich/Manly Pacific murder fame and affectionately known as "The Snake" – asked me for a briefing of what we had. This commander was a very fair man and after I told him what evidence our team had, he asked Lindsay McGillicuddy and I to do a presentation to his boss, the Commander of Crime Agencies as Organised Crime was a unit that worked under the umbrella of Crime Agencies.

The purpose of this presentation was to seek approval for a joint strike force to be formed from our Bankstown detectives' office investigation and The Snake's larger organised crime team.

This wasn't a simple task. Anyone who knew the Commander of Crime Agencies at that time knew that he was not an easy man to present to. He had a reputation for being impatient and quick to anger, especially when the staff involved weren't from Crime Agencies.

I prepared the presentation which we perfected down to a 15-minute presentation of the evidence and the opportunity. The expected challenges came, the Commander of Crime Agencies did not let us down. He challenged us, got angry at us, and attempted to scare us but we answered the questions he asked with our knowledge of the evidence, and we succeeded in getting a joint strike force approved.

This was both a blessing and a challenge. Our young team of detectives from Bankstown was concerned that their more-experienced colleagues from Organised Crime in Crime Agencies would not value or include them in the investigation. I impressed upon our team that Crime Agencies could not ignore them or treat our team poorly. The reason was that our team was the holder of all the information, and only by working together inclusively and respectfully would a good outcome be achieved.

And that was what happened.

About eight months after the original crime occurred, in one 24-hour period, a strike force comprising of the Crime Agencies team and Bankstown detectives went out and arrested the seven men who were responsible for executing two victims at the house on Allum Street.

During those 24 hours, we secured evidence that led to all the offenders being refused bail and waiting for a lengthy court process. The Crime Agencies Team was led by Detective Senior Sergeant Paul Nolan. Paul was a conscientious, hardworking, fair man who treated our team with respect from the time we first met.

Lindsay McGillicuddy, Paul Nolan and I became a close-knit team who worked tirelessly and ethically to secure the conviction of the seven men involved, all the while maintaining the welfare and wellbeing of our team and our witnesses.

What flowed from that point on was like watching a movie.

Once our brief of evidence was received, via covert surveillance we received appraisals of our investigation from the organised crime figures involved. They knew it was a good brief, and unlike pre–royal commission police officers, the opportunity to corrupt us as investigators was not available.

Not long after that we received anonymous information that one of the offenders involved in the executions was seeking to take out a contract to kill Paul Nolan, Lindsay McGillicuddy and myself.

As a result of this evidence, all three of us were issued the authority to wear our firearms 24 hours a day. I have never seen this happen before or since. Our homes and private vehicles were fitted with the latest security measures and our families were given authority to have alias identities created in Drivers Licences and removed from electoral rolls. This rarely, if ever, happened so it was a big deal.

Court cases in NSW that involve jury trials become a partnership and have similarities to what we see on American television. The police investigate the crime, gather the evidence, charge the accused, and then put that evidence in its entirety to the Director of Public Prosecutions (DPP) Office.

When a jury trial is involved, a Crown Prosecutor is appointed. The Crown Prosecutor normally works with a solicitor from the DPP to help assist and manage the prosecution which can involve case conferences and pages of additional requisitions to obtain more evidence that the Crown Prosecutor believes is needed.

By the time this trial was approaching, I had been an investigator for many years. I had learnt that the success of any trial by jury depended on the relationships and trust the prosecution team had with each other.

If the prosecution team was cohesive, then it was a formidable team, but if it was fractured, then the defence would probe the weaknesses of the crown case and succeed in acquitting their clients. In the upcoming trial, we had seven defence teams, all consisting of at least one solicitor and one barrister, all with their own skills, traits and capabilities. We had to be better than good.

The prosecution team consisted of the Crown Prosecutor and their team and the police investigation team, which in our case was Paul Nolan, Lindsay McGillicuddy and myself.

Our Crown Prosecutor was Dan Howard, a dedicated gentleman who was both skilled and respectful. Dan Howard was the deputy Crown Prosecutor to the Backpacker Murders where several hitchhikers were picked up by Ivan Milat and taken to a nearby forest where they were executed. Dan Howard was also the head Crown Prosecutor to a recent high-profile Norfolk Island murder case. He was no slouch. He brought with him his own Deputy Crown Prosecutor, Nicole Noman, an excellent, intelligent, and sharp prosecutor who was an asset to our team and the DPP solicitor Steve Higgins, a tireless worker who handled volumes of work and was fun to work with. We all worked cohesively.

This court matter had twenty volumes of lever arched folders for evidence and an equal number of folders for background information relating to the investigation. Lindsay McGillicuddy and I knew this content backwards. I agreed to create a chronology of the evidence before, during and after the murders occurred, so that Dan Howard and his team knew what the evidence was, and where to find that evidence within the volumes that made up the crown case.

I supported this chronology with a spreadsheet that linked all the phone calls that led up to and after the murders so that the linkages between suspects, victims and witnesses could be established clearly next to the timeline. Through working this way, we gained each other's respect and worked cohesively together to get the best outcome we could possibly achieve.

Then came the Supreme Court trials. What a saga that was; again, stuff out of a movie.

Due to the level of organised crime involved, the fact that the majority of them were in custody, that some witnesses were in witness protection, that intelligence had been received that an attempt would be made on the way to, at or from court to help the offenders escape, we had to put in place a daily routine to protect the integrity and safety of the trial and all involved.

That meant the Special Weapons Operations Squad (SWOS) went to Silverwater Prison every day and escorted the prisoners to and from the court, fully equipped with every weapon they had available to them to deal with whatever issue arose.

Lindsay McGillicuddy and I, together with briefing the Crown Prosecution Team daily, had to brief an additional team of over 10 police officers rostered for additional security inside and outside the courthouse every day before court started.

On the very first day of the court case, we received confirmation in a very real way that the intelligence about an escape attempt was genuine. There was a stolen Toyota van – a large people mover – parked in the side street of the Downing Centre Courts, next to a set of disused glass doors that accessed the street, not far from the courtroom designated for our trial.

The court within the complex had been fitted with the necessary security measures, including bulletproof glass that covered the ingress and egress for persons in custody which barred access to the public areas of the courtroom itself.

Inside the court that day was another offender, not on trial, who had successfully organised his escape from custody at gunpoint in the very recent past on his way to court. This offender was now a free man, having done his time in custody, but having someone of that calibre and reputation in the court on day one of the trial was an unsettling experience. This offender was allegedly there to support his wrongly accused mates, but the coincidences were mounting up. As seen in any good detective movie, there is no such thing as coincidence, just evidence.

This court case went on for seven months with this procedure, oversight and risk strategies implemented every day the trial was on. In the end, we succeeded in securing the convictions of six of the seven men on trial for manslaughter, each receiving lengthy sentences.

The remaining man of the seven, the kingpin of the group had succeeded early on in securing a separate trial from his six co-conspirators. As it turned out about six months later, the kingpin had a three-month trial, which he lost, being found guilty of one count of murder and one count of manslaughter. All of the investigation team and prosecution team were there again for this three-month trial.

Some of the ironies that occur in criminal matters are so unique you can't make them up.

The barrister representing two of the key offenders was never paid in cash. He was paid instead by receiving a black BMW coupe. This was the same vehicle several of the offenders had driven to the crime in and was leased in the same entity as the organised crime shop near Scruffy Murphy's Hotel.

Two of the key offenders in these killings are now dead themselves. One by his own hand, walking into the ocean and shooting himself after crossing a line in the organised crime world. The second offender died in much the same way as his victim died when he brought a knife to a gunfight, gunned down in his own business by multiple offenders who had a score to settle.

Reflections

It was a privilege to be a part of such a unique, challenging and intriguing matter, and come out the other end with a good outcome because of the good work of a hardworking team who succeeded where others had not previously.

It would not be right to start naming all the investigators that achieved this outcome but, suffice to say, their collective expertise, diligence, pride and attention to detail brought about a result through hard, honest work.

Some were experts in the computer side of things and could access detail at the press of a button, some were so diligent with the volume of exhibits we had, and some were just young, solid, honest and hardworking investigators who provided us the complete picture.

When it came time for the arrest phase, some of the Crime Agency personnel were responsible for turning several offenders into witnesses against their peers. Not everyone has this skill but when this occurs, all the evidence that has been obtained has added weight because an offender-turned-witness can fill in the gaps.

Turning an offender into a prosecution witness, whilst a great asset to have, also brings challenges, especially with organised crime at this level. When one of their own provides prosecution evidence against them, the witness and their families can become targets for death.

This means our team must secure the new witness's placement in witness protection and take steps to ensure their safety at that time. There are no second chances. The importance of the information, the wellbeing of the witness and our staff are all crucial. We worked some long hours on this investigation. It is not easy to get a criminal involved in a double murder into witness protection. As an investigator you must know your stuff, your reputation and credibility are on the line if you vouch for the wrong offender who compromises the witness protection program.

The best thing about this group of investigators is that they did work together, using their collective skills to produce an outcome that someone acting alone or in silos could never achieve.

When I dig a bit deeper into my memories, I recall this investigation was a lot of work, probably two years of our lives. Lindsay, Paul and I, and a couple of other key team members spent seven months in the first trial and three months in the second trial focusing on this investigation and nothing else, living it, breathing it, owning it.

In a trial, at the end of every day, the Crown Prosecutor routinely had additional enquiries they want to be investigated and resolved before 9 am the next day since the trial continues at 10 am. For a two-week trial, this is not really a big deal, but for a seven-month trial, it was a massive commitment. This meant a lot of late nights, chasing down additional witnesses or documents that would allow the Crown Prosecutor to be satisfied before starting the next day of the trial. When you mix this with briefing an additional group of 10+ police for security measures inside and outside the court at 8 am each morning for each day of the trial, our days were very full.

For my own sanity and wellbeing, it was important that I did something for myself every day.

At the start and finish of every day, there was not really any time for myself except for lunchtime. The Downing Centre Court Complex is directly opposite Hyde Park, which is the gateway to the Botanical Gardens on the foreshores of Sydney Harbour.

Due to our security measures, I came to know the Sheriff's officers who were responsible for security at the Downing Centre very well. They allowed me to use their shower facilities in the courthouse every day. At lunchtime, I ran every day through Hyde Park, into the Domain, and down into Lady Macquarie's Chair and back again. To be out in the sunlight, looking at the best views in the world proved to be a saviour for my capacity to recover each day and maximise what I could deliver to this massive undertaking.

Not everyone does this or needs this, but I have found over my career that exercise is the circuit breaker that helps me deal with stress. If I exercise, nothing worries me, if I don't exercise, I find the smallest of stupid things can have the capacity to worry me when they should not. Whilst I did the run regularly, I could not go running when there was some pressing enquiry from our Crown Prosecutor that had to be done during the lunch break.

Recounting this chapter of my life with these amazing people focuses my thoughts on how good this team was, and I remember their level of excellence and comradery with fondness and pride.

The quote attributed to Margaret Mead at the front of this book is so relevant to what occurred in this investigation:

*Never doubt that a small group of thoughtful, committed citizens
can change the world; indeed, it's the only thing that ever has.*

There was a lot that went on before the jury delivered a verdict in the
seven-month trial. The prosecutor, the six defence barristers and the
judge all had their turns speaking to the jury about why their advice
is the best advice.

The poor jury must sit through this after seven months of
evidence. It was an excruciating process.

The jury recessed to commence their deliberations and after a
reasonable amount of time, they came back in and recorded six guilty
verdicts against the offenders for the manslaughter of both victims.

It's hard to quantify the feeling of that moment.

After nearly two years of investigative efforts, we had an outcome
against offenders who had never faced this level of judicial scrutiny
before. Up until that moment they had been untouchable.

Our small group of committed citizens, the police, the Director
of Public Prosecutions and all our witnesses had achieved a level
of justice for the victims who were executed so viciously, and we
changed the world for the offenders involved. They had always
avoided convictions in the past, but not this time.

After such a mammoth matter, I decided that I could never repeat
the teamwork and skills achieved in this investigation if I chose to
stay in this field of work. I had already spent over 10 years of my life
in this line of work, so it was time for a change.

I wanted to see if the relationship skills and resilience in the
investigations phase of my career would transpose into other spheres
of policing, to seek other challenges and other opportunities.

But when you walk away from what you know, sometimes you can
take a few steps backward before you go forwards again.

6

The Stalker (2002)

After leaving the world of criminal investigations I went on to do other things.

Some of those things that I chose to do were good, and some were not so good. These decisions all contributed to creating a mind space and a work ethic that helped mould the leader I ultimately became.

Those decisions put me face to face with a young lady who desperately needed my help due to a stalker.

One night I came into work to do my supervisor role in general duties. There had been several officers who had reported in sick, leaving our car crews short of staff. I was asked if I would fill the role of car crew. I was happy to do this as it gave me the chance to work for 12 hours with one of our young constables, and experience what they experience.

We went to several jobs and did them exactly how car crews do jobs, sharing the load, going job for job. Just because I was a sergeant didn't mean I wouldn't share the workload. It was my turn to do the next job. We went to this unit complex and met a young woman who had called the police due to problems she was having with an ex-boyfriend.

I remember this night vividly, more the feeling of this night. It was after midnight when we met the young woman at her front door, she was visibly distressed. She appeared withdrawn, and almost like she had given up. We asked if she was ok with inviting us into her home; as she looked so vulnerable, we didn't want to add to that angst. She was ok and we ended up sitting in the lounge room.

Over the next 30 minutes, the young woman told us of the debilitating horror she had been subjected to by her ex-boyfriend. She had ended the relationship over a month earlier due to his controlling and dominating behaviour.

She had sought an apprehended domestic violence order against him to create some distance between them, so she didn't have to deal with his coercive ways.

He lived with his parents in the inner west of Sydney, and they thought he could do no wrong. Since she had ended the relationship, she started to notice that everywhere she went he would turn up and be outside a café or fitness centre, or following her around in his car. He had been turning up at her home, knocking on windows just to unsettle her. It was working, I don't think I have ever seen anyone so broken. This ex-boyfriend stalked, harassed and intimidated her by his continued actions against her and towards her.

My partner and I had no doubt that this young lady needed help. It was just that the help we could give her was beyond what a car crew could provide that night, but we did put in motion things that could and did help this young woman.

From experience, I knew what we had to do, but a general duties car crew did not have the resources to do what needed to be done.

This type of offender needed to be caught in the act of stalking, and the evidence needed to be clear-cut, that his actions were intended to cause harm. This needed surveillance police to follow the ex-boyfriend around.

In those days, we are talking 2002, surveillance police were a scarce resource and would only be assigned to organised crime, murders and robberies. They would not be assigned to a domestic stalker, or if they were, it may take a month for that surveillance team to become free to do the job, and a month was too long for what was going on.

The job was made more challenging because our police station did not work in the inner west of Sydney. The job needed coordination. If this was 2023, there would be Domestic Violence Teams working at a regional level that targets serious domestic violence offenders, but this was 20 years before that resource ever existed.

Our police station had a proactive unit of plain-clothes police who wore t-shirts and jeans, drove around in unmarked cars, and did not look like police. They were led by a dynamic and experienced detective sergeant who had created a talented crew of young police that could do some good things, but what I wanted them to do wasn't their normal job. This was especially relevant in 2002 as domestics were seen as a first-response job and proactive police officers were not normally assigned to domestic violence cases.

I anticipated the objections to the job: it wasn't a proactive unit task. They go after property offenders and drug dealers, they don't do domestic offenders. That is normally a uniform job.

Once I described the job, the trauma of the victim, the expertise of the police required to place the offender before the court with the offence of stalking and win, the proactive team was on board and relished the opportunity to bring this stalking offender to justice.

It really did come down to the proactive team of police being tasked with this stalking offender that would convict him in court. The team followed the stalker who, whilst causing trauma to the victim, had no clue about surveillance tactics. He was clueless that he was leading a team of plain-clothes police around, videoing him, creating official records of his stalking behaviours to present to the court.

As our victim had described, the stalking offender was following her everywhere, with no excuse other than to intimidate and harass her.

The offender was arrested the first time, given strict bail conditions to not approach or harass the victim and had a hearing date set at court for his matter to be dealt with. As is often the case, this stalking offender vehemently denied the offences and was arrogant enough to continue his stalking behaviours against the victim after he was released on bail.

I think he believed that police from our police station would not go over to the inner west area again to follow him around after they had arrested him once. How wrong this stalking offender was?

The proactive team did follow the stalking offender whilst he was on bail and found him doing the same stalking behaviour towards the victim to harass and intimidate her. He was arrested again, this time refusing him bail, meaning he was in custody, sitting in a cell until the next time he went to court. We won the case, and the victim had a stalking-free life from this offender after the court matter was finalised.

By working together, we made a difference for this young stalking victim. I did receive a letter from this victim, through my boss, several months later. She thanked me for changing her life and making her feel safe again. As a police officer, you treasure that kind of letter, when you really did make a difference in someone's life.

Reflections

The outcome of putting the criminal in gaol when they were stalking a frightened victim is what policing is all about: the ability to make a difference in people's lives.

There is a good quote about the community and the police.

On average, community members will call the police once in their lifetime because they have a situation in which they do not know what to do and they need the help of the police.

When that phone calls come, we as police should not let those people down.

Our decisions in our careers and life give us skills. Sometimes, those skills meet up with an opportunity to do some good.

I am not saying I did anything exceptional, but chance put me in the lounge room of that stalking victim in 2002 when she needed help, beyond what was normally possible for a general duties car crew.

My life and career experiences, rolling with the wins and losses of life, put me in a position to negotiate an outcome for that stalking victim that would not normally be possible in 2002.

The opening two pages of this book have two quotes, one about the results of leadership actions and the other by Margaret Mead.

> *Never doubt that a small group of thoughtful, committed citizens can change the world; indeed, it is the only thing that ever has.*

On that night for our stalking victim, a small group of committed people didn't change the world, but we did change our victim's world. It is rewarding to be a part of that outcome.

The courage of the victim should not be understated given her level of fear. She was terrified. The level of courage it took our victim to call out for help, the night we turned up at her door, was exceptional. When you see that level of courage, you do everything you can to help them.

By the time I was in that young woman's lounge room, and we orchestrated a policing response, I had had a lot of good and not-so-good things happen to me.

I had been successful in winning an inspector's promotion to a role that I had never done before, but which I possessed the skills to do. As was the way in 2002, promotions to inspector were appealable. The incumbent officer for that position appealed against my promotion, and the convenor for the promotion process chose his own staff member over me, an outsider.

I wasn't the only person to lose their promotion to inspector under the promotion system at the time, as that was what the appeals process was all about, but to say it didn't hurt would be a lie.

It was totally up to me how I reacted to this setback in my life.

I didn't carry on like a spoilt child, I always remained professional.

I went back to work and whilst given the opportunity to stay in the same unit as a sergeant I was seeking a new challenge.

I decided to write my own story, looking for the next opportunity.

That was how I ended up as a uniform sergeant supervising the first-response police car crews in western Sydney. That was my next career choice: learn how to supervise our first-response car crews on the street and provide them with whatever help and leadership I could, and at the same time learn operational tactics and skills from them. They taught me more than I ever taught them. I needed to learn some new skills and see if the skills I had already developed would be able to help the people I worked with.

I was seeking to make a career in leading people.

I think leaders should know how to lose.

Leaders who have had setbacks and learn from those setbacks become better leaders.

Those setbacks help leaders to empathise with others on their team who also face setbacks.

From the way I looked at the experience I had just been through, I had been selected for a promotion to a role I had never done before. The appeals process reversed that decision.

I was happy that I had the goods to be selected, and my unsuccessful experience in the appeals process was also a positive. I had learnt what the appeals process was all about should I be selected for another inspector's position.

It was only a matter of time till I would win and secure a permanent inspector's role. Whilst I was waiting for that opportunity to come along, I chose to maximise the worth I had in a workplace by putting to good use the skills I already possessed.

Part 2

Earning Stripes

One of the most important things you do as a leader is to build others up. Leadership isn't about you. It's about how effective you are at empowering other people – and making sure that this impact endures, even in your absence. Leadership is not worrying about your own advancement, but in the relenting focus on other people's potential.

Unleashed, **Frances Frei and Anne Morriss**

7

My First Experience at Empowering Others to Lead (2003–2005)

Between 1996 and 2005, my wife left the NSW Police to do what a lot of women do when their unsupportive husband is too busy working and too busy to come home.

A lot of women who have to care for young children but who still maintain a career are often left with the reality that their working husband and/or partner considers their own career far too important to come home and share the responsibility of caring for their children.

My wife totally had that type of husband in me. My wife was one hundred percent responsible for the care of our children. I was simply a toad.

I am not proud of what I did then, and I will spend a lifetime making up for the selfish man I was then.

My wife and I had just had our second child, our daughter, in 1996.

The NSW Police were in the middle of the Police Royal Commission. Some workplaces had been broken apart and were in the process of a restructure. My wife worked at one of these places, where sections had some police charged with corrupt behaviour. Because of this organisational change, she had no idea where her new workplace would be or who her boss would be to arrange a part-time plan to work and care for our children.

At the time I was a detective sergeant at Bankstown prior to Strike Force Raptor existing. That was created by the executive of the NSW Police about 15 years later to deal with organised crime and violence spilling into the community from Middle Eastern crime gangs. When I was a detective sergeant, there was no such strike force in existence. It was a busy time, and I was a husband who was always at work, and I am ashamed to admit that I did not realise what my wife was giving up.

My former self in 1996 thought it was a good idea for my wife to leave her 15-year career to look after our family. The 2023 me would never let that happen, but that realisation is 27 years too late.

Time, maturity and educating myself about equality in the workplace and the home have led me to have a totally different outlook, especially over the last 10 years.

Raising a family is a partnership. Partnerships are an equal entity, not a lopsided affair. Both partners in a relationship with children should work together so that the other does not feel responsible for most of the work at home, whilst the other forges ahead with their career. There should be and can be balance if commitment is made to achieve and maintain that balance. That conversation on true equality and diversity is another book that I intend to write, as both men and women should be equal contributors to the work-and-home balance. I made the wrong choice in 1996.

After my wife left the NSW Police, her skills and expertise were noticed by an executive sales director for Nutrimetics, a skincare company in Australia that runs home parties, similar to Tupperware.

My wife quickly excelled in this business, building a strong team, developing other leaders, and achieving incentive rewards from the company that included company cars and overseas seminars. She refers to this time in her life as a time when she got her innocence back, going into people's homes to sell them makeup, instead of going there to arrest people or worse.

Due to my wife's level of success in this business, I was fortunate to go on several overseas seminars. At those seminars, Nutrimetics acquired the services of some amazing speakers on leadership. I had never seen this approach before. The NSW Police did not use anything like this level of leadership training to develop their people in 2003.

When I returned to Sydney from one of these seminars, I approached my boss. I asked her if she would allow me to run a three-month leadership workshop for young police officers if they wanted to be part of it.

I agreed that we would conduct the workshop outside of work time and it would be voluntary. We ran one 3-hour session each month with some quality guest speakers both external and internal to the NSW Police.

We had six officers volunteer for the process.

Some influential speakers agreed to be a part of the workshops as I had worked with them at various stages of my career, and they were happy to support my leadership development initiative. These speakers included two deputy commissioners and the Australian Director of Nutrimetics. I included presentations on goal setting and teamwork, along with public speaking. We did the workshops across the road from the police station in the Council Chambers.

I conducted the first leadership workshops in 2003. The feedback from this was extremely positive. The goal of the workshops was to awaken participants with what was possible and empower them to be leaders themselves. When you hear recognised leaders tell their stories, people realise that with a bit of planning, good relationships and support, they can write their own stories and become leaders who empower other leaders.

I was promoted to chief inspector not long after and ran two more leadership workshops in 2004 and 2005. This time the workshops went for 6 months, one 8-hour day each month and my new boss allowed me to run them during work hours.

From 2004 onwards, each workshop had at least 20 participants with the Commissioner of Police or their appointed representative being the guest speaker for the final day.

The most rewarding thing about these leadership workshops is that they were a two-way exchange.

Whilst I imparted and influenced a lot of people in their leadership careers, the participants and other speakers also influenced the path of my life and helped me become a more rounded person.

My goal-setting presentation was all about work–life balance, it did not solely deal with work as it also dealt with relationships, health, educational development, financial development, and spiritual development at a religious or mindfulness level.

I found my work relationships exposed me to different leaders who I admired and who I knew had a story to tell that people would get a lot from.

One such leader turned out to be one of my longest and closest friends but it did not start out that way.

As a chief inspector at Penrith, I was given the crime portfolio of assaults. When I reviewed the assaults in our area, I saw that one of the large local clubs had the greatest number of assaults than any other establishment. And when I looked state-wide, they had the largest number of assaults for any club per month in NSW.

I met with the security manager responsible for this club. When I reviewed how this person and their team managed their staff and their work environment, I was blown away by their skill base and professionalism. Despite the number of assaults each month, each assault had been captured on CCTV and reviewed with the guards involved on how they could improve their performance next time. I had never seen this level of skill or review anywhere before, certainly not in the police.

What I did identify was that the club, with high-capacity crowds, aimed to achieve profits through bar sales. This was 2004 so Responsible Service of Alcohol was not really a thing back then and an Independent Liquor and Gaming Authority did not exist. By filling crowds with alcohol in a crowded environment, a simple bump could turn into a fight or brawl very quickly.

I remember I told the security manager, despite evidence of good practice in some areas, they would continue to receive the attention of police if they did not change the crowds they were attracting.

It was just starting to become a trend in some large clubs and hotels to focus on making venues family-friendly by targeting meals rather than high alcohol sales to reduce their risk and insurance premiums and increase their profits.

The security manager was not happy. He had never had his practices questioned before. They were one of the biggest clubs in the state and he did not like me, the new police inspector in town, changing the way things were done.

The security manager is a big man, he used to be a security guard during the 1970s and 1980s when you only survived because you could outdo the other guy physically. It was not a pleasant exchange.

I gave him space to calm down and later that day I spoke to him.

I thought we could work together to reduce the assaults if he was genuine in his attempts to work with the police. I respectfully shared with him that I was shocked that someone with his obvious leadership skills had reacted to my review of the assaults at his club in such an aggressive way.

He looked at me again, and I wondered what I have I done in raising this issue with this guy. I asked him if he ever read the book *Emotional Intelligence* by Daniel Goleman. I told him that I had found the book invaluable in reviewing my impact on others and it helped me improve my relationships with others by improving what I did.

This security manager, now my friend, did take on board this advice, and over time we realised we had so much more in common than we had differences. We learnt this by treating each other respectfully and learning about the skills and work environments we both worked in. Our experiences were remarkably similar, just in different workplaces.

From 2004 to 2020, my friend was a presenter at every leadership workshop that I led and facilitated, with scores of participants benefiting from his story and ethics in leadership.

I have learnt so much from participants in those workshops both in terms of work and at a personal level.

After one of my presentations on goal setting in the 2004 workshop, one of the young constables came up and gave me some information about an investment property workshop he had just recently done to build wealth at a personal level in preparation for retirement as an addition to superannuation.

The investment property workshop was familiar as one of my wife's uncles had also done it. From that simple conversation with that young constable, my wife completed the investment property workshop, and together we went on to research and buy several properties on the eastern seaboard of Australia in capital cities and large rural towns.

That decision has set us up as a family, to be comfortable in our retirement, highlighting that leadership exists at all levels and is a two-way thing and is not just a work-related thing. That financial decision also taught our own children how to approach investing as a worthwhile strategy.

I remember having the Commissioner of Police speak at the 2005 leadership workshop to close the six-month program. It is amazing to watch this level of CEO speak to frontline people. It is like watching fans worship a rock star. The young constables wanted his autograph in their workshop notes. In 2005, before smartphones were the norm, the ability to take "selfies" was not a thing so the autograph was still the most prized commodity you could get from someone.

I recall when he was signing his autograph for a young constable, he looked at me and told me he had signed his name on my appointment as a commander for my first command and told me where I was going before he was supposed to.

When I was promoted to superintendent in 2005, my superiors knew what I could do in the leadership space. They asked me to run a two-day leadership workshop for supervisors and inspectors for three remote commands. I organised the event at a university in the northern part of NSW. I secured some quality speakers, a high-level fire and rescue commander, and my friend who was now the general manager of a large western Sydney club. There were up to 30 participants at this two-day leadership forum, which included a first-night semi-formal dinner where everyone could relax and mingle.

Reflections

I realised that I had a passion for empowering others to lead and the leadership development workshops had become part of my annual to-do list, to identify and develop new leaders every year. There is nothing more satisfying than seeing future leaders realise their potential to empower others. It is an additive thing to be part of. The more leaders you empower to become leaders themselves, the more leaders they empower. The effect just grows.

The people you meet along the way can and do impact your entire life. That young constable I met who gave me some advice about the investment workshop in 2004 changed our lives. Because of the financial lessons we learnt in 2004 and onwards, our position in 2023 is considerably different from what we could have ever imagined.

Whilst I have never been a financial management expert, each year that I have run the leadership workshops I always talk about work–life balance and the importance of having financial knowledge and independence. In today's age of social media, I regularly see posts about a new investment property or some other investment strategy by former participants of our leadership workshops who are forging their way to achieving financial independence and security. It's wonderful to have been a small part of that journey.

As addictive and satisfying as it is to influence the empowerment of other leaders, I was to learn a valuable and painful lesson. It is not possible to run leadership development workshops if your role as a leader is being distracted by your own performance. I was just about to learn the hard way, that you can't influence anyone in a positive manner if you are failing as a leader.

8

The Good, the Bad and
the Ugliness of Failure
(2005–2007)

This chapter is where the anonymous email at the start of the Introduction to this book becomes relevant.

Before I commence this part of our lives, I will bring you up to date with where we were at as a family at this time.

Kerrie, my wife rejoined the NSW Police part of their Rejoinee Programme in 2005.

This program allowed previous members of the NSW Police to rejoin at their old rank, for Kerrie this was a 'barred' Senior Constable, denoting her 15 years service.

When I was promoted to my first Command as a Superintendent - Police Commander in Western New South Wales, we chose to move the family there, and Kerrie received a 'spousal transfer' by the NSW Police.

What happened to my wife and our 9 year old primary school daughter at this time of our lives, is their story to tell.

This chapter outlines the unintended consequences that can happen when, as a leader, you make decisions that challenge the status quo and create uncertainty. My first command as a superintendent was in the far west of NSW, about eight hours from Sydney. When I arrived there, I was keen to make a difference and was too impatient to introduce new things.

I had been a working detective from 1989 to 2002. As technology started to improve and individual recording devices became more reliable and smaller, I used a personal recorder to record interactions with suspects away from the police station, saving me hours of court time as the conversations were there for all to hear.

I purchased over 20 micro-USB voice recorders for this new command. They were a very compact reliable device that could be carried in a police shirt pocket and used when needed. Some police saw the value in the strategy but take-up was poor with the main reason being a reluctance to change.

The second reason that got traction to not use the recorders was the belief of some staff that I didn't trust the police officers, so I wanted them to record each interaction they had on the street. This was never the case, but such is the resistance to change that facts do not come into consideration.

One night, I decided to get away from the minutiae of being a police commander and wanted to experience what staff were faced with on a Friday night shift at this remote command. I was working with a senior constable, who was the external supervisor, when a nasty job came over the police radio.

An external supervisor is deployed in a normal police sedan, and their job is to essentially go to all the jobs the car crews go to, to provide them with oversight and support.

I believed it was important I worked with our people to understand their environment. We were on our way to a very bad accident about 20 kilometres out of town. When we got there, it became obvious how serious the job was.

I let the supervisor do his thing and run the job. I had a conversation with the driver of the car involved in the accident. I recorded that conversation using one of the audio recorders, with the driver's consent to get his version of events, including admitting to driving and what happened.

That was the only time the driver elected to speak to anyone about what happened and the evidence I obtained that night saved lengthy court proceedings for family and friends.

I highlighted the positives to our staff showing what was possible with the audio recorders, but the message was not getting through. Staff was still reluctant to use the audio recorders in their work as they feared change and feared me.

I would learn that these skills that got me the position of commander would not keep me there.

I did not know what I did not know.

The skills and attributes that allowed me to be successful in securing a promotion to superintendent would not help me be successful at that rank.

As a sergeant and inspector, I was well-known for leading from the front, challenging the status quo, and being prepared to implement change if change needed to happen.

As a superintendent, I had to empower others to do these things. I was clueless as to what would happen if I continued to lead as I had done before. I didn't have the maturity as a leader to know the fallout if I continued to do as I had always done.

As a leader at my level, I had direct reports that were the leaders I relied on to get things done. If I did these things myself, I was signalling, unintentionally, that I didn't trust them to do their job. I was soon seen as a nuisance for changing things up unnecessarily.

When I was a sergeant or an inspector, I always had the support or protection of other leaders above me. When I as the leader implemented change without the support or backing of other leaders around me, I was effectively putting a target on my back and gaining a negative reputation, no matter how good my intentions were.

I have always looked to see how technology can assist us in our work. In 2005, technology in policing wasn't great but it was just starting to show promise.

During my time as a sergeant and an inspector, I learnt how to monitor a whole command, team and individual performance in a pretty simple way. This involved using existing police systems within the police computer network to review performance and provide a snapshot in time of how things were going on a monthly basis. I converted that data to an Excel spreadsheet so the sorting functions could be used across a team, section and individuals. When I introduced the same process to this new remote location it was not well received.

It was viewed as meddling, unnecessary and a sign of distrust. The process I had created, although nothing earth-shattering, wasn't being done at many other locations.

The monthly performance monitoring was something new; it was change, and people fight change especially if there is too much change happening too quickly.

Poor performers can become very noisy, and the system I introduced shone a light on poor performers and more importantly who their supervisors (sergeants) were, and by association who their managers (inspectors) were.

When you have the evidence that there is a poor performer, there is nowhere to hide; you have the data, the evidence, and there is an identified poor performer who has a supervisor and a manager. What is everyone doing about it?

When I introduced this type of confronting change, without the right introduction, support or backing, I just made the target on my back even bigger. I had implemented change far too quickly and effectively made myself a leader of one: me.

The independent reviews of the command performance, prior to my arrival as the new commander, were extremely poor. Using this new style of monthly performance monitoring quickly turned performance around at a global level. But there was a lot of resistance, nervousness and uncertainty amongst staff who did not want the system interfering with how things were always done in the past.

I had not done a good job of explaining the why and bringing people along with me. There was too much change occurring too quickly. Added to this I was the only one who knew how to do the monthly review process using the police systems. I hadn't taught my direct reports how to do the process, so they were not on board, supporting and defending the process. I was trying to lead and effect positive change on my own. A cardinal error, all because I was too keen, too impatient.

People need to know why.

The location had over 100 police and provided policing to 15 police stations across a wide area that covered two to three hours in all directions. Part of my job was to visit those locations and build a supportive relationship with those men and women who worked at these other police stations, doing whatever I could achieve to make their lives a bit easier.

Most of these satellite locations only had a single officer working from there or at most two or three officers. This meant that I was regularly on the road travelling to one of these locations away from the main station, where most of the people of influence, good and bad, worked from.

Our area also had a large First Nations population in various sectors. In some of those sectors, the relationship between the police and the First Nations community was good, but it was very poor in others. I made a commitment to those communities where things needed to improve. I visited them monthly, listened to their concerns and, together with them and other government partners, worked together to improve relationships and outcomes.

The challenge in some of these First Nations communities where relations were not great with the police was because there were individuals who had encounters with law enforcement frequently. Some of these encounters were physical, and allegations of assault were made against the police which converts to complaints and lengthy court hearings. We are speaking about 2005. The body cameras that police wear today were not in use in Australia.

At the same time, again oblivious to how my actions and decisions would be received, I did a couple of other things that just made the target on my back even bigger.

The NSW Police had been through a royal commission about corruption in the mid-1990s. Most of this corruption was around unethical relationships with organised crime but there was an underlying issue with poor police culture and the prevalence of alcohol in the workplace. Alcohol had not been allowed on police premises since the mid-1990s in Sydney.

When I got to my new location as commander, within the first week I was invited to Friday afternoon drinks at a section of the police station where the detectives, prosecutor and inspectors would meet me to celebrate my arrival at the station. When I advised them that I was grateful for the invite, but informed them the beer fridge would have to go and could not return, I never got another invite of that nature. I didn't even think about the ramifications for me, but I would later see the fallout.

A member of staff, who I as the leader had to rely on, proved to be unreliable at a leadership level on several occasions in the early stages. I had a direct conversation with the person involved. I told the person that I did enjoy working with them, but their level of unreliability was an issue. Their unreliability did not stem from a lack of education or ability, it was a choice. I gave that person a choice. Their level of chosen unreliability could have career-damaging outcomes for them. They could choose a different path and work with me, or if they did not want to work with me, I would support a transfer for them. The person chose to be transferred and sought out their own move.

This person was an integral member of the new remote command. I thought I had handled this issue fairly. I believed I could not disclose the content of the conversation between us to anyone else, as it was their private issue, not a public one. In hindsight, that level of privacy hurt me. I had come into their tight-knit remote group and removed one of their people.

The normal way of things at remote locations was when new bosses came in, staff who intended to live there for a long time waited the new boss out. When the next boss came in, the process started again. I had just changed that scenario.

I was the new leader in my first command role, I was looked upon as a city boy who did not know how staff at a remote country location could pull together. I was ignorant of how vulnerable I was.

Sometimes, circumstances dictate that you have to commit to the change anyway but, in hindsight, the lesson I learnt is when you implement change that will be resisted, do whatever you can to ensure you have support so you are not implementing the change on your own. Because I was attempting to bring about change too quickly, I was on my own. If I had a strong leadership team with me, I would have been protected by that team as they would have been making the changes with me.

Sometimes, I had to be the leader and stand up for what was right. I had an instance where sections of our leadership team were making anti-women statements like, "Over my dead body will a part-time policewoman ever be an acting sergeant." Something like this could not be allowed to remain unchallenged, but you cannot fight a war on your own.

Every little change I had implemented, whether good or bad, was viewed as part of the whole package encompassed in the reputation I was making for myself as the new leader of this command. That reputation was bad. When you have a bad reputation, most people walk away from you, very few support you even if they like you.

Despite all the good things we had happening in this new remote command, my personal reputation was bad and everything I did was viewed through that lens. I made the decision to offer to transfer back to Sydney to resolve the situation. I made contact with human resources to make this happen. I was told that the only way I could be transferred back to Sydney was for me to be demoted from superintendent back to inspector. Demotion normally occurs when you have a sustained complaint against you for untruthfulness, criminal behaviour or serious mismanagement. But none of those things had occurred as the command was performing well and continuing to do so with the changes we had implemented. I elected to stay.

The distractions just kept on coming from this point on. It is not reasonable for me to go into what all these distractions were, but how I chose to deal with these distractions only solidified the target on my back making it nearly impossible to lead with any authority. It was nearly unbearable to live like this. I found I could not effectively lead given the level of uncertainty about what the next issue would be, all I was really doing was surviving.

I can't begin to describe what this level of pressure and failure does to you as a leader. All the strengths and attributes I had as a leader going into this position were no longer there during 2006 and 2007. I doubted myself, lacked any kind of courage and was battling to keep my head above water.

Perhaps one of my most shameful experiences during this time was an audit review of our command, and reporting as a leadership team in front of the Commissioner of Police and his executive team.

This process has changed a lot over the years but back then an Audit Team of Inspectors and other experts came to our command and reviewed everything from crime, systems, including human resources, and finances to our links with the community. The report that was produced about a command is about 70 pages long.

I recall this audit report vividly.

The first five to ten pages of the report were scathing, reporting how badly our command was performing. That was the direct first impression you would get if you read the audit report. I was shocked as I knew the results reported were not true.

When I re-read the report, in those first five to ten pages I could see the report was reporting on the previous audit review a couple of years earlier. It was only later in the audit report, from page 10 onwards, that the results we were achieving in 2006 to 2007 were discussed but you had to go looking to find that data. The first impression you got was that the command was failing dismally. I recall my direct superiors at the time asked if I had done anything to upset the audit team leader as the report was slanted to make our command and I look bad.

When we sat in front of the Commissioner of Police and his executive team, I knew if the hits came no one would be coming to my rescue.

As soon as the Commissioner of Police started with his view of the audit review of our command, I could see he was angry and disappointed. He said something like, *"We have never seen anything so bad."* Once this negative momentum starts, it takes someone forthright to change it.

Everyone at the executive table had their say, including my direct boss, an assistant commissioner. He did nothing to support a different view. Allan in 2006 and 2007 was not the same commander as he was in 2020. I was broken and just treading water, quite often gulping in water, not air. I did not speak up for myself or our command. I was and still am ashamed of Allan the Commander in 2006 and 2007. The

Commissioner had to leave shortly after his withering comments for something more urgent than a failing command.

When you get a pillaring like this in front of your executive team, you end up sitting at the table on your own. Everyone shrinks away from you, and no one wants what you have to offer. My boss did come over and speak to me, sharing his views that the experience was bad, but he would speak to me later.

We had spoken before about the inaccuracies and the poor layout of the audit report for our command. My boss did know that the results in the first 10 pages were related to the previous audit reports on our command and not the current one.

My boss looked at me and said, "You know you are right, the Commissioner got it wrong, but we won't be telling him he got it wrong, he's the Commissioner."

In the second season of *The Crown* where Gillian Anderson plays the role of Margaret Thatcher, the first female British Prime Minister, there is a scene that I could totally relate to: Prime Minister Thatcher has just been told by her all-male political party that she no longer had their confidence, and they were going to remove her from the role.

The act was treacherous and well-planned and the Prime Minister, although a skillful political leader, could do nothing about it. Prime Minister Thatcher behaved with dignity and accepted the outcome, leaving the parliamentary rooms and returning to her home.

The next scene sees Prime Minister Thatcher walking through her home, acknowledging all her support staff in a very dignified manner, before entering her bedroom. Once in her bedroom, Prime Minister Thatcher is a real person. She dissolves into a ball on the floor, crying in despair, rocking back and forward.

I have been that human being and it was at the hotel when we were returning from this audit review in front of the Commissioner. Our command was eight hours from Sydney so we, the leadership team of our command, only made it halfway home that night. We had dinner together and then returned to our separate rooms.

As soon as I got into my room on my own, I curled up on the bedroom floor, crying quietly in despair, rocking away the pain. I had never felt such shame and failure. It was devastating.

This only happened twice, once in that hotel room and the other in our family home.

My wife found me in our home, as I always did my best to be strong around her. She had never seen me like this, the pressure was getting to me, and I did need mental health support. She got on the floor with me, and we hugged each other for a long time, consoling each other at the situation we found ourselves in, and assuring each other that we would find a way through this period of our lives.

Despite how bad some parts of this time of my life were, it was not all bad. We lived on a magnificent rural property 40 kilometres out of town. It was a 4,000-acre property that used to be a sheep farm and was now used to farm cotton and other rural crops in large sections.

The property had a magnificent homestead with gardens that would rival a large country town central park. The lawns were huge, and they took me eight hours to mow with a large front-deck mower that had nearly a three-metre cutting width. It was called the Red Roo. The Red Roo relied on three big rubber belts to make it work, like a fan belt in a car. I had to learn to regularly change these belts when they broke in the middle of the paddock somewhere. There were hedges around the entire homestead that would take me a whole day to hedge with a petrol-driven hedger. I loved the work as it was so different from my challenging leadership role.

The property was situated on the junction of two major rivers and was an icon of the area. The owners lived in England and rented it out to suitable tenants. A police commander and his family were deemed to be suitable tenants. The property had a large swimming pool in which we did the occasional skinny dipping as we were in the middle of nowhere, until one day a crop-dusting plane saw us and buzzed us for awhile waving to us.

Inside the home was just as awe-inspiring. It had a massive lounge room the size of a large country town hall where dances can be held. The dining room has this massive antique timber table with 14 red leather-bound chairs, it was palatial.

The property had a butcher shop building, with its own walk-in butcher's refrigerator. This was excellent for family Christmas when over 20 relatives turned up.

We had an amazing life on that property. My wife and I had been horse-riding eventers for several years in Sydney. Eventing is like the Olympics where you see rider and horse do dressage, cross-country jumping and then show jumping. In the Olympics, the jumps can be well over five feet high. We never took on anything that extreme but the buzz of riding a horse at a gallop and jumping fences is something to be experienced.

We had two ex-racehorses that we trained to be pretty good horses, with the help of some experienced riders. My wife's favourite experience on the farm was to be able to gallop her horse, Utah, for 30 minutes in a straight line without hitting a fence. Not something you can do in many places.

One of our favourite experiences with the horses came around our final Christmas in that command. A drover from Northern Territory brought 1,000 head of cattle across the river into our property when my wife was home on her own. He asked her for permission to bring those cattle through our property and onto the *"long paddock"*, the main road.

This guy was a legend, and he came back and helped me with my horse to make him more manageable. After he got my horse to be at fingertip control with me riding him, he tasked my wife and I to ride up the main road a few kilometres and bring back five wayward cattle from his mob that had been separated from the main herd. We had a ball and will never forget the experience.

At Christmas, I had some leave planned when a relieving inspector from Dubbo came up and looked after the command for a two-week period. I also took the opportunity to look after my own mental health during this time and sought professional support without ever taking sick leave.

I received a phone call at home whilst still on leave. It was not from my boss but a senior public servant in the human resources command in Sydney. She had been given the job of advising me that I was no longer the commander of this remote command. I was to report to another assistant commissioner on level 4 of the Police Headquarters in Parramatta in 14 days.

I was not to return to my office or the command and if I needed to pack my office it was to be done under the supervision of the acting commander, an inspector from another command. The interesting thing about this whole period was probably the worst ever time in my life as a police officer. I had never been formally counselled for any wrongdoing, I was not on a performance plan or remedial plan of any kind. I was just that commander who failed.

We have a life and everything that comes with life.

We had three horses that we had to find homes for. We had to find schooling for our daughter back in Sydney. We had to decide what we were going to do with our son's schooling. He was just about to commence Year 12. He was in a boarding school in another town, several hours from Sydney. Do we take him back to Sydney and let him restart at his old school, or do we leave him in his new school where he had forged new friendships and new experiences? We included him in this decision, and he decided to stay put rather than change schools again.

We had to find another house to live in Sydney, as we had tenants in our own home who were on a long-term lease. We had to arrange removalists. We had to break our lease on the property we were staying, with potential exit fees.

One of the first things I did when I received this news was to author a professional email to my staff and the whole command advising them that I had received the unexpected news of transferring back to Sydney for another opportunity that the NSW Police were keen for me to do.

I thanked the staff for their support and listed all the things we had done together, and the fact that the command was soon to be at full strength for the first time in many years due to all the recruiting we had done. It was an exciting time and one I regretfully would not be there to see and help steer in the final changes we had set up. I wished everyone well and thanked them for their support. I later learnt whilst some cheered that I was going, several people cried.

Reflections

The experience showed me that no matter what my intentions were, good or bad, life will throw up challenges. I can honestly say that I have never been so challenged. I was at my wit's end, very seriously thinking about giving it all away and leaving the police forever, but something deep inside me would not let me do this.

No matter how I looked at the situation, I had failed at my first attempt at true leadership. That was difficult to accept, but I had to accept it.

I had made mistakes and those mistakes had not only affected me personally, but they had also affected my family, my staff and the community for better or worse.

As a police command, we had so many good things going on in the town. But the distractions of those who wanted me gone, who I had not taken the time to build a better relationship with, had succeeded in removing me from the town.

It was a bitter pill but if I was going to become a better leader, I had to learn to navigate these challenges a whole lot better.

9

Write Your Own Story (2007)

I was never officially told face-to-face why I was transferred from that remote location back to Sydney.

To the community and the rest of the NSW Police Force, my name was included in an email from the Commissioner of Police detailing the transfer of seven commanders. The Commissioner thanked all of us for our ongoing contributions and looked forward to seeing what we would achieve in our next endeavours. This email helped me explain to our real estate agent why we had to leave our rural rental property early and they generously waived the exit fees.

I learnt my fate upon my return to Sydney. I was to be what we call in the NSW Police the *"Officer in Charge of Corridors"*.

On my first day in this role, I was picked up at home by a peer of the same rank, someone I thought I knew well. I trusted her. She asked how I was and why I was back in Sydney. I gave a summary of what had happened and how it was a torrid time, that I wanted to move on.

Imagine my surprise when I later met with the assistant commissioner who had been tasked with managing me. I was given a dressing down, that I had no right to complain about anything and gave a word-for-word review of the discussion I had with my "trusted" peer on the way into work in that short car trip for my first day as Officer in Charge of Corridors.

I discovered how cutthroat the higher ranks of the NSW Police behaved. It was very alarming. If we treated each other this way, how could our people ever trust us? It was obvious in a lot of workplaces that you couldn't trust anyone, but I couldn't believe a workplace could be like that. I made a conscious decision that I would create safe, supportive and inclusive workplaces where people could trust each other. I would make that my focus. It seemed like a worthwhile goal.

That officer who betrayed my trust that day colleague-to-colleague is a very senior officer now. Sometimes you must accept people doing interesting things, but you do not have to replicate that behaviour. You must be able to look at yourself in the mirror and live with yourself.

Our lives are not all about work and when we find ourselves in a horrible work environment, we have the capacity and power to make the other parts of our lives more fulfilling.

At the time, I had an unfinished master's degree in public administration (policing) and my wife and I were on the lookout for some more investment properties to add to our portfolio. So, whilst I was the Officer in Charge of Corridors, I knew that role wouldn't last forever.

I put my personal time to good use by finishing my master's degree, and from that, I was asked to contribute to a chapter published in a Police Management Educational Book on Performance Management. I also bought several more investment properties in Brisbane and Melbourne for our family's future financial security.

When I returned to Sydney, I learnt that someone I had trusted as a peer and confided in whilst I was working in that remote area of NSW had conducted an entire investigation into allegations against me with only one side of the story, without ever interviewing me and finding me guilty.

Be careful who you trust. Some people are not who you think they are, but I firmly believe the number of good and caring people far outweighs those who are not.

When I found out about this investigation, I was advised that I should make an appointment to see the Assistant Commissioner of Internal Affairs. The purpose of this meeting was to tell them what I knew about the lack of procedural fairness in the investigation that was conducted against me without my knowledge or consultation.

I asked for the investigation against me to be retracted as its outcomes could not and should not stand. I did this, and the investigation was quashed and any sustained findings against me were withdrawn. At least this was what I was told. I was never demoted or counselled because of this procedurally unfair investigation.

I was later told my "stars would never align" for promotion beyond superintendent, but life as a superintendent turned out to be pretty good in the long run. How we view our life is a matter of choice. I decided to be the best superintendent I could be, empowering others to lead and creating supportive and inclusive workplaces.

Reflections

The purpose of describing this period of my life is that bad things happen. My reputation took a big hit, and it was debilitating.

With mental health support, the support of family and friends, and the support of people who treated me as the person in front of them and not the person from the past, my life continued and improved. It was not without self-doubt, it was not without fear, but step-by-step it did improve.

I have an ingrained belief that we can learn from our setbacks, they do not define us if we don't let them. I chose to write a different story. I did not wallow in failure, I did swirl around the drain for awhile, but I did fight against the negative talk in my own head and worked towards a more positive future.

I was and still am a leader.

A leader must provide clear direction.

A leader needs people to travel with them willingly in that direction, a leader cannot walk the path alone.

If a leader introduces significant change, that leader needs the support of a formidable leadership team, the leader cannot survive on their own.

If a leader allows people who oppose change to take the focus off what should be occurring, then when those people who oppose change become too noisy, everyone loses.

Staff lose out.

Communities lose out.

Families lose out.

There is nothing I can do to reverse the storyline of what happened during my first experience as a police commander. I must own it and learn from it and hopefully help others not make the same mistakes I made.

At an organisational level, I did see the NSW Police prepare their commanders to lead in a lot more structured way than I was.

The system at the time allowed me to be the successful candidate in 2005 to become a police commander at superintendent level, without any previous command experience. I was good enough to win the job, but I didn't have the experience base to do the job well without having a very bumpy journey.

What I saw from about 2010 onwards was the NSW Police blooded their up-and-coming commanders in a much better way. It was common for a commander-in-the-making to relieve in command roles across several different and varied commands for two years or more before they were ultimately promoted to the role of superintendent as police commander.

My story is not only for people in the NSW Police. There are thousands of leadership positions across just as many companies and organisations. It may come to pass that you find yourself in the same situation I found myself in that first command. Perhaps the advice I gave a close friend in a similar situation may help.

In the 12 months before I retired from operational duties as a police commander, a close peer in another emergency services organisation had won a promotion at a rural location away from Sydney.

My friend and I had worked closely for several years on major operations and exercises. We knew each other well. When my friend told me of his promotion, I gave him a summary of what happened at my first command.

I impressed upon him the need to build a formidable command team and take time before implementing significant change.

One of the many complimentary messages I received on my retirement included a message from my friend. My experience and learnings from my first command had been used to build a successful leadership story. His message:

> *I have constantly heeded the advice that you provided me about building a formidable team and have to say it paid off. Thank you for your friendship, support, and professionalism over the years we worked with each other.*

Workplaces have a short memory.

If I wrote the story that I knew was me, a professional and caring boss looking to create a productive workplace where other leaders are created, where everyone supports each other, over time no one would ever know the story of my first command and I would become a leader who could be trusted, who created safe inclusive workplaces.

This book is the first time I have ever really shared with anyone how awful my first leadership experience truly was.

I am not superhuman or immune from how much this time in my leadership journey hurt me and hurt my family.

When I returned to Sydney, I was broken, at a mental and reputational level, and I had to build my belief in myself again.

As a family, we were also struggling, so day by day we built our foundation again.

It took a few years to build my internal resilience and certain situations would be like a red flag and put me in that fight-or-flight situation.

I recently took a road trip holiday in and around the area of my first command. Just being in the same environment again, 15 years later, still had the power to bring up all the emotions that existed in 2005. They were not so debilitating, but the feelings were still there.

I sought the help of mental health professionals, family and friends, and there was a lot of self-reflection and awareness. Over time, physical fitness and relationships at all levels of my life would be the keys to building a good foundation to weather any storm, but that took years to build resilience, one day at a time.

I returned to Sydney as the Officer in Charge of Corridors at Police Headquarters in Parramatta. This was a time of high attrition for police commanders. Many were leaving their roles, quite often mentally damaged.

I learnt there was little support for people doing my role, there was little trust amongst peers as things said in confidence would inevitably come back to hurt you.

Peers were trying to outdo each other, and it was embarrassing to watch what some did to earn favour. It was up to the individual to build their own resilience, relationships and reputation as well as look after their own physical and mental health. After several months, I was given an assignment that no one else of my rank wanted.

I was seconded as a Liaison Officer to the New South Wales Department of Premier and Cabinet, Operations Unit. I would work from the government offices with senior public servants identifying areas of risk that may impact negatively on the State Government and the NSW Police.

I knew the senior public servant who led the unit as I had worked with him in First Nations projects at my first command, so I viewed the secondment as an opportunity.

I found the work refreshing and it would forever highlight to me that one government agency does not work alone, we all work together. And the better we work together, the better the outcome for everyone.

A small group of committed people, especially when those people have access to the levers of government, can change the world.

Every situation provides an opportunity, a lesson, if you look hard enough. What I learnt in that 12-month period would be a foundation for every major endeavour I would later be involved with. I just didn't know it at the time.

10

Art or Porn? (2008)

On 22 May 2008, a normal weekday in my second command, I got a call from one of my superiors. They wanted me to go to an art gallery in the eastern suburbs of Sydney. I never had anything to do with art before but my task for this weekday afternoon was to go to an art gallery.

The reason behind this request was that there had been a lot of complaints on talk-back radio throughout the day about a photographic exhibition at this art gallery. The exhibitor of the photos was a well-known photographer who considered their photos art. I had never heard of this photographer before, but I was soon to learn all about their work. Some of these complaints made their way to the police as criminal-level concerns.

The photographer had a passion for taking photos of naked prepubescent children and displaying those photographs as art. Once I started to research the content of the exhibition, I could see why the public was concerned. We secured a promotional pamphlet from the art gallery, and it contained several photos of naked children, including a boy and a girl, in full frontal poses. Several of the photos were taken under a railway bridge or similar location, with the children next to an old, burnt-out car. The age of these children was obviously under 18 years old.

I looked at Section 91H of the *New South Wales Crimes Act*.

Section 91H deals with the offences of production and dissemination of child pornography. It defines child pornography as material that depicts or describes a child under 16 years old engaged in sexual activity; in a sexual context or as a victim of torture, cruelty, or physical abuse "in a manner that would in all the circumstances cause offence to reasonable persons".

Section 91H provides a defence to the photographer and the art gallery that "having regard to the circumstances in which the material concerned was produced, used or intended to be used, the defendant was acting for a genuine child protection, scientific, medical, legal, artistic or other public benefit purpose and the defendant's conduct was reasonable for that purpose."

I found the photos in all the circumstances offensive. I already had at least eight people who had called in their distress at the offence the exhibition had caused them, so I had something to investigate.

I called the members of our team that we would need to attend the art gallery to examine the exhibition and determine what action we would take. I remember that day very well. Due to the media interest generated, we would need to have our detectives attend the job with us to pursue any further investigation and submit the necessary court brief if that was required.

When the detectives first came to my office, they were very negative about why they would be involved in going to an art gallery for a job. It was not something that they would normally do. I explained what the job was, and what we were planning to do. I asked for their opinion and advice after giving them the pamphlet which contained some of the photos. The two hardened detectives who were normally very reserved in showing any emotion saw the photos of the naked young girl, her obvious young age and the lack of any attempt to cover her nakedness, and said, *"That's not right."*

Before I left, I did speak to a person high in rank from the Child Abuse Squad who dealt with such matters. The advice I received from this person was two words, *"Good Luck."*

I went to the job with a group of experienced police including senior detectives and a representative of the Child Abuse Squad.

I walked up to this respectable-looking art gallery thinking this was a very unusual job. It is very rare that the police commander goes to any job as there are several layers of staff with the expertise to handle most jobs.

I introduced myself to the owners of the art gallery, and shortly afterward to the exhibitor. I explained that we had come to the art gallery because of several complaints from members of the public who found the images displayed in the exhibition offensive.

Our purpose at the exhibition was to view and assess the images on their contravention of Section 91H of the Crimes Act. I had with me an inspector from the Child Abuse Squad to help us form an opinion of the images and their level of offence under Section 91H.

We discussed the content of the images we found at the exhibition. The exhibitor was confident that the images that were the subject of the complaints were, in their opinion, art. They captured images of naked, prepubescent children. According to them, this was art that the public wanted to see, and the children involved had their photos taken with the consent of their parents.

Several images were declared as suspect. These images mainly contained the same young girl and young boy, both fully naked, leaving nothing to the imagination. Every photo depicted the young people as brooding individuals. I made the decision to seize those images for further classification with the support and advice of the team and the opinions of the inspector from the Child Abuse Squad.

I had a Police Media Advisor turn up at the art gallery to provide me with assistance as the media interest was going national very quickly. There was a swarm of media crews outside the gallery, very keen to get an update about what the police were doing about all the complaints.

The Police Media Advisor is there to help the police commander who is going to speak to the media. They normally have a journalistic background and therefore the skills to provide support. My media advisor that day was one of the best around, so I was in good hands. The media advisor and I created the phrases I would use in the media conference. The phrases are known as "grabs" or "sound bites" that will be replayed regularly to give an overall summary of what the police were doing.

To say that I was nervous was an understatement.

It was to be my first media conference of such intensity. I remember I had ample time to prepare, and I was pacing inside the art gallery on my own going over what I was going to say, learning my lines. I even had time to say the lines a couple of times out loud. I was meant to say that we, the police, would review the possibility of charging the exhibitor. My script clearly stated *"review the possibility of charging ... "*

When I addressed the media outside and briefed them, I instead said these fateful words for the whole world to hear:

"The items were seized with the intention of charging ... "

I can't explain why I went off-script that day. I would have to put it down to nerves. It is not an unusual thing to see practiced media orators say the wrong thing. Whilst not common, it does occur.

I was clueless that I had said anything wrong when I first walked away from the media conference. I was relieved that it was over. The media advisor came up to me and drew me away to a quieter, more private area. She told me about the error I had made. The error was not in my prepared script. I had made an error in making the statement public.

What I had said to the world was how I would normally do business as an investigator. I had spent my career up to this point, testing legislation and testing case law. In this case, with the photos of a naked young boy and girl I had said what most of the community expected we as police would do.

The issue had a right to be reviewed and should be. Initially, I was disappointed that I had said the wrong thing, but I could live with my error as it had not been intentional. The community deserved the classification of the photos of naked children as art to be tested at a legal level. This was happening.

The situation provoked a national debate on censorship. In a televised interview, the then Prime Minister Kevin Rudd stated that he found the images "absolutely revolting" and that they had no artistic merit.

I was soon to learn that Allan the Police Commander could not act with the same freedom as Allan the Investigator. I have read several articles and books about this day. One book indicated that there was a collective negative sigh at Police Headquarters when I said those words about "charging" and something along the lines of *"Fucken Sicard"* were the next words.

It was an error that I made.

I had been a good and reputable investigator for 14 years before becoming a police commander. I was well-known for "having a go" when others would not, often bringing about good outcomes because I relied on the whole of the evidence and not a narrow interpretation of case law.

That ability to be creative as an investigator was not something the police executive or the art world wanted to entertain. I had spent the last 25 years as a police officer interpreting what would cause offence to "reasonable persons". On the day in question, I had an outcry from reasonable people saying they had circumstances to be offended over the images of naked children at the exhibition. I acted in good faith in those circumstances.

Our team had to arrange to remove the photos of the exhibition that we deemed to contravene Section 91H. There were a lot of photos involved and they were all large, bulky items. They would not fit in the back of a car or a caged truck.

In addition, the items did have a high monetary value, so we had to look after them. If legal proceedings determined the items had to be returned, we could not afford to have the owners of the items say we had damaged them. This involved securing legal documents such as search warrants for us to remain on the gallery premises to finalise these arrangements.

All this took a lot of time, under time-sensitive pressure with the media watching. It took over a day to arrange this process in a secure and professional way as the removal of the photos occurred over a weekend. All this time I was getting continual phone calls from my superiors putting pressure on me to finalise our activities at the art gallery as our continued presence was not helping the NSW Police get off the front page of the newspapers.

I did my best to shield our people from this intense scrutiny and oversight, but the expectation was that I needed to keep my superiors updated several times a day.

This was my first experience with something so politically charged and public.

I had several emails, texts and phone calls congratulating me for the statement I had made outside the art gallery that day. I also had some texts from other persons stating that I had no chance of being successful in pursuing this issue.

The volume of supportive comments far outweighed the unsupportive comments. It was a roller coaster to have the support of most of the community, including the Prime Minister of Australia, but also the relentless scrutiny of my superiors.

What came next showed me that I had entered a different world.

As a police commander, I was to learn we should not do anything that put the NSW Police on the front page in a negative way. This matter became national and international news overnight. The next day, I was summoned to a superior's office in what was to be many such disciplinary meetings where I got placed in the "naughty" chair and was given the "last chance" talk.

I was formally counselled for a poor media interview and to undergo immediate media training to lift my skills in that area.

The next day, one of my best investigators and I were summoned to my superior's office again. I thought we were going there to update them on how the investigation was going. Instead, I learnt that I was about to be formally counselled again. My error this time was that our investigative team had not updated the police official computer network of all the work they had done up to this point. Our work was being reviewed internally by my superiors and I had been found wanting. I took this counselling on the chin and started to get used to how this was playing out.

There was a culture at this time of police commanders and above having a penchant for letting others know that someone in the "naughty" chair had been yelled at and disciplined.

If that occurred, everyone at a superior level was happy. I was counselled at least five times regarding this incident. I had never been counselled in my whole career, so I was learning quickly. To quote a line from *The Wizard of Oz*: "We're not in Kansas anymore."

I could choose how to react to their behaviour, and I could learn how their behaviour made me feel.

I knew the way I was being treated by my superiors was not how it was supposed to be done, but that was what worked for them. I would later see the same behaviour by others at The Mosman Collar Bomb and that behaviour is not the way to get the best out of people.

That trip into my superior's office the second day with my senior investigator to be counselled and told off for not putting information on the police computer system fast enough could have been so easily done another way. A simple phone call to my senior investigator would suffice. That would be the decent thing to do. Instead, the message had to be delivered in the "naughty" chair for everyone to see.

I then chose to do something I have never done before and have never done since. The regularity of unpleasant phone calls from my superiors became so frequent, I chose to put a ringtone on the call so I would know who was calling me.

I have some nice ringtones for those nearest and dearest to me, "A Kind of Magic" and "Sweet Child O' Mine" and "Burn It to the Ground" which is my favourite Nickelback song for someone else who is very close.

The song I assigned to unpleasant callers was the Bon Jovi hit "Bad Medicine". The opening riff is so distinct it is almost like an alarm bell.

The song itself made me laugh and put me in a better mood to deal with the inevitable bad news phone call.

I didn't do this all the time, but I found it to be a very powerful thing for my own wellbeing, to not answer the call and let it go to message bank as my own way of managing the ongoing scrutiny and oversight. Nastiness and bullying are not the ways to inspire loyalty and a good relationship, it is all about power.

I found out after one of my many visits to my seniors' offices that there was another police commander who had such visits. It was a relief to know it was not only me getting disciplinary meetings, and once I knew the number of police commanders in the same situation, it became quite funny.

Some leaders teach you how to lead, others show you what not to do.

Our investigative team put a good brief of evidence together. My top-down scrutiny and oversight did not stop there. I walked that brief of evidence to the Director of Public Prosecutions Office and met with Senior Crown Prosecutors to seek an urgent review of the brief we had compiled. I was harassed daily by my superiors to get the status and outcome of this review as soon as possible; they wanted the issue to go away as it was making the NSW Police look poorly.

My job as the leader of our people was not to put them under the same pressure as I was being subjected to. They were doing a good job under challenging circumstances. A couple of people close to me knew what was going on, on a daily and sometimes hourly basis, but I believed that I did not need to put our people under the same pressure. It would not have been helpful or productive.

Commentary on a talk-back radio station at the time highlighted what the opposing issues were. Aside from arguments of artistic merit versus decency, there were discussions of child abuse, of whether the 13-year-old girl's parents had the right to engage in such a contract with the photographer on her behalf. As for protecting the underage girl, there was not only the issue of the photos' exposure but also the public's reaction that had thrust the underage into the spotlight, whether she wanted it or not.

The NSW Department of Public Prosecutions (DPP) announced in early June 2008 that its official recommendation was that no charges be laid regarding the gallery's collection of photographs by the artist who took the photos.

Media coverage of the decision not to prosecute the photographer or the art gallery contained the following quote: "The court is not the place to decide matters of art."

In 2010, NSW Parliament announced that artists and photographers will face expensive fees to have their work classified, under reforms to NSW child pornography laws that will scrap the "artistic merit" defence. NSW State Attorney General introduced the new laws saying that they would help authorities better distinguish child pornography from art, protect victims and make it easier for police to prosecute cases.

The legislation was created after the public furore over the pictures of nude children taken by the photographer who took the photos as art, and flowed from a working-party examination of the state's child pornography laws and sex offences sentencing.

"Currently, a clear line does not exist between child pornography and art – a situation that is not ideal for the public or the artistic community," said the Attorney General. The laws adopt commonwealth provisions where the court looks at the artistic merit of the material when deciding whether it is child pornography, rather than relying on the defence of artistic purpose.

Reflections

When I gave that press conference that day about seizing the art exhibits, I believed the images of children displayed would in all circumstances offend reasonable persons.

My intent, as scripted, was to say we would "review the possibility of charging the photographer".

I instead delivered the words, "The items were seized with the intention of charging the artist, the Gallery, or both with 'publishing an indecent article' under the Crimes Act." My words placed me and the NSW Police in the spotlight that day.

I have come to accept that it is in my DNA to challenge when things need to change. Change brings fear, anger and challenges. I have come to live with that, and I accept that but change also brings true progress. I was to get better at taking on issues when things needed to change, learning that change didn't always have to be a fight. If I could build momentum for change, then with good support the change became more harmonious and long-lasting.

Sometimes an issue needs to have a spotlight on it so that something changes. You must back yourself and be part of that change if you feel something is worth it. Although what I said in the press conference was an error, I had to own what I said. The opening quote of this book from Commodore P.M.J. Scott says:

> *Your decisions, words and actions will directly impact not only on yourself, but your people, your command, and your navy [or police force], for better or for worse.*

This was a living example of the truth behind that statement.

This period of focus that I brought upon myself was uncomfortable, and at times very scary after "last chance" edicts wondering whether I would be sacked overnight. It taught me that I could only ever do my best and provide the best work environment for the people who worked with me.

I didn't need to mirror the bad behaviour I was getting from my superiors to the people who worked with me.

This period as a police commander also showed me that it is not a good enough motivation for me, or the people who worked with me, to simply keep ourselves in the good books of our superiors by avoiding doing something that attracts their disapproval.

There must be more to life than the fear of upsetting your boss.

Empowering others and creating a workplace that is supportive and inclusive was something worthwhile to focus on.

This is not a whinge or a "poor me" story about working for bad bosses. I am by nature a loyal employee and I like to support the team in any way I can. When I was managed the way I described, I was unsure of where the next "smack" would come from. I was no longer supportive of the actions of my superiors and believed their continued actions and zealous scrutiny were unnecessary. I knew our people were doing a good job under unrelenting pressure.

My superiors in this story did me a huge favour.

I knew that this method of managing people did not motivate initiative or any sense of trust, and as such moulded me to not manage people that way in any situation. In the short term, ordering and disciplining people to get an outcome might work, but people never forget how you make them feel when you resort to tyranny to get what you need. There is a better way.

I would get this right for the rest of my career, most of the time, but we are human, and we still make mistakes.

During this chapter of my career, I met a gentleman called John Threlfo. I say gentleman, sincerely as in my view, I came to believe that John was the last remaining true gentleman in the NSW Police. John was the Local Area Manager for my second command. He and his team, looked after all things finance and paperwork that related to Human Resources, and Work Health and Safety. John was the longest serving Public Servant in the NSW Police with up to 45 years of service. John was not a lover of technology and could be regularly found twirling his glasses, with a HB lead pencil in his hand, writing all over a budget report that you would normally review on a computer.

His office was full of bits of paper, but he knew where every one of those pieces of paper was. As a young commander, adept with using computer systems, our clash of working systems initially grated on me, until I looked at the whole picture. John had more knowledge in his head about where the NSW Police had come from and how we got there, than any other person. He was a respected leader across all his public service staff and had a reputation of empowering his people to reach their full potential. A lot of senior public servants in the NSW Police have been mentored and supported by John.

I came to respect him, his agency, and his dignified manner towards everyone, despite how some other people treated him. He was always respectful and a true gentleman in every sense of the word, John taught me, with his pencil and papers, to become adept at reading the budget reports for a Police Command, and how to interrogate them when needed, to address uncontrolled spending.

John taught me above all, the most valuable lesson of all. A leader, and a workplace needs to treat everyone with dignity, regardless of their stage of career. Over the remaining years of my career as a Police Commander, I had several conversations with younger police leaders who wanted to move on the older person in the workplace. Each time this situation arose, I could impart the lesson I had learnt from John. We all get old, but that doesn't reduce our contribution, or our knowledge, and it is our collective responsibility to ensure that everyone can contribute to a workplace to their own abilities and exit their career with dignity, when the time comes. One of my proudest days was John's retirement function at his beloved City Tattersalls Club in Elizabeth Street, Sydney. Despite having several other police commanders after I left his command, the police commander he wanted to speak at his farewell, was me. Such a privilege.

11

The Mosman Collar Bomb (2011)

Despite receiving several disciplinary counselling and the "last chance" warning, I was still a police commander. I was not held in any esteem by some of the superiors above me, but I was still there. Some senior police above me would turn the other way when I walked into a room and if they were forced into the humiliation of shaking my hand in public, they would physically turn their head away each time. I can honestly say that I have never seen that particular trait before or since, it is unique to some senior police leaders.

I still held to the principle that we write our own stories, and we learn from past mistakes.

It was no good sitting there thinking, *Poor me*. I knew I wanted to get better at being a leader, and someone who created a kind, safe and inclusive workplace. I looked around both inside and outside our organisation for mentors, confidantes and role models. I knew if I sought out the right level of support, I would get better at leading leaders.

I asked one person who I considered to be an outstanding leader to be my mentor. A mentor is someone who has the skills to guide you, to offer you suggestions and advice but is not your boss. It is a relationship of trust, and the learnings can and do happen both ways between the mentor and the mentored. Thankfully, that person agreed to be my mentor and this person was former Assistant Commissioner Alan Clarke.

It is up to the mentored person to pursue the frequency, the location and the topics discussed at meetings. My favourite is to do this away from a workplace, and normally in a coffee shop, any coffee shop, preferably one with good coffee.

We would spend many hours in those meetings and talk about all kinds of things. My mentor shared some very private stuff with me and vice versa. I think we mentored each other. This private stuff involved some of our deepest police-related fears, and some family and personal issues. We trusted one another implicitly. We are still friends to this day and share a level of trust that is rare and treasured.

I learnt so much from my mentor. He had the ability to connect with people, anyone. It was not uncommon to witness my mentor start up a conversation with someone in an elevator on the 40th floor and by the time we arrived at the ground floor, we knew the life story of that person.

It is often the little things we change about ourselves that make the biggest difference.

The biggest thing I learnt from my mentor was connection with people.

Once you start to focus on doing things differently, change seems to happen around you.

There were changes in the senior people I reported to. They operated differently and did not employ the "naughty" chair strategy. I remember this was like a breath of fresh air.

We went to our first group police commanders meeting after the "naughty" chair period was over and they started the meetings with bacon and egg rolls and cappuccinos. Such a small and simple gesture to start our relationship. And then came these words: "You have been treated like children, you will be treated like men and women from now on."

Under new leadership, I was given a chance to build belief in myself. Under their guidance, I was offered several opportunities. These opportunities changed my level of experience, my reputation, my ability to work with others and my resilience. I was no longer being threatened, bullied or counselled; I was allowed to develop at my own pace.

I started to do external police commander roles for events at the Sydney Football Stadium and the Sydney Cricket Ground as well as some other major events in the Sydney CBD including the Sydney Marathon and the Mardi Gras. After watching how my mentor connected with people, I changed the way I acted as a commander as staff came into the briefings for these major events.

I learnt to develop a skill with all staff as they entered a police commander briefing. Some Commanders only come into a briefing room when everyone is gathered. I made it my business to be in that briefing room at least 30 minutes before and greet everyone as they came into a briefing.

Typically, groups of police come in together from one station. This way, I could greet them and speak to them about where they came from. Because I had been around for awhile, I had worked with or knew people who worked at the stations they were from. We talked about common points, and we formed a connection. I did this with every group that came in and would often shake their hands and thanked them for coming in to work at whatever the event was.

How this level of connection helped me was like any public speaking engagement. If you can make it personal, you connect with your audience. In this case, the audience was a large group of police about to go out and work for you, representing themselves, their station, and the NSW Police with other stakeholders.

Their main task was to ensure the event community had a safe and happy experience, and that the non-event community is not negatively impacted. All I did during my briefing was make mention who was in the briefing, the relevant skillsets they brought to the event and thanked them for their presence.

When you do enough large events, you start to know the event regulars who are good at what they do, and the greeting process becomes more like meeting an old friend. I could write a whole book on some of the large events that I was a police commander in charge of but I will give a summary of what I did before the Mosman Police Collar Bomb.

I was given opportunities to relieve as the police commander at Eastern Beaches and Kings Cross. I led large police operations with other stakeholders for:

» Future Music Festival at Randwick Racecourse with 30,000 people

» Good Vibes Music Festival at Centennial Park with 30,000 people

» Australia Day at Coogee Beach.

At the Future Music Festival, the year before, organisers and police had been unprepared for the number of outlaw motorcycle gang members who came to the event with bumbags full of drugs.

These gang members were big and fit men. Their numbers and behaviour led to several assaults and clashes with the police. Once they were in the venue, it was difficult to stop their activities, as any approach required a significant policing response, which led to a negative outcome.

When I read debriefs of what had occurred and viewed photos of the gang members, I could see the challenges that police and event organisers faced the year before. But with enough talented personnel and planning you can come up with some good solutions. The Randwick Racecourse is a large, licenced venue. The licensee or the event organiser can refuse entry to any patron for any reason.

Working together with event organisers and the security/events team of Randwick Racecourse, we publicised on every ticket sold and every communication message about the event that illicit drugs would not be permitted in the venue.

There would be a large contingent of drug dogs and police at the venue, which was in the early stages of this policing strategy in 2008. It was imperative we come up with a strategy to prevent the outlaw motorcycle gangs and other organised crime gangs out of the event. If we could identify them before they entered the venue, we could deny them entry, refund their ticket, and send them on their way.

Normal police who do first-response duties do not have the expertise to identify organised crime gang members who are not wearing their "gang colours" but members of the Organised Crime Squad can.

I learnt the power of relationships in that job. I knew the boss of the Organised Crime Squad. I shared with him what my challenge was and what the possible solution could be. To my delight, he guaranteed at least 20 members of their squad to attend the event. They met and challenged several outlaw motorcycle gang members that day. Each patron was told they were being denied entry to the event and their ticket refunded. There were no drugs and assaults at the event linked to organised crime.

I still remember the best officer at doing this. She would walk up to the gang member with a smile, said their name and then told them the bad news for them and the good news for the safety of the event.

To my delight, I had the pleasure of meeting that young officer after I retired. She came up to me at a local shopping centre and said to me, "You probably don't remember me."

I said, "Of course I do" and recounted the story of her at Future Music.

Up to then, I had done all I could to prepare myself for the next big challenge. In any case, my mentor used to say, *"Sometimes the job chooses you."*

On a relatively quiet August weekday afternoon in 2011, the job did choose me.

I was sitting in my office doing some of the paperwork that comes with being a commander when I heard a police radio broadcast from one of our car crews at Harbourside Local Area Command. Our police command looked after everything on the coastline from Balls Head in Waverton to the Spit Bridge in Mosman. We also looked after St Leonards, Northbridge, Cremorne and North Sydney.

The summary of that radio broadcast was one I will never forget. Our car crews were at a job in Mosman. It was an affluent area that we rarely got called to. Apparently, a man wearing a balaclava went into the home of an 18-year-old woman and calmly told her he was going to put a device around her neck, which was a collar bomb.

The man, who was later identified as Paul Peters, proceeded to secure the device around her neck leaving her with clear instructions in a typed written note attached to the bomb that he was an expert bomb maker and that her father was to contact him to arrange a payment. He would afterward assist her father in safely getting the device off of his daughter.

The note claimed a powerful plastic explosive has been attached to the girl's neck in a booby-trapped case by a former special forces' munitions specialist. "So, act now, think later or you will inadvertently trigger a tragically avoidable explosion," the note stated, making numerous references to a man in the United States who was killed when a collar bomb exploded. "You will be provided with detailed Remittance instructions to transfer a defined sum once you acknowledge and confirm receipt of this message."

The note also referred to the fact that the offender was like the main character Dirk Straun in the novel *Tai-Pan* written by James Clavell. Dirk Straun was a pirate, an opium smuggler, and a master manipulator of men.

As the note and its contents were being read out over the police radio, there was complete silence, almost a chill, as the note left a feeling of evil and horror. I made the decision there and then that this was a real job and advised the police radio that I as the commander of the local area command would be attending the scene within the next 20 minutes.

As I prepared to go to the job, I made a call to my superiors. It is good practice to let superiors know when a big job is occurring, so they can get ahead of the job and keep people like the Commissioner of Police and the Premier of NSW informed on what is occurring and what is being done about it.

Once I told them what the job was and the fact that we had a young 18-year-old woman with what we believed was a bomb around her neck, there was silence for quite awhile before the response, "Ok Al, let us know what we can do."

It was suggested to me to consider ringing the police negotiators to the job to help the young woman.

When I called the police negotiators, they responded that it was not their type of job to attend to. This initial decision was not due to indifference but was based on a clear set of guidelines for the deployment of police negotiators. A person with a bomb around their neck wasn't one of them.

I explained to the person making the decision that I wanted the police negotiators to help the 18-year-old woman to remain as calm as possible. The negotiators were probably the best qualified specialist resource the NSW Police had to help this young woman stay as calm as possible in such a situation. Shortly after this conversation, they were on their way.

Not long after that, I made my way to the job.

Once I arrived, I was impressed by the organisation two duty inspectors had set up in a short period. We were in for an extended job that would require many specialist resources and inevitable media attention. We needed space to work that afforded us confidentiality, whilst at the same time letting the rest of the suburb go about their business.

Our duty inspectors had set up a large inner and outer perimeter with an area for media briefings whilst creating a traffic plan with our traffic supervisors to allow the rest of the suburb to go about their normal lives.

The first cars to arrive was a Harbourside car crew with a senior constable, herself a mother of two children, and a probationary constable. I recall that the young probationary constable was later admonished by her mother for not coming home to the family dinner. After she explained to her mum where she had been all afternoon and evening, all was forgiven by her mother.

Our officers were met with a visibly upset and emotional young woman with the reported device around her neck. They were never in any doubt that the device was believed to be real, and that the 18-year-old girl was not some student embarking on some hoax to get out of doing her HSC exams.

I recall seeing a photo taken of the young woman that day with the device around her throat. The photo showed an extremely distressed young woman, with her hair a dark brown colour and drenched in sweat. The young woman normally had beautiful glossy blonde hair.

Shortly after our first crew was at the job, their external supervisor also came to the home. Upon seeing what the job was and the risks involved, the supervisor made the decision with the consent of our senior constable for the latter to stay with the young girl. This occurred for two reasons: we could not let the device go mobile in the community and, more importantly, it was the decent thing to do to leave the young girl with support.

When I arrived at the scene, declaring on police radio that I was now in command, I also took on the accountability for the outcome of the decision to leave an officer with a young woman with a device around her neck.

Each of us who made that decision felt a high level of anxiety regarding that decision. There was no rule book, emergency manual or regulation that had ever considered a situation such as the one we were faced with.

I recall the deafening silence I got when I briefed my superiors about the decision to leave our senior constable with the young woman.

After the silence, I was asked, "Are you sure about that, Al?"

I said, "Yes I am." My peer didn't question me any further, we were in uncharted waters.

As I was getting briefed on what had been done so far, I could see we had a good and spacious inner perimeter set up with which we could amass the resources we needed to resolve the situation successfully. Ambulances and the fire brigade were already on the scene, with room for the bomb squad and negotiator resources, and additional investigative resources should they be required.

The initial briefing was that the bomb squad was out of Sydney on this day doing training exercises and it would take longer than normal for them to arrive.

Shortly after this, a bomb squad technician who was not out of Sydney on the exercise came and spoke to me. I will never forget this briefing for the rest of my life.

The bomb squad tech said, "Mr Sicard, I have three points to highlight to you. Firstly, where your policewoman is, she will die if the device explodes. Secondly, the success rate for removing a collar bomb worldwide is zero percent. Thirdly, on the information contained in the note from the offender, referring to another collar bomb incident in America, that device was on a two-hour timer."

I remember thinking at the time, *That's the worst briefing I have ever heard, can I go home now?*

I had no control over the content of the briefing, all I could do with the people with me was work together to do our best to resolve the situation to a successful outcome.

In the last three years from 2007 to 2010, I had been the police commander for several large public events. I knew I had this training, structure, experience and network to rely on.

There was a bomb protocol we had to follow and that involved proving whether the device was a bomb or not. It would involve several steps, resources and other agencies.

It was already on my mind that the note left by Paul Peters had stated, "Don't call the police." It was clear from the media coverage that the police had been called and we were on the scene. Despite this, the device had not been triggered. Was this because it was not remotely controlled or was this because it was on a timer?

When the first negotiators arrived, there was not enough bomb protective gear available for them to be kitted up to provide close support to the young woman.

The police negotiator supervisor almost had to fight with the young negotiators not to go down to relieve our senior constable without the correct protective gear. There were enough shields for the early negotiators to go down to where our senior constable was to provide her some protection. Despite the precarious nature of the situation, our senior constable elected to stay with the young woman for a lot longer than she needed to, because it was the right thing to do.

There are several steps to proving whether something is or is not a bomb. I learnt all this on that day and night. Whilst I can't go into all those steps, one of the steps involves using bomb dogs.

This all sounds straightforward until you put the device around someone's neck.

The problem was that bomb dogs had never been trained to detect and indicate explosive material when the device was on a person.

Emergency services personnel are solution-orientated, not problem-orientated. The bomb squad handlers, who had all arrived by then, enlisted the assistance of one of our intelligence officers. It turned out this officer's next career goal was to work in the dog squad, so she volunteered to assist by training the bomb dogs to indicate explosive material attached to a person.

One of the most important aspects of a multi-agency job like this is communication.

It was my job as the police commander to engage and enlist all specialist representatives in regular briefings so we were working towards the same outcomes using our collective expertise. During this entire incident, I held a briefing every hour. These briefings included senior representatives from ambulance, fire and rescue, bomb squad, negotiators, local council, State Emergency Service, police investigators, and other specialist resources.

It was in the first briefing that the superintendent from the ambulance asked me to consider a trauma plan. I had never heard of it, and I asked her to explain. She advised we needed a plan to deal with the outcomes if the device around the young woman's neck did explode. There would be injuries and it was logical to plan for that outcome.

When photos were reviewed of that night, fire and rescue staff were kitted up in breathing gear and helmets. They were to be the first personnel to go in if the device exploded, extinguish the fires and assist paramedics in removing casualties who needed treatment.

There is always more behind any picture and any story.

The fire and rescue staff can only stay in their breathing gear and helmets for 30 minutes before they need to be rotated out so they can recuperate, refresh and be ready to return when their colleagues are exhausted. Several years later, in the Grenfell Tower Fires in London, there was extensive criticism that fire and rescue staff were lying down amid the mayhem. This is the reason why: they had already been in the fight, they were beyond exhausted, and were recuperating to go back in.

One of my other considerations on that night was the post-job review.

That review could be in a Coroners Court, by media or by some other review agency either internal or external to the NSW Police.

As police commander of that job, I had total accountability for what happened, good or bad. That review would hold me solely accountable for my decisions. I have never been one to let that paralyse me. Decisions must be made under the prevailing conditions, and we all do our best to make the right decisions. That has always been my focus.

In a job like this, it is physically and mentally impossible to do everything. I have learnt that my job as the commander is not about me or my ego, it is about creating an environment where people can do their best.

In these jobs, the best of the best, come to do their specialty, whatever that is. As a commander, I listened to their advice, agreed on a plan, owned the plan, and move forward.

If we feel comfortable and valued in our work environments and personal lives, we will do our best. If we feel discomfort, due to the conditions imposed by our work environment, we will not do our best. A leader can influence, comfort or cause discomfort.

A good example of comfort and discomfort was the bomb squad commander getting regular phone calls.

Those phone calls were challenging, as whoever was on the other end was talking so loudly and aggressively that the bomb squad commander was regularly moving the phone away from his ear.

My job was to work with the bomb squad commander. It was not my job to emulate the angst and aggression of the phone calls the bomb squad commander was receiving. We had to work together productively to achieve an outcome. I would not add to the angst of the situation by being unreasonable in my own behaviours and actions.

But I was reassured by the level of expertise and support our bomb squad was receiving. The commander was taking calls and advice from experts all over the world, such is the network of bomb squad technicians. It is a rarefied collective of brave individuals who take on that line of work. I could see we were in good hands. It is not often you see first-hand experts from all over the world helping each other in real-time.

I needed someone to answer my phone, take my calls over the police radio and record my decision-making as to why we did or did not do certain things. If I did these things myself, I could be distracted when crucial information came to light.

I enlisted a talented young constable to assist me, to allow me to focus on resolving the situation successfully. One of the first things we recorded in that decision-making log was why I decided to leave our senior constable in place with the young woman with a device around her neck.

The second thing needed was identifying whether the device was a bomb or not a bomb. There were several steps that we had to go through to minimise the risk that the object around our victim's neck was a bomb.

I referred earlier to the best of the best turning up at these jobs to do their best.

An example of this was the negotiator supervisor who briefed me regularly about how his team was going and how our victim was holding up. Things were going as well as could be in the circumstances. The team of negotiators was kitted up in protective clothing, making their time with our victim limited due to the amount of energy those suits tax from a human body in an intense situation.

As I talked to the negotiator supervisor throughout the night, it was impossible not to notice he had one of the most gravelly and coarse voices I had ever heard.

Police are known for their black humour at times, and to bring some lightheartedness to a challenging night, I told the negotiator supervisor that he had been to too many jobs to have a voice like that. His response made me feel like I was being insensitive, but the level of dedication the people we were working with that night had equally inspired me.

The negotiator supervisor's voice was like that due to a job in his past that had not ended well. The outcome of that level of stress affected his vocal cords permanently. The only way he could talk was to have a large steroid needle into his vocal cords every six months, so he could continue to communicate in his life and his job like the rest of us take for granted.

It was a privilege to work with people like the negotiator supervisor and the bomb squad commander on that night, people doing their absolute best no matter the challenges.

Our crime manager of Harbourside was on site as well. He took over the liaison role with the victim's family and we allowed them to stay as a group at a table outside the bomb squad truck that showed on a large television display their daughter in real-time.

This again was my decision and would be questioned by some as to why. In my view, we were all in this together, and it was the right thing to do to include the victim's family into the mix, witnessing what we were all doing to resolve this incident successfully.

This job was the first of its kind in Australia. It was potentially a terrorism-related job. This made the job an international event, almost immediately.

Something I was unaware of, but learnt quickly on that night, was the NSW Police must be reassured that the commander in place is up to the job and that the NSW Police will not be embarrassed or questioned by the actions of that commander later.

I was a commander who had been at two previous commands and did not have a good track record. I had been at my new command less than a year at North Sydney, hardly the crime capital of NSW. At first glance, I did not have the credentials to manage a job like this one.

I didn't appreciate this concern until my direct boss came to the job.

He brought with him a team of other officers, one of whom was the designated commander of a team of investigators from our terrorism response strike force, trained in all things terrorism and tasked with responding to terrorism-related incidents. They train annually and a small group of police commanders is included on the Strike Force Pioneer cadre to lead terrorism-related incidents. I was not a terrorism-trained commander.

My boss's first briefing to me was that the Commissioner of Police had instructed the terrorism strike force police to attend the scene and be on standby. They were to take over the job if and when the bomb squad technicians advised that the device around our victim's neck was a declared explosive device.

It could be said having a team of other resources, including your replacement commander on site, ready to take over from you, is disconcerting, but I viewed the situation for what it was. I couldn't change what I couldn't change, so I just got on with the job.

A clear and small detail that my boss did not do was declare that he was taking over command. I knew the subtlety in that omission, and I knew my boss would not make that omission in error, it was deliberate.

His presence would to some staff signify that he was in charge, but it was technically still me who was accountable for the outcomes.

The interesting thing, at a public level and for many years to come, was that anyone who was not at that job did not know my role that night. I am comfortable with that. It was not until I gave evidence at the Coronial Inquest for the Lindt Café Siege in 2015 that the public knew of my leadership role in this incident.

One of my core beliefs is that a leader influences others to achieve outcomes.

Those outcomes could not be achieved without others doing their best. My job as a leader was to create an environment for others to do their best. It was not about creating an environment where I was in the spotlight. As my leadership career continued, I was comfortable in this role. My job was to put the right people together, guide them, and create the right environment for truly effective change to occur, often without my name on it. This is one of the most satisfying things about being a leader. Influencing others to create long-lasting change or successful outcomes.

One thing my boss did do was take over the family liaison role with our victim's family. Having someone of his rank and status was reassuring to them and demonstrated we were all in this together.

The other thing my boss did that I will be forever grateful for was that he did all the media briefings, with a pack of media that was ravenous for information with a story going all over the world.

Over the next few hours, I held the multi-agency briefings on the hour with my boss and his terrorism response commander present at all those briefings.

In the meantime, the bomb dogs were trained to detect explosive material attached to a person. Once trained, they went in and did their job. The bomb dogs did not indicate any explosive material so just to be certain, the bomb squad recommended the bomb dogs repeat the exercise. They did and the result was the same.

So, about eight hours into the incident, the bomb squad supervisor came up to our leadership group and said, "I need authority to cut the device away from the victim's neck."

I will never forget what happened next.

It was like I was in the nursery rhyme game "Piggy in the Middle". Every other person in that leadership group who was with me took a large and pointed step backward, leaving me on my own in the middle. It was my decision to make.

Without a pause, I said, "I give authority to cut the device for the following reasons," then listed four strategies that we had used to minimise the risk of the object being a real bomb and finished with "Go ahead."

What followed this was the longest wait of my life.

The fire and rescue agency was responsible for removing the device from our victim's neck. I felt isolated as I waited for what felt like an hour after giving the order even though it was closer to 30 or 45 minutes. It was almost unbearable waiting for a cheer or an explosion. I was kicking stones or anything that took my mind off the outcome.

It was at this stage I learnt the value of supporting your mate or your colleague. Another colleague saw that I was struggling and came up and simply put a hand on my back and said, "You made the right decision Al."

That's all I needed at that time.

I was alright after that small gesture. Not long after that, we received confirmation that the device had been removed successfully.

I had requested the State Emergency Service so they could set up their resources and assist with welfare and breaks in the form of food and tea and coffee.

The ambulance has a chaplain service, who is not only there for ambulance personnel, but everyone at the job. I regularly saw the ambulance chaplain offering support to the victim's family.

We also set up an evacuation centre in a nearby council-owned community hall where the displaced neighbours near the job site elected to stay. There was a lot going on.

At the end of the job, my boss asked me to provide him a two-page summary before I went home that night, so he could brief the senior members of the NSW Police Force and government on what had occurred during the job, and the steps taken to resolve it.

I went home about 3 am that night and really couldn't sleep because even though the job had gone better than we could have hoped for, the "What if?" thoughts did start to float around my head.

I recall waking up around 5 am that same morning unable to sleep.

I have found exercise to be a good clearer of negative thoughts and emotions, so I donned my running shoes and went for a run with our German Shepherd around a nearby park.

I didn't know it at that time, but I had glaucoma, a condition where pressure builds up behind your eyes, causing blurred vision. For me, if it was dark, any light had a halo effect around it. I found exercise and drinking water would relieve the symptoms in the early stages of the condition. I used to think the condition was stress-related. When I went for my run that morning with every streetlight ringed by large halos, I thought to myself, *It's just the stress going out of my body after such a big job. Keep running, clear your head, and go back to work and make sure everyone is ok.*

When I got to work, I found the first three officers who found our victim back at work, all in our training room in North Sydney, just talking to each other. I was so impressed and proud that these three officers had just been to one of the most challenging jobs ever, and here they were the next day, supporting each other, debriefing each other, and getting ready to go back out and do their job again. No fuss, no fanfare.

Once my boss shared the two-page summary I had prepared, it was clear the level of bravery our senior constable had demonstrated by staying with our victim. Once this became known publicly, our senior constable was in huge demand from the media. She started doing media interviews the day after the job. Her modesty, professionalism, and genuine care for our victim above her own safety came through loud and clear.

I started a lengthy report not long after to highlight the bravery and professionalism of all the people involved from all services. The National Bravery Awards were considered but this awards process takes years before the awards are given.

The true heroes of the job are the first five response officers, then the negotiators and the bomb squad officers including the dog squad. These specialists are trained for the job, but all these people put themselves in harm's way to get a successful outcome.

The most impressive person on the whole job, who also received a National Bravery Award, was our victim. A young person with no training put their trust in their family and the emergency services in one of the most confronting of situations anyone would ever be faced with.

Our senior constable received the following awards for that job:

- » International Women in Policing – Bravery Award (awarded in Johannesburg, South Africa)
- » National Bravery Award
- » Commissioner's Courage Award
- » Commissioner's Unit Citation
- » ACWAP Hellweg Bravery Award
- » Pride of Australia Bravery Award (2nd place).

Something that I am very proud of is the two emails I received the following day. This type of feedback is rarely, if ever, given to the police, particularly for this type of job. People do not normally want their opinions in writing.

Having worked with several region and local area commanders during various emergencies, I just wanted to say I thought your leadership and organisation was excellent throughout the evening.

Staff Officer, State Emergency
Operations Controller (SEOCON)

I am sorry we don't have more dealings with your LAC (although I'm sure you are not of the same opinion!). I can honestly say I have never seen a smoother run bomb incident than the Mosman job. Very professional on your part.

Commander of Rescue Bomb Squad Unit

Reflections

What these emails taught me, and the simple act of support by my colleague when he just put his hand on my back after I had made the decision to cut the device from our victim's neck, was that each of us can support each other.

If we feel we are supported, I really believe we can and do achieve the most amazing things. Sometimes, like this job, we can be in uncharted waters, and we must back ourselves. Hopefully, we have done a lot of foundation work to have the confidence to back ourselves when the time comes.

It is important in challenging jobs, and more importantly in life, not to feel isolated. It comes down to relationships – to have meaningful relationships and interactions with other people is an inherent foundation of being human.

A good illustration of this point about providing support when you are not even involved in the job occurred at the start of the Mosman Collar Bomb and the Lindt Café.

When the Mosman Collar Bomb was first broadcast and I advised I was on my way via the police radio, one of the first phone calls I received was from another commander. He said to me about the collar bomb, "Al, that sounds like a shit job. If I can do anything to help, just ask me."

Four years later, when I was on my way to the Lindt Café as the commander, the first phone call of support I got was from that same commander. He said, "Al, that sounds like a shit job, I have thirty police heading your way to help, use them how you need to."

This type of support goes a long way in policing and in life. That type of support gives you the courage to carry on.

Bad and challenging things happen regularly. If we reach out and provide support so people are not alone, we can make a difference.

If we create that culture in a workplace, in our group of friends or family, then such simple gestures can make significant positive contributions.

A job like the Mosman Collar Bomb never leaves you.

I was asked to invite all relevant personnel to a debrief of what occurred and review what went well and what could be improved. I invited all the relevant spokespersons for all the agencies that were represented at the job, and they appreciated their presence at the debrief, as it was not common for them to be attending a police-related debrief.

As I walked into the debrief about two weeks after the job, I heard some senior police saying, "We can't defend what Sicard did" – referring to my leaving our senior constable in such a vulnerable position.

I learnt throughout my career that for every job, no matter what it is, people will conduct their own review and pass judgement without all the facts. That's just what humans do; we are wired that way. I can't change the way people think.

There was no policy or regulation that provided guidance on whether to leave our senior constable to support the victim. It came down to the leader in that situation with what they can live with. It was the decent, moral, and right decision to make, even though others thought it was not.

A good recent example of decisions outside the rule book or what the manual stated was the unprecedented floods in northern NSW from 2021 to 2022. This crisis required a multi-agency response as it was beyond what any one agency could do.

During this crisis, one agency initially asked for the community to help rescue other people in need using whatever boats they had, as the situation was beyond their capacity to rescue everyone. Shortly after this reasonable call for assistance was made, the request was rescinded by other senior emergency services people due to the risks involved since the community was not trained in rescuing people.

Whilst I understand the logic behind not wanting the community to rescue others when they are not trained to do so, the emergency was unprecedented. The required multi-agency response was beyond what it could do effectively and did need the willing support of the community. The community and the emergency services were in this event together and needed to work together.

The community nonetheless went ahead and rescued those in need of urgent assistance with boats, social media communications and even three helicopters, all outside the purview of the multi-agency response. Open-source media accounts and subsequent enquiries gave examples of how the community felt abandoned. All it would have taken is one of those emergency services leaders to back themselves, work outside of their normal parameters and do something different.

That decision and act of courage, to work willingly with community members who wanted to help, would have been a positive step in building some trusting and lasting relationships out of a challenging emergency.

That decision was never made and the multi-agency response was officially reviewed. Rightly or wrongly, emergency services at the leadership level had critical findings of what was done and what was not. It is a real-world example of how relevant the following quote is.

> *Your decisions, words and actions will directly impact not only on yourself, but your people, your command, and your navy [or community and state], for better or for worse.*

The perception of success or failure is such a fleeting thing though.

The entire country of Australia continued to be challenged by the worst flooding the nation had ever seen in 2021 and 2022. The unprecedented level of flooding just kept happening. The future responses to ongoing emergencies at a local, state and federal level improved as each emergency unfolded. Humans are experiential learners. Mix in some high-level emergency and disaster skills and that level of learning is expedited and improved upon. The outcomes for your people, your community and your state do improve when you have a core group of committed people making that happen.

12

Homelessness (2013–2020)

In the NSW Police, every superintendent at a police command level has sponsorship. Sometimes, these sponsorships are assigned, and sometimes we volunteer for them.

In 2012, I was sitting in a meeting where all the other commanders like myself were being updated by our superiors. A request was made for a volunteer from within our police commander group to take on the Sponsorship of Homelessness. This had never been a sponsorship area previously and most police viewed homelessness as a non-police issue. The looks around the table indicated that no one wanted to be the Sponsor for Homelessness.

For me, our command had just had two homeless people who died in caves in the local area. Our area incorporated all the harbour surrounds of the northern suburbs from Waverton through to the Spit Bridge so to have homeless people die in such an affluent area was a surprise to me. The deaths were not suspicious, they were more tragic for they had died from long-term exposure to the elements. I volunteered for the sponsorship, and it was one of the best decisions I had ever made.

The next eight years gave me the privilege of working with some amazingly dedicated and kind people who genuinely wanted to make a difference in people's lives. Much the same reason most police become police.

When I took on the role, I was keen to learn as much as I could about this issue. The NSW Police at that time had this quarterly educational journal that highlighted topical issues.

The most recent magazine had a detailed article on homelessness, and it was written by Professor Catherine Robinson from the University of Technology in Sydney (UTS). I arranged a coffee date with Catherine and the rest is history.

Catherine told me that most homeless people are victims, some have been victims since before they were born. Some were in their mothers' womb when their mother was assaulted. They were born into environments that were both violent and poor, where mental health issues and addiction were prevalent.

Catherine told me about the peak bodies that coordinate activities to reduce homelessness such as Homelessness NSW and similar organisations. Once you knew where to look, homelessness was everywhere, people just chose to ignore it, or worse shunned them as people who welcomed this state of social exclusion.

I quickly learnt that anyone could become homeless. It just takes one, two or three things to happen in quick succession and you can be homeless. This can be as simple as a parent having a business fail, unable to pay mortgage or rent. Add to that some traffic fines that have not been paid that prevent the parent from driving the work van and a whole family can become homeless overnight.

The paths to homelessness are many and varied. The most common one is domestic violence. If your parent has a mental illness, the path to homelessness is hastened.

I once met this intelligent young woman in her late teens or early-20s at a youth homelessness fundraiser. This young woman could have been my daughter. The ex-Liberal Federal Treasurer Joe Hockey was there as the patron of the charity raising money. I saw Joe Hockey and this young woman in a lengthy conversation, and it had the vibe of a politician getting briefed by one of their policy advisors.

What I was to learn shortly after was this young woman had been homeless. Her mum had separated from her dad. The mother started a relationship with another man, who liked the young woman's sister but not her. An ultimatum was given and the young woman's mother chose the new partner over her, so the young woman became homeless. The young woman was intelligent and looked online for organisations that helped with homelessness. She found herself in a refuge that was well-known to police as it housed a lot of drug-addicted men with lengthy criminal records.

The young woman spent several nights in this place. By pure luck, she found a flyer for the youth homelessness charity in the refuge. The name of the place was Phoenix House in Crows Nest. The charity provided the young woman with a platform to get her life back on track.

As I spent time in the homelessness space over the next eight years, I came to learn that the story of this young woman was very common. Many parents, when faced with the choice of a new partner over their older teenage children, will often make the choice of partner over their own child, sentencing their children to the perils of youth homelessness.

Youth homelessness is often hidden. Young teenagers rely on friends' families to "couch surf". Some families are wonderful, but some are not. If they choose to stay at a house where there are addicts, either drug or alcohol, or those with mental health problems, then then the situation can deteriorate quickly.

In other homes, there may be opportunists. Once they have a young person in their home, the adult demands some form of "payment" from the young person for staying in their home. This can often take the form of sex. These stories are common and once a young person enters this kind of life, their mental health suffers, along with their self-esteem and they commonly end up with addiction and mental health issues.

The statistics are scary. Once a child has experienced homelessness, there is a high probability as an adult that they will also experience homelessness.

What I came to learn was that Allan Sicard was never going to solve homelessness as it is known as a Wicked Problem that has several social and political factors.

I spoke to people in the homelessness sector who were icons of the work they achieved. I met with them over coffee and started to see a pattern. Everyone was working on their own. There were meetings held, normally monthly, by an agency without any real traction achieved. It was common for organisations to receive funding for a particular issue and they only accepted clients in the narrow field which excluded others.

I went to one of these meetings and came away dismayed. The meeting was scheduled for 1 pm. There was no agenda, no real summary of what had happened at the last meeting. There was no time designated for the end of the meeting. What transpired was a discussion about how hard the whole issue was, no notes were taken and no actions were allocated. Everyone left in a depressed state and accepted this was how things were.

From experience, I knew the value of talented people working together to get outcomes that were not viewed as possible if each party worked in isolation. So I approached the people who I viewed as the leaders in the homelessness space. I asked them if we could hold a meeting, which I would chair with an agenda that would give the stakeholders a common purpose to work together to reduce homelessness in Sydney CBD.

I became famous for holding the one-hour meeting, where despite the many attendees, everyone had a chance to talk and we all walked away with an action item to achieve before the next meeting.

The meetings became popular because things happened. It soon became clear that if we worked together, we could provide homeless people with a home due to our collaborative approach that took advantage of our collective expertise.

In those early meetings, I was frustrated with the quality of people who were nominated to attend on behalf of Family and Community Services (FACS). The people who were coming from FACS were like modern-day politicians. A lot was said, but no clue what was really said with no outcomes or actions contemplated.

I had a good relationship with a director in FACS and met with them regularly over a coffee to see if we could not get someone who could work with our eclectic group.

We did eventually get the right person, Jamie Brewer, who had the right awareness and the confidence to work with other stakeholders to make a difference. The result of all these meetings was that we agreed each month to identify a location of high need where "rough sleepers" were known to congregate. We agreed as a coordinated group to meet at these locations at around 5 to 5.30 am, normally the coldest and wettest day of the month, and work together to identify people who needed a home. We did this every month and started to get good outcomes where people were housed.

We also questioned how things were done. Why did a rough sleeper have to fill out a 50-page document before they were considered for housing? A lot of these people couldn't read or write. If we had people from housing with us, they could streamline applications and their processes using vacant homes immediately rather than sticking to old practices.

The 50-page application was gone, and a tech-savvy housing representative with a web-based tablet would do the housing application on the spot at 6 am. This same group of people formed a coordinated group, of which police were a part, known as the Homeless Assertive Response Team (HART).

From the information and intelligence the group collated throughout each month, some individuals needed more long-term efforts to get a successful outcome. The HART coordinated what needed to be done and through that approach, we housed 300 people in the City of Sydney in 18 months, without any extra funding, just by working collaboratively.

I received the following message about the HART recently:

The HART is alive and well and the State Government have formalised their housing outreach based on our model.

City of Sydney Council, 2021

From small things come big things and people who need help get it. I was happy with the outcomes we had achieved in the City of Sydney, but my command was not in the city. I wanted to see if we could replicate the outcomes we had achieved in the city.

I held monthly meetings with all the relevant stakeholders from the Sydney Harbour Bridge to the Northern Beaches, including Hornsby and Ryde. We did the same thing, we identified where our resources were needed most and targeted those locations on a quarterly basis for a HART-style approach. Homelessness was not as acute in the City of Sydney, but it was there and more widespread and hidden.

What we achieved with the Northern Suburbs Homelessness Group was even simpler. Anyone from the group – which included Mission Australia, Youth Homelessness Refuges, Ryde Homelessness Agencies and Manly and Hornsby Homelessness Agencies – would email me as the chair of the meetings. All I had to do was send a group email to the rest of the group, which included over 50 people with the right skills, and ask, "Can we help?" Normally, within a week we housed the person or persons with the support of specialist homelessness services.

I remember vividly one of our first 6 am starts in North Sydney, working across agencies in the same style as HART. A council worker, along with a nurse from Royal North Shore Emergency Unit, brought in a man who had lived in the caves in Waverton for 20 years. (That was the reason I started the journey into working to improve our response to homelessness.) Today was the day this man made up his mind, with the right level of support to never be homeless again. A home was arranged for him that day. There is no better feeling than this. A small group of committed citizens had changed the world for this wonderful old man. I will never forget his smile.

The power of a collective is never to be underestimated.

Each year, Homelessness Week occurs in August to raise awareness of this issue. The Northern Suburbs Homelessness Group proposed to do a 24-hour walking relay across the Sydney Harbour Bridge on the walking deck, with posters and balloons to highlight homelessness but the group didn't know how to go about this.

In my role as police commander, I knew the right people and got the right authorisations. For the next three years, we conducted a 24-hour relay across the iconic Sydney Harbour Bridge in August to raise awareness about homelessness. One year we were on Channel 7's *Sunrise* due to the interest raised.

I used the momentum of Homelessness Week to show police had a heart. Every police officer has at least two or three pairs of police boots. Many boots have been retired but are in still good condition. I arranged for every police station in NSW that wanted to take part to gather all their old police boots for Mission Australia to collect. They then distributed them to rough sleepers, many of whom do not have shoes that would ever protect them from the elements. I still have the photos of the first rough sleepers down in a park around the City of Sydney when they were given their first police boots to wear. I arranged that Boot Drive to happen for several years and the police who took part loved being involved.

Sometimes, the line between Homelessness and crime can be a very fine line. If a homeless person commits a crime, it's usually because they are after money for food, or sometimes drugs to numb the pain of their existence. One day, a homeless man broke into a local aged-care home stealing several items. It turned out the homeless man was a very young fit man and the ensuing foot pursuit with police chasing him all over the countryside went on for awhile till they finally caught him. When the police had a good look at their apprehended felon, they found he was wearing recently donated police boots, which made him incredibly nimble.

I got to know some influential people in the homelessness area. They sought my placement on state-level committees tasked with updating and rewriting the Homelessness Policy for NSW. I went to the first meeting of this group. I was the police representative and there were several other agencies. The organiser of these meetings inferred that we would not have to do much as nothing was really going to change.

I questioned this statement and gave some quick facts and figures about why we should do something to change the status quo. I was told that I should have the awareness to know what I could change and what I couldn't by the person convening that first meeting. Thankfully, I did not listen. I stuck with the idea that together we could make a difference and many people in that room that day were instrumental in changing policy.

At that time the policy on homelessness needed improvement. The homeless person had to navigate their way around a horrible system to be considered for housing, and good luck getting any support services for your mental health or addiction problems. Best practices across the world showed that a housing-first approach was the most effective strategy. Simply put, you provide a house first, and then the support services go to the individual at that house to help keep them from being homeless.

After many years, the Homelessness Policy is one where people are now given housing with support. I have met with several policy advisors to ministers on this issue accompanying representatives from agencies such as Mission Australia to get better outcomes for homeless people. Collectively, the power of good people working together does get some amazing outcomes.

One of our homelessness leaders proved to be a "Margaret Mead tragic quoter" as well, so I immediately knew that anyone walking around using the same motivational quote I used had to be someone I could work with. That leader, Trina Jones, was the driving force in the creation of the HART and is now the CEO of Homelessness NSW.

I originally saw this quote due to my affliction of being a tragic fan of the band Nickelback. One of their music videos had at the end Margaret Mead walking along with a large group of women in Ireland in The Freedom Marches saying this quote, and it has always stuck with me as it is so true.

> *Never doubt that a small group of thoughtful, committed citizens can change the world; indeed, it's the only thing that ever has.*

On learning of my pending retirement, I received some wonderful messages from the homelessness agencies I had worked with. The one below is my favourite.

> *You have been a dedicated and genuine voice for people who are vulnerable and have advocated with all levels of community and government to have a system that responds efficiently and provides support holistically, to anyone who is in need. You have been a leader in addressing rough sleeping in the area and allowing us all to be part of the rapid and easy response. Over the last few weeks, some of us have been involved in the street count across the district and the numbers have been low. Whilst we do know that so much homelessness is hidden, the numbers on*

the street are indeed low and we would absolutely credit you with leading the way in this. Your emails to the wider group were met with immediate response and you chaired your meetings with purpose and thought. So thank you – for being such a leader of change, so passionate for those who don't have a voice and so inspirational in the way we work together.

Rachelle Elphick, Mission Australia 2020

Our homelessness partners in northern Sydney were always looking to raise money and awareness for youth homelessness. So, in the city on a Saturday morning in November 2016, we had to abseil as a team down a 42-storey building on Market Street overlooking Darling Harbour. What was impressive about our team was the three other people I was with. They had never abseiled before and they still did it. I had been in police rescue back in the 1980s and had done hours and hours of abseiling but that was 30 years earlier and 42 storeys above the ground is ...well, 42 storeys above the ground. That is really really really high. I had more than one moment of *What are we doing here?* But we did it together. There was a lot of screaming, laughing and sheer relief when we all got to the ground again, but we did succeed with many other people that day to raise awareness about youth homelessness.

One final point to highlight the importance of people working collaboratively together is the only real thing that makes a real difference.

I was at an Affordable Housing Conference in 2018 in my role as the Sponsor for Homelessness in the NSW Police.

A former rough sleeper from the Hawkesbury area, in the northwest of Sydney, asked me if I could help introduce, a Homelessness inter agency group, like what we had done in the city and the Northern suburbs. He said that homelessness was on the rise in the area and the support services response was struggling. He was quite distressed.

I made no promises, but I undertook to research what was happening in the area and see what I could do if need be.

Upon researching the status of rough sleepers in the Hawkesbury, homelessness, was indeed on the rise and beyond what existing strategies could manage.

The Local Council was struggling with the number of rough sleepers in tents along the Hawkesbury Riverbank, and the amenity of the area was being impacted. This meant rough sleepers and the wider community could be heading towards a confrontation.

I approached the relevant directors of Family and Community Services along with the heads of Specialist Homelessness Services, the local council, volunteer organisations and the Police Commander of the location.

I asked if they would mind if I chaired a couple of interagency meetings with the relevant stakeholders to see if we could replicate the successes achieved in the city and northern Sydney simply by working together more collectively and cohesively.

This was approved and I chaired a couple of meetings at the local police station with all the stakeholders present.

This was all it took. I provided advice and examples of what worked in the city. The stakeholders in the Hawkesbury area then did the rest with the same adage applying, when a small group of committed people work together, amazing things happen.

I was invited back 12 months later to this now highly functional Hawkesbury Homelessness Interagency Group for an update.

The invite was from the Mayor of the Hawkesbury Council who was now the chair of this amazing group of people.

Collectively they were housing homeless people ending their vulnerability just by working more collaboratively.

This group is still recognised as an example of good practice in what can be achieved in making homelessness rare, brief, and non-recurring.

Reflections

I have done some amazing jobs as a police officer, but I think my experiences within the homelessness community give me the most satisfaction. It sums up who I am at my core. If something needs to change, then I change it. It is really that simple.

Homelessness is a heartbreaking issue.

Homelessness is not viewed as a police problem to solve. It is often seen, incorrectly by some, as merely an enforcement issue. It is not ok that homeless people are viewed as failures and are excluded by many in society. Homelessness can be solved, at least for some, simply by saying it is not ok and then working with committed people to resolve the issue.

We created a group of people that questioned the status quo and, through that approach, we housed hundreds of people. And the model we created was used as an example of best practice across the state of NSW.

Homelessness will never go away.

To summarise Trina Jones' address to State Parliament in March 2023.

In 2023, homelessness should be rare, brief and non-recurring. We cannot end homelessness without housing. There are three key areas that can assist.

Twenty-five thousand social housing homes a year need to be created across Australia to end homelessness. People are increasingly being pushed to the brink of homelessness at unprecedented rates.

The increase in disasters, the long tail of the COVID-19 epidemic, and now the cost of living crisis is pushing people to the brink of homelessness more than ever.

What this looks like in reality is working families are living in tents on the south coast of NSW. Older women who no longer have enough money to live in a home are living in their cars, and circling the car park at large metropolitan hospitals in an attempt to get free medical care.

There are high rates of youth living in dangerous conditions, and people fleeing family violence, choosing between living in a home where they may be injured or killed, or leaving that space with no safe place to live.

Housing should be a critical infrastructure.

If the federal government provides funding to state governments for social housing, the state government should match that funding to maximise the amount of housing that can be produced.

To give context around how dire the situation is in 2023.

In NSW, there are 57,000 families on the waiting list for social housing. Every year, 35,000 dwellings get built in the state. Approximately 700 of those dwellings are social housing properties. At that rate of investment, it will take over 80 years for everybody on that list today to have a house over their heads. The list is not a 10-year waiting list, it is an 80-year waiting list.

We all have a shared responsibility to ensure everybody has a safe home. A home is the foundation of good health, education and employment.

We cannot ignore the fact that the current rate of funding for social and affordable housing to end homelessness is not enough.

There is a need for courage and compassion at a leadership level to address this crisis that is affecting those most vulnerable in our society. There is an opportunity here to fund and leave a legacy across intergenerational boundaries.

Some things are too important not to fund.

The worth of the community and its officials can be judged by how they look after their most vulnerable.

13

Empowering Other Leaders
(2011–2020)

As a police commander running a large inner-city command, with the challenges and tasks that come with that role, committing to a six-month leadership program every year was a huge commitment. The task was outside of my job description, but the rewards were immense and sometimes unforeseen.

If you have ever watched the movie called *The Old Guard* starring Charlize Theron, you might get a sense of what I mean. In that movie, there are five soldiers gifted with immortality. They save particular people throughout history from being the victims of violence. After centuries of doing this work, this group of immortal soldiers question their relevance until a researcher tracked what the people these immortals had saved went on to do. Without exception, each person that they had saved went on to do some earth-shattering experiment or implemented change in human history that made a fundamental difference.

Whilst I cannot claim that level of outcome, nor wish to, I do know that many participants of our leadership program from 2011 to 2020 have gone on to become outstanding leaders, changing the lives of others. It is a humbling thing to be a part of.

These leadership programs were not an organisational requirement or resource-supported initiative. I ran these workshops from within our own command, often securing placements for other commands to join our own leadership crop of future leaders.

There were some special people amongst those 240 participants and some equally special presenters. Commissioners were still a regular final speaker for the last day, as was Deputy Commissioner Jeff Loy. I don't think he missed a final day for the last four years.

Deputy Commissioner Mick Willing was also a regular, in one particular year giving two presentations during the six-month program. Participants wanted to know more about him.

I had speakers from all walks of life, since every leader's journey is different, and every participant derives inspiration from different speakers. I presented to each group on goal setting and teamwork and, as time went on, my experiences and learnings in the Mosman Collar Bomb job and the first two hours of the Lindt Café Siege.

From 2011, workshops had a structure. Each year, the participants were split into four or five smaller groups. Their task as a team over the six months was to formulate a 10-minute presentation on a current issue in the NSW Police that they thought they could make a difference. If the presentation had potential, they may have to present the same content to executive roles within the NSW Police Force.

There were many good presentations during those nine years but two stand out.

The first group did a presentation on the perils of not searching offenders coming into police custody well enough. Accompanied by news photos and narratives of searches gone wrong, it was a hard-hitting presentation. The presentation was so relevant I approached the Principal of the NSW Police Academy to allow our group to present to the graduating classes. For classes in that period between 2011 and 2013, this group went to the Police Academy and gave this presentation.

One of our guest presenters was Tony Crandell, now an assistant commissioner. He had the sponsorship responsibility of the LGBTQI communities' relations. When he gave his presentation, it was just after NSW Police had received very bad media coverage of their overuse of force on members of this community during the Mardi Gras celebrations of that year.

A group from that year's participants made their presentation on raising police awareness given their responsibility of managing and supporting LGBTQIA events. This presentation was so good it was used by me in all LGBTQIA events and by Tony Crandell to brief staff tasked with overseeing and supporting those events. It was put forward to other police as an awareness tool to understand what this community had gone through in the very recent past and supported by the NSW ombudsman.

The presentation included recent NSW history that homosexuality was viewed as a crime and a scourge on the community by previous Commissioners of Police. Where Mardi Gras was celebrated now, it used to be a protest march on how unfairly their community was treated over their sexuality. Researchers have recently learnt we even had a gaol at Cooma to rehabilitate queer men from their supposed afflictions. The group responsible for this presentation also went to the Leadership College for Police at Richmond and showed what was possible from frontline police when given the opportunity.

I had a presenter who was a police officer that represented the Japan recovery mission after the 2011 tsunami. That same police officer was the police forward commander when the police went into the Lindt Café to end the siege. There has been a lot written about this fateful day but none of those stories tell you what it would be like to be the police forward commander who authorised tactical police to go in and end the siege.

Once the siege was ended, my fellow police commander and friend had to endure the following briefing: two civilians are dead, one from the offender and one from friendly fire, two other civilians are injured from gunshot wounds, possibly from police fire, and one police officer has a gunshot wound to the face, possibly from police fire.

Every time I have heard this presentation, it has the same outcome. To this leader's credit, he presented each year to our new group of leaders, telling his story and his pain. Each year, there was the same stillness in the room and the same level of respect for his leadership under the most difficult of times.

Other presenters included people I had met in my various aspects of policing.

One young woman was one of the best young leaders I had ever come across. At that time, she was in her mid- to late-20s. She had the ability to influence others to work together and across agencies. We worked well together. Her story was outstanding. At the age of 16, she had been a night club manager in Ireland and later attended university. She then came to Sydney and started doing amazing things in the homeless community showing outstanding leadership qualities for someone so young.

One of the groups she spoke to had a sergeant from Sydney city command. The sergeant had a passion for understanding and working with homeless people. Our presenter emphasised that each homeless person was an individual with their own story. If you took the time to know their story, a better working relationship could be achieved between police and rough sleepers. This sergeant took this on board and got to know the people in his patch.

In August 2017, this same sergeant was the police officer who averted an unnecessary confrontation between police and rough sleepers when the Martin Place Tent Embassy in the Sydney CBD was about to be forcibly removed at the request of the NSW Government.

State government legislation had been expedited to the police so that force could be used on vulnerable people to deconstruct the Tent Embassy. None of the police wanted to use force as homelessness is not a policing issue, it is a societal issue where government policy, over decades, has let down those most vulnerable in our community. Unfortunately, around the world, policing is the tool used to make homelessness go away through enforcement. But it really doesn't go away, it's just hidden.

This sergeant knew the main organisers, had a relationship with them and through agreement with the organisers, the rough sleepers in those tents at Martin Place agreed to pack up their tent city and dispersed without confrontation. Creating and empowering other leaders has far-reaching implications on how they improve their own workplace, their environment and their community.

Another strategy offered to each participant each year was mentoring. Participants were tasked with finding their own mentor and through that relationship expand their potential.

Without exception, each year I was asked to mentor either one or multiple participants. I never said No as I found these relationships to be equally enlightening for me. I always made time. In the final year, I mentored a policewoman who was a supervisor, and who had parental responsibilities and held herself back from what she could be to meet those parental responsibilities.

At that time, I was running large training exercises in auditoriums, conference rooms and school halls to prepare our staff, our stakeholders and our community for the next big event like a Lindt Café Siege or Mosman Collar Bomb. I would arrange to have up to 200 people in an auditorium, all with the skills needed to work together to get an outcome for something bigger than they had ever thought of.

Some of the scenarios revolved around a murder in an emergency ward at a big Sydney hospital with the fallout flowing into an incident involving a major shopping centre and the transport interchanges that service those big shopping centres.

Because of those exercises, we learnt each other's capabilities and what actions were needed if something bad went down. The sergeant I was mentoring came to every one of those training exercises.

I think Steve Waugh is one of the many leaders attributed to the saying, "There is no such thing as luck, it is when preparation meets opportunity."

In January 2019, preparation met opportunity.

The sergeant I had been mentoring was on duty at Chatswood when five young Middle-Eastern men thought it would be a funny thing to walk into Westfield at Chatswood with five fake but very real-looking pistols. Their presence sparked alarm and concern amongst the communities and emergency services.

The sergeant allocated her resources to key points once she was aware of what was going on. This allowed for clear descriptions and locations of where these five young men were. With that information, other leaders on the ground, who had also been at the same emergency training events, resolved the issue without incident and without anyone being shot or killed.

The outcome of this incident was put forward as a great example of best practice for a new education component proposed by education services. What is most satisfying about this incident is that I wasn't even there. The training and the relationships I had created to empower others prior to this incident occurring, saw other leaders utilise what they had learnt in that training.

One of the most satisfying strategies I employed during these workshops I learnt from one of the guest presenters, at that time the commander of a large police area command, was called the Career Planning session.

He had this simple process where he drew a line on a piece of paper starting with the age of the person you were talking to, and the end of the line was when they envisioned retiring. Then you ask the person what they wanted to achieve in the sections between their age now and their retirement.

Once people started to voice their aspirations, a timeline or a plan with strategies was created. After he showed me how to do the process, I offered the process to each participant of each leadership workshop every year after that. Not everyone chooses to undergo the process, some are happy where they are at.

Some people did elect to go through the process and I never said No. Some people were less than 10 years out from retirement, some people had 40 years to go. The outcome and content were always different because everyone's story is different but the awareness that came out of those sessions was amazing. The sessions taught me how to listen and be aware of what people really wanted to do.

Not everyone wants to be a police commander, but they all want to be good at what they do and be satisfied with that choice. I used to include a line underneath the work line and make that the life and relationship line. I emphasised the importance of prioritising family, no matter how much we wanted to achieve in our working lives. I remember one guy who was very good at what he did. When we were doing his plan, I asked him what his top five priorities were. We did all that and spent a good two hours with each other. I knew he had a wife and three young children.

Before the end of the session, I tapped the one-page plan and said, "What about your wife?" He looked at me crestfallen.

I said, "You have told me how much your wife helps you and how insane your family life is with the three children. Would it be good to arrange a regular date night with your wife to say thank you?" Date nights went into the plan.

As I write this book, I have been retired for over three years.

Only recently, one of the younger participants of the last leadership workshop sent me a message via SMS. I had done the career life plan process with them. I still remember the meeting; the person was keen attentive and engaged. They were just starting their career, but they had skills, ethics, humility and spark. The message was a simple one. A picture of the career and life plan I had prepared with this young participant was sent to me, with the accompanying words: "I still review it often."

Reflections

I am very thankful that I took the time to create the leadership workshop program. Not only did I have an impact on several future leaders' lives, but they also taught me so much. I still get emails and text messages of updates about what a lot of these participants are up to now, such is the level of relationships we created. I still receive messages like, "Thanks for teaching me it's ok to make my workplace safe, I promise to pay what you taught me forward to the people I lead."

One of the most humbling things about the leadership program was that I needed a cohort of talented, authentic leaders each year to present and empower our future leaders. When I asked these leaders, from private contractors to business owners, to deputy commissioners and commissioners, they all agreed to be part of the program no matter how busy they were.

I was very careful of the leaders I put in front of our participants. I did not want braggarts or leaders who were all about them and not about the people they lead. The most sought-after content from any leader was an insight into their own personal story, when things did not go right and how they got through those bad times.

I would like to acknowledge the presenters our program had over the years as their collective message and influence did change people's lives.

I have learnt that leaders like all of us are human. Leaders get impatient, worried and even scared like everyone else. A leader who let their emotions get in the way becomes too involved in the process to bring about change, creating a level of unnecessary angst and sometimes anger at the level of change occurring.

We all do it.

When I saw these leaders who had a reputation for becoming involved in the process and causing unnecessary angst give personal presentations to empower future leaders, we got to witness firsthand who they were at their core, at a very personal level. Unfortunately, the pressures of leadership do bring about less-than-perfect outcomes. Some leaders choose to force change to happen, causing unnecessary angst, and some leaders chose to empower others to lead and through that process positive change can and does occur.

That's the core value of empowering other leaders. It takes support, kindness and care to empower other leaders. If those conditions exist, then there will be people within the leadership group that will have a quiet word with the leader who is becoming too involved in the process and perhaps micromanaging and tell them they are doing something stupid. I know I had a team of people in our leadership group that was quite confident to tell me, "That's a stupid idea, Boss." People need the confidence to tell a leader that advice without fear of losing favour, and a leader needs to take that advice on board and truly reflect on how to progress.

14

Kokoda (2014)

One of the most amazing things about the NSW Police is how they look after the families of police officers who have died, either on or off duty. Police provide ongoing welfare support, group outings, school scholarships and financial support. The charity that looks after police families is New South Wales Police Legacy. Like any charity, they fundraise above and beyond its business model which sees nearly all police employees contribute a small percentage of their wage towards the fund.

One of the best known fundraisers is the Kokoda Track in Papua New Guinea, following the path of our soldiers in World War II when they faced the Japanese army, intent on using Papua New Guinea as a stepping stone to Australia.

The NSW Police Legacy Kokoda Track runs every year just before Anzac Day. Although April 25 commemorates the thousands who died at Gallipoli, Turkey, during World War I, Anzac Day also commemorates all Australian and New Zealand soldiers who had served and died in wars and other operations.

Let me provide a short history lesson regarding the Kokoda Track.

During World War II, Japan invaded Singapore and made its way down the islands toward Papua New Guinea. The idea was that the Japanese army would use the Kokoda Track from the northern side of Papua New Guinea to make their way to Port Moresby, where they would take control of the harbour and begin preparations to invade Australia.

The Japanese forces were battle-hardened, up to 2,000 strong, and up until the Kokoda Track had never been beaten by any opposition. There were merely 300 Australian reservist soldiers sent from Port Moresby to meet the Japanese. They were referred to by regular army soldiers as "Chocolate Soldiers".

Whilst the name Kokoda Track sounds quaint, there is nothing about the location that is easy or quaint. It is a diabolical place, with mud, rain, heat, rivers and the steepest hills you have ever seen, both uphill and downhill. When you add to this someone shooting at you and there are 2,000 of them and 300 of you, it lets you know the dynamic. The result was a lot of soldiers died on both sides. Reinforcements were sent to aid the Australian soldiers, but the initial 300 soldiers did stop the might of the Japanese forces when it counted.

To undertake the NSW Police Legacy Kokoda Track, I had to make an application to be included and agree to do the necessary preparation for the experience. I intended to do the Kokoda Track with my son, Kirk. He was 24 years old at the time. Kirk is 6'6" tall and extremely strong and fit. I was 52 at the time at 5'10". My physical fitness was the most important preparation that I needed to do, to give myself the best chance of completing the track in one piece and uninjured.

We were advised to do group and individual training months before the Kokoda Track. These training sessions involved hours of walking through our extensive national park systems throughout the Sydney and Blue Mountains area, slowly building from two-hour walks to six-hour or longer walks. When you do the Kokoda Track, it is done with a guide who is authorised by the villagers to be on their land, providing compensation to villagers who have an extremely low standard of living.

The guides give you the option of carrying your own backpack, with up to 25 kilograms of equipment and stores, or employing a porter to carry your backpack. The porters of Papua New Guinea have a long and honoured history, with many historic photos depicting them helping injured and sometimes blind Australian soldiers away from a war zone to get urgent medical help.

In early January 2014, we started the group training through some thickly forested terrain in Sutherland National Park. It was obvious early on that some were extremely fit, and others were not. We all had our place as being fit or not fit, and I soon identified with the role of staying back with those not so fit, to make sure they did not give up and enjoyed the satisfaction of finishing each challenging training session. One thing played on my mind as I prepared for the actual Kokoda Track: nothing we could do in the Sydney area could replicate the heat and humidity of the Papua New Guinean mountains and jungles.

My son and I would make it a weekly thing to go to the sand dunes at Kurnell. I had always read about what these sand dunes were and used to see photos of elite sporting teams in anguish during their preseason training sessions on these hills.

Kirk and I lived in the Hills District in the northwest of Sydney, and the Kurnell sand dunes were on the other side of southern Sydney, closer to Wollongong. When we arrived at the sand dunes for the first time, we were struck by the sense of community. There were family and community groups of all shapes and sizes, walking and running their way around these hills. Some of these sand dunes are 100 metres high and extremely steep in some sections. Kirk and I gradually increased the weight of our backpacks from 10 kilograms to 25 kilograms over the weekly sessions in these hills.

There was one section we found that was about 100 metres from top to bottom and the incline was insane. Once we found this section, we used it as our training ground doing repeated inclines and declines to build up our endurance.

This incline was so steep that you had to hold your hands in front of you to stop falling forward. The sand itself was so soft that our feet sank and our GP soldier boots filled up with sand, making the task even harder. Kirk could always do this training way easier than I could. Some days, I was gasping for air, sweating profusely at the top of the hills and gathering myself for the next run, whilst I watched Kirk do two runs to my one. But I was getting fitter and making progress.

I had a good location near my home for practising hill sprints. Our German Shepherd Bill used to accompany me on those hill sprints. A German Shepherd is a very fit dog, and my goal was to make him run rather than walk as I made my way up this 200-metre hill. If I could pass Bill up the hill, I knew I was getting fitter. I used whatever I could to motivate me to improve during these sessions. I found the song "Kickstart my Heart" by Mötley Crüe had the best beat and cadence for me. Even to this day, when I hear that song, I am taken back to those hill sprints with my dog getting ready for the Kokoda Track.

One of our final sessions as a group before we departed to do the Kokoda Track was a very unusually hot April day on the sand dunes at Kurnell. This was the first time we met all our NSW participants for our Kokoda Track experience. We were a wide and varied group, with huge differences in our physical capabilities. That last day on the sand dunes of Kurnell showed what we would be like on the Kokoda

Track. Some took off and left the group, with the sole goal of being first, with others who were not as physically gifted left at the back of the pack struggling on their own. I made the decision to help those at the back, as there is nothing worse than thinking you have been left on your own, feeling that you are not good enough. We all need support. I soon realised, when I got to the Kokoda Track, that I would spend my whole time at the back of the pack helping and supporting others.

My last training session was in the back stairwell of the old Redfern Police Station. This was across the road from the Redfern Railway Station and was eight storeys high. I had been asked to relieve as the commander for Redfern for April, just before I did Kokoda Track. That month was one of the highlights of my career. The normal commander of Redfern had formed a partnership with local First Nations elders, creating the Clean Slate without Prejudice Boxing Fitness program in a local community gymnasium that ran three mornings a week with local youth from 6 am to 7 am. It was about local youth mixing with local elders and community leaders, doing boxing fitness and at the same time committing to a routine that they would need if they were going to seek employment. Three mornings a week I took part in those boxing sessions. It was a special thing to be part of, helping create the future leaders of their community.

So, my last training session for Kokoda was to spend an hour and a half, in full police uniform climbing up and down the stairwell of the eight-storey building, non-stop. It was a very hot day, and the stairwell was not air-conditioned. At the end of that 90 minutes, my once light blue police shirt was completely dark blue with sweat. I wasn't tired and enjoyed the training session as the up and down of the stairs was what I would experience in Kokoda.

When I booked my spot on the Kokoda Track with my son, I also asked my wife and daughter to come along. They laughed at us and told us gleefully they were planning a getaway in Hawaii. The day we left for Kokoda, my wife and daughter sent us a photo of them travelling along the Hawaiian coastline in a Chevrolet V8 convertible with the roof down. I remember looking at that photo thinking their holiday may have a few more comforts than what we had planned, walking up mountains in high temperatures and heavy rainfall.

Our Police Legacy group was to be dropped off in the village of Kokoda, with the plan to arrive in Port Moresby the day before 25 April 2014 after nine days of walking the Kokoda Track. When we landed in the small airport near Kokoda village, we were picked up by three Toyota utes with canvas-covered trays and wooden seats. All of us fitted into the three vehicles and it was a very bumpy ride, but way better than walking from the airport to Kokoda village. We went through a couple of villages before we got to Kokoda.

In each of the three cars we were travelling in, we had a Papua New Guinean local police officer sitting at the very back with a sawn-off shotgun strapped over their shoulder. It was a very real awakening of the potential for violence there.

Apparently, the gun-toting extras in our cars were protection for us as some of the local groups were currently having violent confrontations. Such is the nature of Papua New Guinea: a beautiful place but with issues that sometimes occur between community groups that boil over into violence. We were very fortunate; our guide was a well-known and respected regular on the Kokoda Track who was soon to clock up 100 trips as a guide. Our guide always brought donations to villages and local hospitals and knew to only use porters that were approved by all the villages along the Kokoda Track.

We set out the following morning from the village of Kokoda making our way to our first night's campsite on the top of our first mountain climb with our 25-kilogram packs on our backs. I will never forget that first day. It was to be the hottest day of the whole experience.

The full afternoon sun blasted our climb up the steep side of the first mountain. I remember that climb vividly, it nearly killed me. It was so hot, my backpack was so heavy, and the incline was so steep that I had to rest multiple times to make it to the village.

That first afternoon really made me doubt I could do the whole Kokoda Track to Port Moresby. I had done a lot of training, but I found I could not last without resting. I finally made it to the first campsite, with most of our group already there. Hardly any other person in our group had found that first climb difficult and they were excited about the next few days.

During that first night at the campsite, after eating and bathing in a nearby waterfall, someone in our group who had done the track multiple times gave me some advice that transformed my whole experience and ability to do the Kokoda Track. The reason I had struggled so much on that first mountain was that I was trying to take large steps up the mountain, often looking to go straight up in the most direct line. The advice I got to make the experience easier was to take small steps and zig-zag my way up any steep sections. As soon as I did this, I found my ability to do the Kokoda Track infinitely easier.

We were on there for nine days and each day I would walk with different people who were struggling. I shared with each of them the advice I had been given, and then their experience of the Kokoda Track also became easier.

Our guide was well-prepared to help us all complete the Kokoda Track. He had two ex-special forces medics in our group to help with any medical needs. They ended up being two inspirational people who were an asset to our group. This preparation by our guide had earned him the distinction of everyone who had started the track with him finished. No mean feat as the Kokoda Track is not a kind place.

The Kokoda Track is a demanding place and is always looking for a way to take back control over the persons walking on it. I found with regularity, if I did not look where I was walking, I would inevitably fall. There was always a piece of mud, rock or large tree root that would jump out and make you stumble, and the next thing you knew you were on the ground. I lost count of the number of times I fell over. This was an old person problem as my son would run, using his 6'6"-frame to jump down uneven steps. I would have to stop and climb down, such was the difference in people's experiences. I would see him at the start of each day, and then towards the end of each day when he would invariably come back to meet me, offering to carry my backpack during the last part of the track for that day.

One day in particular is etched in my brain. I was starting to get sore knees when I trained and, at the time, I thought it was just a sign of getting older. No matter how much I trained I couldn't go downhill for any length of time without experiencing an immense amount of pain in my knees. On this day, the second part of the day was all downhill for what seemed like four hours. I had never been in so much pain. After about two hours, I felt like I could not walk any further as each step was so very painful. I didn't complain, but I was so slow getting down that mountain that afternoon.

In the last hour of that day, we had torrential rain and what seemed like rivers of mud. The rain and the mud took my mind off the pain in my knees and when I made camp that afternoon, I just sat in the rain for about half an hour, very glad to be at the end of the day's journey.

What I was to learn about knee pain on the Kokoda Track, after I had finished it, was that several other people in our group also had sore knees but they used painkillers like Voltaren. I would have been grateful for this gem of knowledge, but I made it without drugs so all was good.

A few years later, I solved the problem with my knees. Our daughter had been on a plant-based diet for several years and on an overseas holiday with her, she shared a podcast from Simon Hill who does "The Proof" podcast. We had a long layover at Hong Kong Airport between connecting flights, so we used that time to learn about plant-based eating. I was to learn and experience that all the dairy and cheese I was eating, although I absolutely loved it, didn't love me. As soon as I cut out dairy and cheese in my diet, and went plant-based, I could walk up and down hills all day long with no pain at all. I wish I knew that before I did the Kokoda Track.

I still shudder at some of the river crossings. They were raging rapids, with some having two trees tied together to form a bridge and you balanced your way across. The native porters would guide you across these crossings, balancing our way over the raging river below. There were no guide rails to hang onto, just the hand of the native porter. You had to totally put your trust in them. Other rivers were so fast-flowing that if I didn't have a big, strong Papua New Guinean porter next to me, who grabbed me, I would have ended up in some waterfall somewhere. My feet were swept out from below me within a second.

About two days from the end, another person in our group did what I had done multiple times every day and fell, just whilst walking along. That simple act of falling, with a backpack on, saw this person put their hand down to break their fall. When they did this, they broke their wrist and were immediately in an immense amount of pain.

Our medics went into action straight away, splinting the injury and placing a sling to carry the injury around the person's neck. They also loaded them up with painkillers. This person was offered the opportunity of being helicoptered out but declined. We had all been on the track for seven days and had grown a strong bond. Two of the front runners who always finished each day well ahead of everyone volunteered to help the person with the broken wrist make it to the end, walking with them to guide them across river crossings and the unforgiving landscape. With someone else carrying their backpack, this person did make it to the end.

Several other people were also struggling. My son and I spent the last two days with another person in our group who had started the Kokoda Track with a shoulder injury. They had a couple of falls and were struggling on those last two days. My son and I stayed with this guy the whole way, just taking our time, taking breaks, offering food, and any other creature comforts that this person needed. Our toilet paper and wet wipes were a much-needed luxury at one point on those final two days.

We finished the Kokoda Track just after dawn at the Port Moresby end. The final hill was just as steep as any others we had taken on, but we knew this was our last hill, and with our companion who had an injured shoulder, we finished it. It was a special moment and one that I will always cherish. My son was not tired at all and to show how much energy he still had left, he picked me up sideways, grinning from ear to ear, under the arch that commemorates the end of the Kokoda Track. We have a great photo of that moment.

Whilst I and several others in our group had found the Kokoda Track challenging, we had all chosen to do the track as an experience. It was a sobering thought to remember that our soldiers had willingly risked and lost their lives whilst fighting the might of the Japanese army on the same track. Our soldiers were not equipped with the right uniform, boots, or weapons to do battle on the Kokoda Track, but they did it anyway, against a stronger military force and succeeded in stopping the Japanese advance. We had nothing to complain about, and everything to be grateful for our soldiers' sacrifice and bravery.

At the end of the track, it is tradition to give away a lot of your kit to the porters so that they can share it amongst their families. All of us who had done the track thought nothing about giving something away that we had used once, most of us were just glad it was over. But to the local porters who did not have the access to money that we did, the array of items laid out on the ground to be given away was a source of goodwill to them and their villages.

Upon arriving in Port Moresby on 24 April 2014, we showered and had a decent meal or, in our case, several meals. I remember Kirk and I had hamburgers, pizzas, chips and beers multiple times that afternoon, whilst we were sitting around the hotel pool. It was heaven.

The Police Legacy Kokoda Track takes nine days to complete but it takes at least 6 months to prepare. That preparation was required to maximise the chance of completing the track without injury, as well as to work as a group.

There were many people in our group that year who had not prepared enough and were injured for many days. That didn't make these people bad people, it just meant they couldn't enjoy the experience to the same level as those who had really prepared for the Kokoda Track. We were all there together, we started together and we had to finish together.

Reflections

I remember how confronting it was for me personally that first afternoon climbing up the first horrible mountain to our first campsite. I was done. It was hot, I was exhausted, and I wasn't anywhere near the campsite, I was hours away. I was fit, I had trained for six months but I was still in a world of hurt.

It came down to one step, one small step at a time will get me up that hill. That became my ethos for the rest of the nine days we were on the track.

I didn't have to be first; I didn't have to be the fittest, I was there to help others who were not as fit as me to make it all the way home. There was no rank on the Kokoda Track, we were all just doing our best to collectively complete the track that our soldiers had defended so valiantly against a far superior force.

We all have our strengths and our weaknesses. I could help others find the headspace to put one foot in front of the other all day and go from one campsite to the next in one piece. Often, between those campsites were challenges that would scare the pants off me.

One of these challenges was this raging river with rapids and foamy water that just roared. The river had one crossing between two large boulders on either side and two very thin tree trunks had been tied together with jungle vine. My job was to balance walk across these extremely thin trunks to the other side, carrying my heavy backpack with me.

I watched my son, dance across it like it wasn't even there but my headspace wouldn't let me do it.

I am ever grateful to the two Papua New Guinean porters who were there at that crossing. One came out onto the tree trunks, took me by the hand like a child, and backed his way across the tree trunks holding my hand to get me across the crossing. I was terrified but oh so grateful that I was across that raging water crossing. If that local porter was not there to help me, I would still be there.

There were so many similarities between the Kokoda Track and leading a police command. Whilst I was good at helping people take the next small step to make it all the way home, I was less than inspirational at leading the way across a raging river.

This showed me that you don't have to be good at everything.

We all have skills, and we all have areas we need to improve on. But others have the skills we lack. We must trust those who have the skills we don't have and together we can achieve something we will never be able to on our own.

The next morning, Anzac Day, 25 April 2014, we woke up in the dark, got dressed in our police uniforms and left by bus to Bomana War Cemetery in Port Moresby for the dawn service.

There is nothing like the moment when the Australian National Anthem plays, and we are standing in full uniform saluting the Australian Flag to the dawn sunrise in an Australian War Cemetery where 3,000 white grave headstones of our fallen soldiers are.

It still sends shivers down my spine thinking about it. It is like our own smaller version of Arlington War Cemetery in Washington; the aura and stillness of the place have the same feeling. The extra special memory of that moment is that I got to share that experience with my son. I spoke about this moment at my son's wedding, during my speech to him and his intelligent, smart wife. My son and I have a large photo display of some of the moments we shared on the Kokoda Track, but my favourite is us standing arm-in-arm at Bomana War Cemetery in Port Moresby with all the white headstones of our soldiers in the background.

15

"Buttercup"

I had been doing boxing fitness in the cells underneath the Surry Hills Police Centre with other similar-ranked peers for several months when we arrived back in Australia after the Kokoda Track.

I decided to put myself forward as a possible boxing participant in the Police Legacy Boxing. This was a big deal for me and way outside my comfort zone. Anyone who knows me knows I am a lover, not a fighter. I am a small bloke, reasonably fit, but no boxing skills at all. A lot of boxers have that alpha-male quality about them, they must be the best and dominate. That is not me at all, I am happy being in the background, and do not crave centre stage. The boxing ring is all about being centre stage.

I used to meet up with an assistant commissioner most mornings around 5 am in the old cells area of Surry Hills Police Station. It had been converted to a boxing training area with a very small boxing ring in one of the old cells. This bloke is a big man with a busted nose and about 20 kilograms heavier than me. Thankfully, he is also a kind man and did not attempt to really hurt me or crush me, letting me improve each session.

Despite all this, it used to take me an hour to drive to the training session each time. I got up just before 4 am, took the dog for a quick walk or run, and then made my way in for a session in the boxing ring. On those one-hour drives into training, I used to wonder each morning why was I volunteering to get into a boxing ring with him. This bloke used to love boxing with me and laugh about my lack of skills because I never moved my head, and as such, I was a very easy target. Despite my fears, I did improve little by little every day.

The Police Legacy Boxing Team all offered advice and skills that helped me improve. I used to get hit regularly, used to find myself on the mat regularly looking up wondering what had just happened. One second I was standing, the next I was flat on my back on the floor.

No one ever unleashed on me to the extent that they could if they wanted to. It wasn't until I was to fight another superintendent in the boxing card for the big night that I knew I needed to do more. The person I was fighting was good. He had boxed before, and he had the capability and skills to hurt me. I had seen him train, I had seen him in the ring the previous year and I had seen videos of him punching people. He had the capability of hurting me with one punch.

I needed more specialised help. A sergeant at our command had prolific boxing skills but was also kind with how he trained a beginner like me. He was so quick in the ring you never really knew where he was, and I can honestly say in that first year I never hit him once in all our sparring sessions but I did learn a lot from his skills. I also sought out and paid for the aid of a professional boxing trainer who was the resident boxing trainer at the North Sydney Police Citizens Youth Club. He had trained world champion boxers before, so I was in good hands.

My skills and fitness did improve. I was a left-handed boxer known in the boxing trade as a Southpaw. That made me more difficult to handle although I am not an aggressive person, so my punches were never knockout-worthy, just short and snappy.

My trainer taught me how to be a counterpuncher, which means to throw your combination and get out of there. If your opponent rushed you, you could throw another couple of punches from wherever you were, because of the footwork my trainer had taught me. My opponent in the Police Legacy Boxing Match was a fighter who would always come forward, so my trainer taught me what he loved to call "The Matador Move". The Matador Move is based on the premise that as your opponent charges at you, intent on killing you, you step to the side and throw a combination at the same time as they go past you, then reset and repeat.

When you are not a fighter, or someone who enjoys being hit, training for a boxing match for four to five months every weekday means you get hit every day.

There were some funny stories though. My son had been doing Brazilian Jujitsu (BJJ) for several years and they do a lot of mixed martial arts with that training, including boxing.

At 6'6", my son was then and still is a bit of a weapon. He volunteered to spar with me in the backyard every Wednesday night to help prepare me for the fight. I used to dread those sessions as my son was just too big and too quick. I always prayed that he would have overtime on those Wednesday nights just so I didn't have to do it, but somehow he always turned up to flog his dad.

I remember that I rarely ever hit my son. The hit ratio was at least 10:1 in his favour. My daughter recorded one session but the video was shaking too much as she was laughing too much at the inequity of the boxing match occurring in our backyard.

In the end, to make it so I had a chance of getting through, my son would spar with me with one hand behind his back. Anyone watching would have died laughing, and in truth, I still got flogged. Even with one hand behind his back, my son was way too good for me.

I started to enjoy sparring in the small ring at the old police cells as I familiarised myself with being in the ring and improved my ability to think beyond being scared out of my wits. As I became more familiar with that arena, I relaxed, breathed normally, and was able to sense my opponent's moves.

Since I had been taught to be a counterpuncher, I found my punch would flick its way out before I ever thought of it. Sometimes, I amazed myself when I had a stunned sparring partner looking at me after I had collected them square in the face. You could see them with the look of "Where did that punch come from?"

I hadn't even thought about throwing the punch, it had just happened naturally.

I learnt you didn't have to be a knockout puncher, sometimes it was all about timing. If the punch was snappy enough and the opponent is walking into the punch, physics does the rest.

About two weeks before fight night, I got in the small ring in the old cells with the wrong guy. He was way too big and had a reputation for breaking peoples' ribs. I lasted the first round, but frustrated him because I was left-handed, stinging him a few times with my counter punches.

Each time I got him I could see him grinding his teeth more and more and I knew my time was coming. He figured me out in the second round, all he had to do was monster me into the corner of the small ring, and even though I was pretty good at getting out of corners, he just man-handled me, and threw me back into the corner and then gave me a massive hit to my ribs.

Everyone heard the punch and there was a collective sigh ... then a pause before someone asked, "Are you alright Al?" I nodded and I lasted the rest of the round but later in the day, I knew something was wrong.

I went to my doctor, had an x-ray and found I had a broken rib. The injury meant I couldn't throw a punch effectively; I couldn't even sneeze without cringing in pain. It didn't look good, it looked like I would renege on my promise to fight in the Police Legacy Boxing two weeks before fight night.

For the next two weeks, I just did footwork in the ring. My trainer had taught me footwork to essentially spin and turn all the way around the ring for three minutes.

Our fight was only two-minute rounds so this training would prove to be the foundation for me if I was to survive. Without being able to throw a punch, I would do multiple rounds of footwork, and eventually started to throw punches without my ribs hurting. I did my footwork routines around North Sydney Oval and on an oval in Goulburn when I was down there for a Passing Out Parade. The footwork drills became a sense of security and reflex, whilst building up my fitness and endurance.

Before you can fight in a boxing match you have to be signed off by a doctor declaring you are fit enough to do so. My doctor had only just seen me two weeks before with a broken rib so I didn't like my chances of getting him to say I could fight.

I initially went doctor shopping and visited someone I didn't know when I asked him to sign off on my fitness to fight. He just shook his head and showed me the door. I had to eat humble pie and go see my doctor. When he saw me, he did all the doctor's small talk and then asked me what I was doing visiting him again so soon.

When I told him I wanted him to sign me off as fit to fight, he burst out laughing and looked at me saying, "Only you would come in to ask me that."

We bantered on, I laughed with him and told him what I had been doing in the training sessions with my footwork, and that I could now throw punches again. He looked at me and said, "What if someone hits you in the rib, how will you go?"

I told him my training strategy of "The Matador Move" and he just laughed, shook his head and signed me off as fit to fight with his final words being, "Good luck, you are going to need it."

By this stage, I had raised more than $10,000 in sponsorship, so I wanted to follow through and do the fight.

On fight night, I was allowed to have my son as one of my crew in the corner with my trainer. Nothing prepares you for your first fight. The minute you step inside those ropes it is just you and your opponent. I can say without a doubt, of all the scary things I have done in policing, that stepping into that boxing ring scared me beyond silly.

Everyone has a fight name, but as I am not a fighter and I didn't feel right naming myself with any mean boxing name, I named myself Allan "Buttercup" Sicard.

I had a great fight song, using Nickelback's "Burn It to the Ground".

It's all quite civilised initially, you are in your corner with your trainer and crew telling you everything you want to hear. Then you meet in the middle of the ring with your opponent and the referee, who I remember was a well-mannered young bloke. You get told to go back to your corner, and then the bell rings for the start of the first round.

I knew my opponent; he was a nice bloke. I had rung him when I first broke my rib, concerned that I would have to pull out of our fight. He said that he had a similar issue the previous year and two weeks was a long time and to give it time. He "promised not to hit me in my ribs" and I believed him. This bloke, who I met in the middle of the ring ready to fight, had a level of intensity about him. He didn't seem like the same nice bloke who had made the nice promise not to hit me in my freshly recovering broken ribs.

I used "The Matador Move" repeatedly in the first round, and I wasn't getting hit that much. I was that relieved I had got in there and boxed, and I honestly thought that it might be a good time to go home now. One round was enough and, in my head, I was ready to go home but then my son stuffed up any notion of me doing that. He leaned over the ropes, whilst I was sitting on the stool, after round one and said, "Proud of you, Dad." Those words did it, I had to stay for another two rounds.

I was exhausted, my Matador tactic was annoying my opponent, so in rounds two and three he threw me in the corner and started pummelling my ribs. Any promises were out the door. The sergeant at work had taught me well how to get out of the corner, it normally only took a massive step along the ropes and punch the guy on the way out. It worked most times, but on two occasions I was stuck.

I was getting belted, and I turned my head away twice, as I did not know what to do. The referee told me that I wasn't allowed to do that. My inexperience at this boxing caper was shining through, but it didn't happen again after my second warning.

My opponent was a good guy. He was very popular and had the nickname "Silver", the whole stadium was cheering "Silver". There was another police officer from our command also fighting, so together we had a lot of people from our station, but you couldn't hear them over the "Silver" chant in that last round. Anyone yelling out "Buttercup" didn't really have the same quality to it.

We were about the same age but he was a way better boxer than me and we were exhausted at the end of three 2-minute rounds. I was just happy the fight was over and didn't really care who won or lost. I thought my turning my head away those two times would mean I would lose the fight as it was not a boxing thing to do. The referee did say to me at the end of the fight, "Great footwork." I was happy with that compliment, as I was the guy who everyone loved to box initially because I was so easy to hit, so to say that I had learnt some sort of boxing skill was enough for me.

The judges had a split decision and awarded me the fight.

The picture of "Silver's" corner team in the background of the referee raising my hand in victory says it all. They had their hands over their faces looking to the sky, saying "How did that happen?" I don't really know how it happened either, but it is a nice photo to have.

The adrenalin and nerves took a toll, and I was tired after the fight. I stayed and supported other people I had trained and boxed with and ended up getting home around 11.30 pm.

My only problem was that I was the police commander for the Sydney Running Festival the following morning, which included a full marathon over the Sydney Harbour Bridge and all over the streets of the Sydney CBD. I had to be at the Sydney Police Centre for a 2.30 am briefing in three hours. Both the fight night and the Sydney Running Festival were set in stone, I just had to deal with it. It was only two days.

I did not sleep a wink, I just laid there in bed with the adrenalin of my first fight flowing through me for one and a half hours till 1 am. Then I got up, got dressed, travelled to the city and gave multiple briefings to over 200 police and other stakeholders.

I agreed to fight the next year. My opponent was a Macquarie banker called Marcus Drago. He was a beast and gave everyone he sparred with trouble with a capital T, even the big guys. I should have known with a name like Drago, the Russian fighter from *Rocky III* who killed Apollo Creed, that it would be an omen.

So, this is how the story went in my second fight.

Allan "Buttercup" Sicard was the pre-card fight against Marcus "The Destroyer" Drago. The fight after was former Australian boxing champion Danny Green against Mark Bouris from *The Apprentice*. It was the one and only time I would ever be in the opening fight on a fight card, before a major boxing name like Danny Green.

I was so much better than the previous year. I was fitter and had trained hard, sparring with bigger guys, with the plan to wear down "The Destroyer" by using my fitness, footwork and left hand.

My trainer had taught me some great new combinations that I even managed to hit my old sergeant trainer with. I wasn't complacent, and I always knew "The Destroyer" was going to be hard. There is a saying in boxing: "The plan goes out the door once the first punch connects."

"The Destroyer" was also trained by a former heavyweight champion trainer. They had done their homework on my left-handed style and viewed footage of my first fight.

When the first round started, I was hit five times in the face in the first minute of my fight. I didn't see any of those punches coming at all, they just rocked my world. I have never been hit so hard in my life. My plan of footwork and getting out of my opponent's path went out the door, and I knew I was in trouble.

I made a poor plan in the moment of getting flogged that if I am going to lose, I will lose throwing as many punches as I can. My memory is I threw the best combination of my life at him: I hit him in the face with a left straight and followed that with a right hook to the side of his face. They were perfect punches. I think I must have stood there a moment too long admiring how good my combination had been because the next second I found myself looking up at "The Destroyer" from the floor.

It was about the fourth time I had hit the floor in 90 seconds. The referee stopped the fight and gave "The Destroyer" the win. Six months of training over in 90 seconds. He was simply too good. My head was already ringing, and it took my brain a good two weeks to settle down and feel normal after that fight. In hindsight, and even when the decision to end the fight was made, I was ok with that. If I had kept going and traded punches for whole three rounds, who knows how my 55-year-old head and brain would have been?

It was a fight for charity. Fight crowds love seeing boxers get knocked down, so I had set the scene for the first fight of the night.

That same night, two other police from our station also fought. One of these fighters I had trained together for six months for this fight and together we had reached an incredible level of fitness. This was his first fight. No one tells you what it is like to wait in the dressing rooms before a fight. Normally, your opponent is warming up right next to you, and some of the other fighters have a different mindset and are intimidating to be anywhere nearby.

I knew my mate's fight was late in the fight card and he would be waiting on his own for his turn to fight. I went and sat with him for an hour before his fight, talked about everything but the fight, doing my best to calm his nerves, as nerves drain all your fitness away. The same lesson was coming through in all my collective experiences. With support, we can nearly do anything.

My mate was a champion in his fight and was declared unanimously the winner.

My ego wanted to have another go in next year's competition, but my commonsense came through. It was not a smart thing to be doing, to learn how to box in my mid-50s taking hits in the head with regularity. It was more than possible but not smart, so I never stepped into the ring again.

From 2015 to 2020, I still did boxing training most mornings before work with staff and had a great time. At my last station, we had a large accessible flat rooftop. We used to do boxing fitness on that rooftop every Tuesday and Thursday at 6 am for one hour. Some of those sessions were incredibly hard but everyone loved them. It was fun to hit the boss as hard as you could and pass the old guy running up and down five flights of stairs as we did sometimes during an exercise called the "Animal".

Those sessions became known as "No Rank on the Roof" and they remain some of my fondest memories of my working life as a police officer. When you play with your staff, you get to see another side of them and they see another side of you.

One of the backstories to the fighting adventure is that your activities influence others to do something different. One of our sergeants started to train with us in the first year. He was overweight and wanted to turn this around. I have never seen anyone train as hard as he did and eventually became fitter than all of us. He ended up being the conditioning trainer for our team for the second-year fight night. He was a bigger man and sparred with me a lot in preparation for my second fight with "The Destroyer", crowding me, pushing me around wearing me out.

This sergeant became a very good boxer and ended up getting a silver medal in the Men's Masters Boxing titles in Queensland in 2015. We ended up having a team of people who would come along for several years to do the fitness sessions together, and all of us would have fun and it made our working lives better.

Reflections

Whilst this account of my foray into the boxing world is a good side story, how does it fit into leadership? There are two main points that relate to leading people.

It is never too late to learn something new. If you need help to learn, then go to the people who know their stuff. It's ok to say you don't know.

Our environment should have as much fun as possible, no matter how serious the task is.

Boxing was a good example of learning something new. I knew nothing about boxing. I knew it was a very hard sport to be part of. Boxing took a degree of courage to even contemplate doing, let alone the sparring and then getting into the ring on fight night. It took a lot of discipline and sacrifices, in small increments every day to improve to a standard where you could be considered competitive. If I replaced the word "boxing" with "leading", the same descriptors apply.

I knew early on that I needed an expert trainer to help me, firstly, to survive and then thrive in the boxing ring. The trainer I found was a perfect choice for my character and fighting style. My trainer broke down boxing into small bites, that included muscle memory training like transfer of weight, how your body moves, how your shoulders and hands move, and how they are all connected to what your feet are doing.

Again, if I change the term "boxing trainer" to "leadership mentor", the same correlations apply. Leading is about those little instinctive things we do every day that make a difference in people's lives, how we empower them and make them feel supported and included.

The second point is to have fun with the people you work with in whatever way you can.

I started to really change my approach to my fitness in 2013. I was invited by a close friend and my mentor to join them in their daily sessions in the old cells of the Sydney Police Centre where they did an hour-long session of boxing fitness drills called "Old Man Boxing". The name of the session was misleading as there was nothing "old man" about it. There were several women involved in the sessions and the intensity of those sessions left me exhausted for several months till my fitness improved.

What I noticed from these sessions was that I was with several peers, superintendents, and some assistant commissioners, inspectors and sergeants all training to the limits of our abilities with the intent of becoming fitter. But there was something else at play at a deeper level.

We were having a lot of good clean, harmless fun together.

That was the core outcome of what the Old Man Boxing sessions were about.

It was about having fun together.

We never talked about work, and we would regularly ring each other throughout the day laughing about whatever session we had done that morning. The work was still done and done to a high standard but there was something else going on. In the high-risk environment of policing, in which a lot of us were involved at the pointy end, we were building a support network of lasting relationships and improving our own physical and mental health at the same time.

There is one funny image I will never forget.

Part of my role in these sessions was to bring the music playlists to whatever exercise regime we had going on each morning. There was one song that nearly always had us in stitches: "I'm Shipping Up to Boston" by Dropkick Murphys. A lot of boxers use it as their fight song. Within the song is a distinctly Irish theme that brings images of Irish Dancers jumping up and down and pointing their toes in a very fancy style.

What used to happen when this song came on, no matter what drill we were doing was this: our boss, a well-known assistant commissioner with a bald head and a very smashed up nose, and well over 6-foot tall, would start doing the Irish jig with his boxing gloves on, doing the best impression of a professional Irish Dancer. This song always takes me back to the old cells, laughing at our boss doing the Irish Jig.

Part of leading is paying it forward.

I learnt the value of how much fun these sessions in the Old Cells at Sydney Police Centre were, so I replicated them at our workplace. We had a lot of men and women who wanted to train together before work, so every Tuesday and Thursday morning we would train together and do some insane sessions in the North Sydney Police Citizens Youth Club, with the underlying theme of having fun.

I continued this pre-work training regime through to my last command where we were fortunate enough to have this large rooftop area to train on.

For nearly three years, we trained on the roof of our police building, laughing, sweating, running, and falling to the ground in exhaustion. The staff called these sessions "No Rank on the Roof". They remain some of my fondest memories about working in the NSW Police. There were no barriers to who took part in those sessions and the drawcard was you got to hit the boss (me) in some of the boxing drills.

I always found that it was ok for me to admit I didn't know what to do, but I did know who to source to learn what to do quickly. I learnt that it is a must to have fun in the workplace. It is a key ingredient to building a supportive and inclusive workplace.

16

The Lindt Café Siege

In December 2014, I was relieving as the police commander for Sydney City Police Area Command for three months from December 2014 to the end of February 2015. Around 8 am on Friday 15 December 2014, I was driving in my police commander's car across the Sydney Harbour Bridge heading towards North Sydney for an emergency management meeting with other stakeholders.

I had the police radio on, listening to what was going on in the city. Some commanders never listen to the police radio, some do. I liked to have it on all the time as you get to know which crews are on and who is supervising them.

By listening in, I could get a feel for who was capable, who was keen, and who was not acknowledging jobs. More importantly, if something did happen that I needed to know about, I was already aware of the job. It's impossible to listen to the police radio all the time as a commander due to the work schedule and activities involved, but it is still healthy to be across what is going on when the opportunity arises.

That morning I was very glad I had the police radio on. What I heard I will never forget. There was a lengthy description of an offender, wearing a backpack with wires coming out of it, armed with a shotgun taking hostages at the Lindt Café in Martin Place, directly opposite the building that housed Channel 7 and the NSW Government bureaucrats and ministers. It was not a good location for the risk it posed to any future activities in and around that area.

I heard the inspector responsible for that location broadcast that they had tried to ring the Lindt Café but received no answer, which was not normal, as that is where police in the area normally got their daily coffees from.

It was obvious that the job was a real job from those first broadcasts. I decided to return to the city and lead our response. I did a U-turn on the northern end of the Harbour Bridge and broadcast over the police radio that I was on my way to the job as police commander of the Sydney City Command.

I requested two things:

1. I asked for the traffic commander for the Sydney City Region to take over the traffic plan so that the perimeter for the job was secure, but the wider Sydney CBD remained flowing and operational so that the rest of the city could function. At an economic level, it could not be allowed for the city to become gridlocked. At an operational level, we needed clear access to the site as multiple emergency services resources would be required to manage this job to a successful outcome. I knew also from the Mosman Collar Bomb that it didn't have to be me to prepare this traffic plan if I could delegate that task to someone with the right skills.

2. I requested that the ambulance commander on site prepare and implement a trauma plan should outcomes go that way. What I didn't know was that when the Tactical Operations Unit (the unit with the guns and explosives for ending sieges) deploy to a real job, they take a paramedic crew with them to develop a trauma plan, so this task was already in hand.

As I drove to Lindt Café, I couldn't believe I was on my way to another job of this magnitude after having done the Mosman Collar Bomb. I was grateful that I had that experience, as it had me planning what we would need to do before I got there.

I called my boss whilst still on the Harbour Bridge to let him know what was happening and what was developing. My boss at that time was Assistant Commissioner Mick Fuller who went on to become Commissioner.

I outlined what I had heard over the police radio, and what I was doing, and that it was, in my opinion, a real job. My boss thanked me for the call and said he would be in touch again soon and to keep the updates coming.

What came from that phone call highlighted the value of communicating early and often. When you are part of a committed group of people, the load is shared. I was just about to learn how that load was to be shared. From my phone call to my boss, he went from his office on the seventh floor of the Sydney Police Centre in Surry Hills and went to the Police Operations Centre on level 4. There he set up, in a time, a Police Commander Incident Management Team to lead the NSW Police response. My role was to be the forward police commander on the scene at the Lindt Café.

On the way to the job, I heard the inspector and sergeant in charge of the shift working together at the Lindt Café managing the crews already on site. I knew this pair. One was a former homicide squad team leader, and the other was one of the best young sergeants I had ever seen. They were providing updates on the radio and giving advice about what they had seen and what they were doing. It was a professional, calm response.

When I got to the briefing location at around 9.30 am, everything was relatively calm. I let police radio know that I was on site and I was taking over command at the scene. The atmosphere was a lot calmer than expected. I met with our inspector and sergeant.

There was also a highway patrol motorcycle officer who briefed me. This officer had been up to the window of the Lindt Café and counted 15 hostages, with a man wearing a backpack that had wires coming out of it and carrying a shotgun.

We all thought we were dealing with a bomb in the backpack. The motorcycle officer was on his own, witnessing a confronting situation. Several of the hostages had looked directly at him, seeking his assistance. I could see he was distressed that he could not act on his own to save them, but the quality of the briefing he provided gave me a reliable picture of what we were facing.

I met with the officer responsible for the tactical response who was to be tasked with resolving this. He briefed me about what they knew, and I could help consolidate that information with the briefing I had just received from the motorcycle officer.

I offered advice that it would be useful for some tactical response police to speak to the motorcycle officer about what he had seen. The possible existence of a bomb being carried by the offender meant that any action would have to include that consideration.

I knew from the Mosman Collar Bomb job that a bomb is a bomb until proven otherwise. The steps involved to eliminate an object as a bomb were many. A bomb being worn by an offender made the situation even more challenging to both hostages and any tactical team seeking to end the siege.

I took a call from my boss around this time, briefed him on what was occurring, and he asked that I let him know should we decide to execute an urgent response.

At this stage, I was still not a counter-terrorism-trained police commander despite requesting placement in the program several times. I did know that the tactical response police would be responsible for entering the Lindt Café to resolve the incident.

I told the officer responsible for the tactical police what my boss had said and requested. He told me that if we had to enter urgently it would be his call with my authority, and there may not be time to advise upwards. I accepted this as it sometimes comes down to the people on the ground to make the call.

After leaving that first briefing with the tactical officer, I met with our Sydney City team. Two other inspectors and two additional sergeants had arrived on site. One was one of the best operational leaders I had ever worked with, and the other was a former police prosecutor. I put the operational inspector and the inspector with former homicide experience together. They were my planning and operational people.

I tasked them with evacuating buildings in line of sight of the Lindt Café. This was due to the risk from the firearm the offender had. I also tasked them with evacuating other locations adjacent to or above the Lindt Café due to the risk of a bomb being carried by the offender in his backpack.

In conjunction with these activities, I requested the operational inspector set up a working inner perimeter for the forward command police team to operate from with fire and ambulance. This required a mobile police command bus, and a sergeant to provide a level of security about which police and other response teams were allowed inside the inner perimeter.

When you have a major policing or emergency incident, everyone wants to be near the command post. I had learnt from the Mosman Collar Bomb that security around the command post was something to be protected and cherished. Unnecessary people around the command post only clutter the area, create more noise, and attract more people thus making it difficult to do your job.

I emphasised the need for us to provide a large inner perimeter, so that the necessary resources had room to move as well as to look professional. If you view images of what that site looked like that day, the inner perimeter was orderly and functional.

This all happened quickly, and we ended up with a good forward command post. I held regular briefings with tactical police, negotiators, and other specialist police from this command post. The traffic commander I had requested set up his form-up point for all his traffic resources at the end of Macquarie Street in Hyde Park. From that location, he did exactly what I asked him to do. He closed the streets which we were operating our inner perimeter from, whilst at the same time having a traffic plan that let the rest of the city function.

Another inspector from Sydney City came to the site. He was one of the most experienced and methodical senior detectives we had in the Sydney region. The perfect person to have at a job of this magnitude. He had the responsibility for all investigations responses from Sydney City Command. He set up a location for taking witness statements at the nearby NSW Rugby League headquarters.

Also at the site was our manager from the Sydney City Command who controls all things related to finance. He turned up at the site with his work credit card, ready to approve whatever we needed to help maintain our staff, such as mobile phone chargers, record-keeping materials, and additional laptops. People with the right skills were doing their jobs to the peak of their abilities and doing it well. This allowed me to remain focused on what we could do to end the siege.

Over those first two hours, I met with police media liaison officers to arrange to stop the media being displayed on the news and on the front window display of Channel 7 directly opposite the Lindt Café. This would limit the level of information the offender in the Lindt Café had from the outside world. I was aware that the offender was allowing hostages inside to communicate with police using their own mobile phones to update them on what was occurring. This was unusual. Our police were not actually speaking to the offender.

One of the demands the offender made through one of the hostage's calls was that he wanted to speak on a talk-back radio program to list his demands in exchange for the release of some hostages. I had advised my boss of this, and we entertained the idea of securing the release of some hostages that early was a positive thing.

The value of relationships came true that day. We needed a plan for the building. Because we had worked closely with the City of Sydney Council, one of their managers came to the Lindt Café site with an architectural plan for the building, all within the first two hours of setting up our command post. It also turned out that the building manager for the Sydney City Police Command and the Lindt Café were the same person so we also had him on site to assist tactical police to formulate their tactical plans.

As we were between briefings, one of my staff tapped me on the shoulder and then pointed upwards to windows on the first floor above our command post at the intersection of Martin Place and Elizabeth Street. The Lindt Café was up on the next block at the intersection of Martin Place and Phillip Street. There is a large downhill slope between these two intersections. What I saw when I looked up at the windows above us were several people standing up against full-height windows with handwritten signs: Help Us. What we were looking at was a solicitor's office waiting area. This waiting area was on the same level as the Lindt Café, and only had a foyer with swinging unlocked doors separating them.

Our specialist police were on site and planned how to get these people out. I recall that some people in the office wanted to make their own way out via other stairwells in the building. We did not allow this as we had not definitively secured the rest of the multi-storey building and could not account for additional offenders in the area. We secured rescue squad police with ladders to climb up to an awning outside the windows of the waiting area, and got all occupants from that area onto the awning, then down the ladders and onto the safety of the street.

Two hours go by quickly in a situation like this. I was satisfied with the progress we were making. At around noon, I saw another police commander who I knew well and he was trained in counter-terrorism.

I knew immediately I was about to be relieved of my role as the forward police commander.

This commander did it graciously and invited me to remain to observe if I wished to do so, which I did. One of the first things the new commander did was move the forward police command post to a more secure and larger site. This site ended up in one of the many levels of the NSW Rugby League headquarters. I remained at that location till around 11 pm witnessing briefings and updates till that time. I had no official role for this period.

What I did do was ensure that the police on the ground were supplied with refreshments, sustenance and information during this time. The people doing the mundane things like guarding an intersection or similar regularly get overlooked. Many of the police who were doing these duties had been there since the job started around 8.30 am and had started their shift at 6 am. As the job moved into the afternoon phase the logistics team from the Sydney Police

Centre supplied meals to the forward command post, but those meals never made it to the police on the ground.

A large contingent of fresh investigators and other support services consumed any meals and refreshments before they made it to the police on the ground. I ensured replacement meals were ordered and secured for these frontline police, but they didn't turn up for some time.

I had learnt from the many large events I had commanded that if you make sure your frontline police are fed and looked after, they will do anything for you, beyond what you would think they would do. This was one of those jobs where we needed that mindset.

The offender lost control of his hostages throughout the siege with groups of them escaping at different times. At one point during the night, the offender made the manager of the Lindt Café, Tori Johnson, kneel on the ground and shot him in the head from behind with a sawn-off shotgun, killing him instantly. There was a gap in time when Johnson was seen to be kneeling on the ground and the fatal shot. A police sniper did communicate what was occurring via secure police radio, but that message was not received or not received in time for urgent action that could have saved Johnson.

Tactical police did enter the Lindt Café and ended the siege by killing the offender. Regrettably for all involved, a ricocheting projectile killed one hostage and injured another two to the extent that they required lengthy hospital support and rehabilitation.

The tactical police did not enter earlier as they, like me, believed that the offender was carrying a bomb. A bomb is a bomb, until proven otherwise. When tactical police prepared to enter the Lindt Café, both themselves and their commanding officer believed that they were going to their deaths because of that bomb. Messages were sent to families saying goodbye as they really believed they were going to their deaths. Very brave actions for all involved. The tactical commander later said, "It was the bravest thing he had ever seen."

The forward commander that ordered the tactical police to enter and end the Lindt Café Siege was a colleague of mine. He was and continued to be after the incident a regular speaker at our annual leadership workshops, sharing his insights, experience, humility and vulnerability making him one of the most sought-after speakers in our program. When he retells the personal story of what the Lindt Café was like as the forward commander, it is a "you could hear a pin drop" type of story.

My colleague was on holidays when the Lindt Café occurred. He was up on the central coast with his wife. As the job was evolving, he contacted the police commander of the job and offered to come back from leave. My colleague was one of the most qualified counter-terrorism-trained police commanders in Australia at that time, with over a decade of training in that and other fields.

He was the only Australian police officer to go to Fukushima, Japan, after the 2011 tsunami with a search-and-rescue team, made up of fire and ambulance officers. He was used to big jobs. He came back from leave and knew with certainty that by being the oncoming forward police commander after 10 pm, it was more than likely the siege would come to an end under his leadership.

My colleague talks of the despair he felt as the briefing came in after the siege ended. His briefing was one offender deceased, two hostages deceased, two hostages injured by projectiles, most likely from tactical police, and one police officer shot in the face also from friendly fire. What we believed to be a bomb in the backpack of the offender was actually stereo speakers with wires coming out, made to replicate the appearance of a bomb.

No matter the training, none of us have ever had to deal with a briefing like that. My colleague knew with certainty that when the ultimate coronial review occurred, he would be seen in a negative light and he prepared himself, his family and his staff for such a reality.

Over the next few days, Sydney and the rest of Australia came to terms with the Lindt Café Siege and its terrorism-related issues. Terrorism was no longer something that happened to the rest of the world, it also happened to Australia, to us.

An event like that affects everyone differently. Some of the images show a group of plain-clothes police in a line making their way to the window of the Lindt Café as the siege was first evolving. They intended to do something, something that NSW Police were not trained to do then. You can see from the footage that they decided to withdraw despite their best intentions. I can understand that. They were not trained to breach. They were just regular frontline police who did their firearms re-accreditation and weaponless control annually. Training at that time did not equip them to enter a siege situation against an armed offender. Some of those police needed some time off after that day to deal with what they were confronted with.

After that day, I made some regular foot patrols on my own through the streets of Sydney just to show that we the NSW Police were still out there. The positive responses from the public were encouraging. The community was shaken but recovering.

I went to a city-wide debrief that called for all persons affected by the incident to attend if they wanted to. The debrief was organised by the counter-terrorism command in conjunction with NSW Health. The venue was a large community hall in the centre of Sydney. There were emergency services and community members present. It was a big crowd. The NSW Health representative gave a good summary of what everyone would be feeling after such a major incident. There would be sadness, nothingness, nervousness, avoidance, anger, relief and a whole ambit of emotions, until we came to accept what had happened. Each of us would deal with the situation in our own way.

As people were invited to ask questions or to provide feedback, one man came forward and provided his views. He was angry, very angry. He had been in the solicitor's office waiting room directly opposite the Lindt Café. He was furious about the length of time it took to get the people out of the solicitor's office waiting room and upset that he was not allowed to lead people out of that waiting room using the stairs available rather than be rescued out the window using ladders. He was obviously an educated man, and a good orator. The whole room was silent as he spoke.

He said something like, "What fucken idiot made that decision? We could have been out of there a lot sooner." There was a long silence. The police running the debrief looked a bit lost for words as they could not address this issue.

I was at the back of the room in a suit as I was not in command of this briefing. But I responded to the organisers and this man, "Sir, that idiot was me." The whole room turned to look at me, with some of the police organising the debrief looking at me and shaking their heads.

I then provided the reason why I made the decision I made. It came down to controlling what we could control, we did not know whether other offenders were within the building and it was not safe for civilians so close to the actual siege to attempt to make their own way out. The only safe way was to allow tactical and rescue squad police to facilitate the exit from the solicitor's office waiting room using the ladder and the awning roof. That was the safest option.

The man then just looked at me, took a breath and went back to his seat without a word. I got the impression he accepted my explanation.

As for me, I felt like I was on my own as my fellow officers didn't want anyone to say anything.

The coronial inquest date was set, and all involved in the response were called as witnesses. The coverage of the inquest was like nothing we had seen before in Australia, with many differing opinions being given as to what should have occurred.

I was grateful for the support I received in being part of this process. The NSW Police had employed a large legal team to prepare us for what lay ahead, with many meetings with legal counsel and coronial counsel. It was daunting but I did not feel isolated.

I was also provided with the opportunity to meet with senior police psychologists and peer-support psychologists. This support was also made available during the inquest, where a police psychologist sat with me prior to my giving evidence, during my evidence and after it was over. I took the option of having my wife come along and provide familial and professional support. She was a serving detective inspector at that time responsible for overseeing the management of police complaints across a large sector of police.

An event like the Lindt Café Siege impacts your colleagues and how we are all different. We supported each other the best we could but, for some, the continual hourly and daily criticisms of police actions were too much to bear. The incident and the subsequent scrutiny did damage our people, who had done their absolute best, both physically and mentally.

I have firsthand stories about some of my colleagues' reactions when they heard the coroner give their findings live on media. When the coroner declared the outcome, that no one individual in the police response was responsible for the ensuing deaths that occurred, several of my colleagues just broke down and cried. Their next action was to reach out to their peers and staff involved and break down and cry again. No one prepares you for this eventuality.

Reflections

There will be another event like the Lindt Café, it is inevitable.

Mick Fuller went on to become the new NSW Police Commissioner. He acknowledged the NSW Police could have done better and made commitments that frontline police would be trained to enter active armed offender situations to resolve this type of incident at the first available opportunity. Mr Fuller provided advice that even though police would be trained to enter siege situations in the future to end them more expeditiously, the outcome may prove to be a lot worse than the Lindt Café. Nevertheless, he provided assurance that police would act differently in the future.

The very sad reality of the Lindt Café Siege is that the state of NSW lost a lot of talented and skilled police officers because of the very public and critical review of what occurred.

The coronial inquest went on for months, with every word said by each witness dissected and commented upon by the media and social media. Often, those making the comments about what police did and did not do had never had to be in a life-or-death situation, and probably will never be in that position. Every police officer and support staff who was part of the Lindt Café Siege was there doing their absolute best, with what they knew and because of the training they had up until that point in time.

Could things have been done better? Yes. Could they have done better with the training, knowledge and technology at that time when they were responding to the first real terrorist act on Australian soil? Probably not. They still responded anyway, did their absolute best – two civilians lost their lives, and one offender lost his life with several others injured by ricocheting projectiles, including one police officer.

The ultimate finding of the coronial review of the Lindt Café Siege was that no police officer was personally accountable for the deaths of the two civilians killed, one by the offender and one accidentally by police. But the cost to many seasoned police of that very public inquest was that many never went back to work again. Some were shunned by the organisation that asked them to step up at this critical time.

What the incident taught me personally was that we must look after our people better when bad things happen. We invariably experience the debilitating reality of isolation. The reason for this appears to be purely political and self-serving. Senior leaders in the NSW Police do not reach out to their people to make sure they are travelling ok during the most challenging of times.

Once the inquest proceedings were in full swing, I was never contacted by a colleague at any time to make sure I was ok. Despite this isolation, I was regularly in contact with others during this ordeal to make sure that they knew they were not alone.

I was included in the future training of police commanders for counter-terrorism. I learnt new skills and was requested as a guest speaker in other jurisdictions because of my experiences.

I made a commitment to myself, our staff and our community that we would be prepared as best we could for the next Lindt Café. In the words of a World War II general, "The best form of welfare for the troops is first-class training."

Someone will have to lead the police into the next Lindt Café. Now that our police are trained in active armed offender training to effectively end any siege as soon as possible, the reality is that police and other emergency services who support police may also lose their lives in their endeavours to protect life and property.

Those police leaders who are there will find themselves before an enquiry, not only justifying why their actions may have resulted in the loss of life of civilians and offenders, but also the loss of life of their police colleagues whom they authorised to act. Are we ready for that reality? I don't think we will ever be ready for that reality and all the costs that outcome will bring with it.

Part 3

Learning from the
Past and Paying It Forward

*The boldest and most effective leaders, use a combination of
trust, love and belonging to create spaces where people can excel.*

Unleashed, **Frances Frei and Anne Morriss**

17

The Courage to Act
(2015–2020)

In early 2022, I was at a large formal farewell for a well-known deputy commissioner. In his farewell speech, he referred to the police union, known as the NSW Police Association. They are a powerful entity, having over 18,000 members and they have existed for over 100 years representing the rights and welfare of officers. It had been my experience in my command/leadership journey that the union was not there to help some commanders, instead making a commander's life difficult with the goal of having them removed from a command.

In his speech, the retiring deputy commissioner referred to a colleague of mine who went to Northern Region Command as the police commander at the request of the police executive to bring some stability to a long-term location where the union and commanders were traditionally in dispute.

Several commanders at this location ended their careers due to the stresses, pressures and high-profile nature of the location. The location was a highly sought-after place for police to work, and once there they rarely sought further transfers, opting to see out their policing careers there. This made the location challenging.

When my colleague was sent there, the deputy commissioner delivered a message to the union telling them to leave him alone, that he was a good commander, so let him do his thing. It was a nice compliment to my colleague but at the same time an acknowledgement of what the union could do to a police commander's longevity.

When I had the decision to act on an issue, when I saw examples of exclusion and an unwillingness to lead change, I had to really dig deep to decide and act on this issue rather than let it slide.

In a previous command, the morale, productivity and outcomes achieved were better than ever. Not because of anything I had individually done, but because everyone was working well together. Crime was on the decrease. We were talking, interacting, and arresting criminals, and the level of professionalism our staff displayed was admirable. Almost every day our staff were responding to people with the intent of taking their own life on the sandstone cliffs of Sydney. They were truly heroic.

I had no inkling anything was amiss. There were no grumblings to either me or any member of our leadership team. I took a couple of weeks of annual leave with a relieving commander looking after the place.

On the day I returned, I learnt that in the previous 24 hours, the police union had lodged an industrial dispute involving my superiors about the unsafe working conditions at one of the police stations that came under my command.

The police station in question was a substation. Some units worked from there with the station constable working as a single unit in the old courtroom section of the station.

Several years before my appointment as a commander, there had been one incident where an offender had entered the station at night with the intent of assaulting the constable working on their own. There was nothing in place to protect the constable, as there was just a counter that allowed access to the public. I learnt about this historic issue as the industrial dispute progressed, but I had never heard about it until the police union started their industrial action.

My superiors were less than impressed. I was counselled that I should have known about this issue. Ignorance was no excuse on my part, and I was left with no doubt it was up to me to fix the issue quickly, without any counsel, support or advice on how I might do this. The simple instruction from my superiors: "Fix it."

At the time, several members of my leadership team asked the union officials why they chose to raise the issue in my absence and after being there for several months already. There was no real explanation given other than "It's just what we do."

The way a union dispute is supposed to work is there are supposed to be discussions and negotiations, and it only goes to dispute if either party, normally the commander, does not agree to some reformative outcomes. None of that had occurred in this situation, but that didn't seem to matter. The edict from my superiors was simply to fix it.

Over the next eight weeks, the matter was resolved.

I consulted with the region expert on work, health and safety matters and sought their advice. I met with staff representatives, an executive union representative and a representative from police properties soon after. It was easy to rectify by building a security access door restricting access to the station constable.

The conduct of the executive union representative at the first meeting was nothing short of deplorable.

It was my first exposure to how union officials behave when they are not under the scrutiny of more senior police. If they were talking to a Commissioner, they were the epitome of professionalism. If they were acting alone, without scrutiny, they were abusive, rude and used language that was more akin to a street fight rather than a professional.

What was worse was that I knew the person. We had worked together before at a previous command and I thought we had a good working relationship. I learnt again there were no rules, it was all about the "performance".

What I was starting to discover was that decency and forming respectful relationships do win out in the end. When people behave badly around decent people, others who witness the bad behaviour want to help decent people, not rude people.

The representative from police properties expedited work orders and had the necessary work completed within an eight-week period by installing a series of protective barriers. The delay was not an issue as meetings had occurred, a plan had been created and work orders put in place. The union moved on having shown their members they forced an outcome, albeit outside of the normal channels of decency and diplomacy.

I had a couple of other negative experiences with the police union over the next few years, again with similar disruptive strategies. Normally, when our command was starting to get a positive momentum, the police union representatives would attempt to disrupt this positive momentum.

I also had a personal disappointment with their lack of action in my first command. I had gone to the executive police union a couple of times to enlist their support for one of their members when their member was going through a nasty and unsafe time. The representatives involved just shrugged their shoulders, smiled and said, "There is nothing we can do."

As already stated, I made it my focus to build strong and united leadership teams. As in any endeavour, you do not achieve the perfect outcome straight away, but over time it does happen. The benefit of a strong and united leadership team is that the leader is not the only target.

The whole team takes on an issue if it needs to be taken on. The benefit is that each leader within the team has the support of the people they lead. That depth of support is well-earned, as every leader is focused on creating a strong supportive environment for our staff.

Experience is a good master but, at my core, I still had a level of apprehension if there was another union intervention. At one command later in my service, another union issue did arise.

We had built a very effective leadership team. We were all different, but our differences made us stronger and wiser. Together we had navigated significant change in our command and the strength of that positive change was well known.

One unit within that environment resisted the change. It wasn't even the whole unit that resisted the change, it was some individuals within that unit. The unit was a support unit to frontline police and the community by offering specialised skills that were essential to policing. The unit was resourced well, and part of the change entailed this unit working a 24-hour day coverage, 7 days a week. We had a simple purpose as a command, anything we did had to benefit frontline police and benefit the community.

It was obvious to the leadership team that this unit was falling behind in the change. Their rostering, particularly of the individuals concerned, of which there were several, was not achieving coverage over the weekends or the afternoon periods of the day.

Upon review, I learnt that several individuals concerned had not worked a weekend for at least six months, whilst the rest of their team carried the responsibility. I sat on the findings for 24 hours. I viewed the actions of the involved individuals as an attempt to block the proposed changes for the team, which impacted the support the whole command and community received.

I was aware that if I chose to take this matter on, our successful management of change for the whole command could blow up and derail the whole process. I also knew, with a degree of certainty, the dispute would be escalated to the police union. Given my old wounds in that area, did I want to go there again?

It was tempting to let the successful change management process we had already achieved be good enough and rest on our laurels.

I spent those 24 hours contemplating … *Will I, won't I, will I, won't I?*

After that, I still had the same view. We had to do something about the unwillingness of these individuals to effect the change needed to benefit the whole command and the community.

I raised this issue with the manager of this group. We looked at the evidence and came up with a strategy to create a change over a six-week period.

We made the agreement that the unit's manager would meet with most of the individuals involved on their own, but I asked to be present for some.

The reason I wanted to be present is that I believed there were underlying issues around exclusion that I wanted to address. The sources and victims of these exclusionary experiences did not want to make a target of themselves and elected to let the behaviour go on unchallenged. I viewed these meetings with these individuals as an opportunity to put all issues on the table. I could see that there was a pattern of resistance occurring that did not benefit the wellbeing and safety of the whole team.

As we anticipated, the meetings ended up confrontational when I was involved. The meetings I was at raised issues that the team in question had a negative culture towards some members of their team. The response to this issue by the individuals involved was that the culture could not be changed because that was just how things were.

We were told it would be detrimental to the morale and output of the team to attempt to implement any change. I advised the involved individuals that change would be implemented, and they had a choice to be part of that change and lead it. Alternatively, if they chose not to be a part of that change and lead it, I would support them with a transfer with no hard feelings.

What I did do differently with this situation, compared to my past experiences with implementing change that I knew would be resisted, was that we had a strong and united leadership team going into the decision.

We had a whole command that had successfully taken on and committed to a positive change that benefited the frontline and the community. The wellbeing and support of the whole command were the best I had ever seen. As such, I was of the view we were in a strong enough position to challenge the resistance.

I put in place a level of support for this change. The manager with responsibility for leading this change would be assigned a "critical friend" from our leadership team who had top-level skills at leading people, both internally in the police and externally. Both these managers would have my full support and I would address any executive-led union issues that would inevitably come.

Predictably, there was executive union engagement. It took the traditional part of raising issues around parenting responsibilities, long-distance travel requirements and the inability to do this with the rostering proposal on the table. The union never met with me, they went directly to my superiors instead. I received two emails from the executive union officials, essentially asking me to reverse the rostering proposed.

I took the emotion out of the issue and applied the same theme in both of my responses.

I told the union what the purpose of our command was. Everything we did revolved around benefiting the frontline and benefiting the community. The roster I was proposing intended to do just that. If we had the capacity in the roster to achieve 24-hour coverage, seven days a week, surely that should be implemented.

There was some heartache, there were tears, there was some aggression, but we stayed with our strategy supporting the manager of this unit and the people within the unit who wanted to change to occur.

The executive union officials provided the feedback that the change had merit and that the issues raised to engage the union could not be defended.

The outcome was that some people who opposed the changes chose to leave the command and pursue their careers at other locations. Other individuals chose to go to locations that had a Monday-to-Friday roster. The rest of the team united and became a dynamic group of truly remarkable people that valued inclusion and supported each other to an exceptional level.

Sometimes the best measure you can get about the impact your actions made is in the personal messages you receive.

What a ride, thank you for your faith in me. I think we have created a great product at our command. You smashed it.

Bill

Just a little gift to show my appreciation for the support you have given me since arriving at our command. You have helped make me stronger both professionally and personally, and I thank you for taking the stand you did to make my workplace a happier place to be. I have learnt a lot from you which I promise to pay forward throughout my career."

Marcus

Reflections

What I have learnt about any organisation – whether it is a team, division, company, command or union – is that they are only as good as the people selected to represent them, how consistent those people are, and ultimately how you are treated by those individuals.

I have had some shocking experiences with the police union during the span of my police career which have coloured my feelings toward the union overall.

Before I went to Goulburn Highway Patrol in 1984, I was working at a far south coast location in NSW after transferring there from Sydney. At the time, the union had mandated to not issue traffic tickets to roadside offenders to put pressure on the government over a pay dispute.

We as operational police were supposed to do a lengthy summons report instead, which protracted the process by making each traffic offender go to court instead of receiving a ticket.

As a very young police officer, I had never had any dealings with the police union. As police on the street, we have discretion whether we enforce the law or not. I remember I stopped this very disrespectful young driver who had been doing some stupid stuff in their car. The driver promptly told me that I could not issue him with a traffic ticket for his driving offences as he had been following the newspapers. I issued him several traffic tickets, educating him that I still could issue them if I wanted to and then sent him on his way.

I thought nothing of this interaction until I came to work the next day.

I was relatively new to this new command and I was one of the youngest officers at that station. When I entered the station for my next shift, I could feel the mood of the whole place had changed.

When I went to my pigeonhole, I found a large sign over my correspondence tray with the word "SCAB" written across it. I was shattered. This treatment went on for nearly a month and was a lonely and isolating time.

I just kept on being me, it was just the way things were. I did have some support and advice to just ride it out, and I kept in contact with some of my former peers in Sydney who had never heard of such behaviour.

The police union does some amazing work and the conditions that they have fought for and won for their members, me included, are exceptional. Publicly, the police union is all about programs they have implemented to support officers going through hard times in the disengagement process from their policing careers. The thing I find frustrating about the union is this same process is not followed for every one of their members, even when they ask for support or recognition.

On my final days in the NSW Police Force, I received a farewell gift from the police union to recognise my service. This is a normal ritual that all retiring police officers who are members of the union are supposed to get, whether the retirement is medical or optional. The ritual involves a photo in the monthly union journal of all the retiring members who get presented with their police union watch.

I was presented with my watch by a union representative who I regarded with a high level of professionalism. This person had just recently come to work in our command. The union representative cried when she gave me my watch. I cried too because I was going to miss working with this officer.

I know of more deserving officers than me on their retirement from the NSW Police who never got an ounce of support from the police union and never had their service recognised. Even after requesting they would like to receive what other union members receive on retirement, a police union watch to commemorate their membership of the union after years of service to the NSW Police, that watch was never presented to these officers.

If you forget to recognise someone when they exit the police force, they feel forgotten.

People can only judge you by what do or do not do.

At a holistic level, the reflection of various stages of my life and my policing career looks at the role of unions and sections within any business or organisation that resist and are hostile against any change.

It is the expectation of unions that the leader and their leadership team have the skills to take them on.

If the union and their similar entities smell any kind of weakness or uncertainty, they will exploit that and test the reserve of the leader and their leadership team. If the leader is a team of one, then the union's job is easy to displace the leader. If the leader has a weak leadership team, the job of the union is still easy. If the leader and their leadership team are united and strong in their leadership, then there is little need for the union to become involved.

It could be said the union is like the sharks that circle the Navy SEAL recruits when they are in the freezing waters of the Pacific

Ocean trying to pass their selection challenges. They say the best recruits see the shark being curious around them and then punch them straight in the nose, showing confidence, courage and skills. The unions are just like those sharks, they are sniffing around for weakness in leaders and their leadership teams, and they will test the confidence, courage and skills of that leader and their leadership team until a weaker candidate comes along.

I was told early on in my journey as a police commander by a respected senior police commander, in a room full of junior commanders, that we should all be careful about what we wish for. If you want a promotion to the role of police commander, you might just get it. And if you do, you will have to deliver on everything that is expected of that role.

I clearly did not know the role I was selected for as a police commander in those first couple of years to the level I should have. I paid the price for that lack of knowledge and had to play catch up to become a better commander and leader.

18

Support (2015–2020)

I was relieving as the commander of the Sydney City Police Area Command for a three-month period. During this period the Lindt Café Siege took place. Whilst I was on this secondment, there was a committal hearing of several young police officers at the Downing Centre Court Complex. Several months prior, an incident occurred in the city where a young man under the influence of drugs conducted himself in such a way that attending police used their tasers and capsicum spray to subdue him. The young man died during this arrest.

An independent investigation occurred on behalf of the coroner, with the outcome being the police involved should have a committal hearing in the local court to see if the magistrate was of the opinion that they should be committed for a criminal district court trial for their actions. In layman's terms, was there a criminal case to answer in the death of the young man whilst being arrested by several police officers?

There were several police officers from Sydney City in that hearing, both as accused persons and witnesses. A few of them had since transferred to other stations in NSW. Some were still working in Sydney City.

I believed that it was important that these police officers had the support of their colleagues whilst going through one of the worst times in their lives. Our court system is built on the foundation that one is innocent till proven guilty. Sadly, it is not the vibe those who find themselves in that situation get. I have often seen police in that situation looked upon as pariahs and left to their own devices.

Each day of the hearing I ensured we had a senior member of the command present to meet with and sit through the evidence and offer support to our officers and their families. I attended two days of the hearings.

What I learnt from attending the hearings and speaking to the police officers involved and their families was both concerning but not surprising.

I learnt that some of the officers who had since transferred from Sydney City had been told by their new superiors that they would have to attend the committal hearings, out of work time, and that they did not have the support of their new command.

It was only when these officers and their families sought the assistance of the police union that the officers were allowed to attend the court hearings as a rostered shift.

The outcome of the hearing was one officer out of the four officers accused was found guilty.

Each of the officers was charged with assault-related offences, not murder or manslaughter. The officer found guilty was not found guilty of using their taser, but guilty of using capsicum spray beyond what was reasonable. The magistrate determined that even though the officer was guilty of assault relating to the use of capsicum spray, they were not convicted. Since that fateful day, the officer involved had suffered mentally and had never been the same.

It costs nothing, other than time, to provide support. Once that time is past, it can never be regained and the people involved will always remember the support that was or was not provided. Each of the officers involved, and the witnesses who had to give evidence, knew they had the support of Sydney City Police Area Command, even on their worst day.

A second incident that will touch on support deals with a police supervisor who was charged with Perverting the Course of Justice upon recommendations by the Director of Public Prosecutions for conduct whilst off-duty. This conduct related to the police supervisor tricking or coercing a young probationary constable not to do something they should normally do at a criminal level and then bragging about it via text to a group of other police from their team at a local hotel.

This district court trial meant that an entire team of officers who were at the bar drinking with their supervisor would have to give evidence about what happened, including during and after they had been at the bar. Three officers were crucial witnesses relating to the behaviour alleged, with the probationary officer as the main witness.

In my 40 years as a police officer, I have never seen anything like this case, where mates must give evidence against a member of their team on such an issue. When this matter came up, I had just concluded the Lindt Café Inquest giving evidence for two full days about my role as the police forward commander for the first two hours of that job.

What happened regarding my involvement in the Lindt Café Siege is written in chapter 16, but the aftermath and the support I received going into that inquest are relevant.

Prior to giving evidence for the Lindt Café Inquest, I was offered the services of a police psychologist, a senior police peer support officer, and other levels of support. Interestingly, before my evidence, no one at a senior level above me offered any support whatsoever. Some of my peers who were also involved in this inquest were doing it on their own. They had opted to not seek the support of any work-related welfare assistance. My wife, also a detective inspector but not related to the Lindt Café Siege, sat in the back of the inquest to provide me with personal support.

Prior to giving evidence at the Lindt Café Inquest, I sat with a senior police psychologist before each session started. I walked with them to the courtroom and they sat in the courtroom listening to my evidence, staying with me for most of the time. They contacted me the next day and several days after to make sure I was ok. I never felt alone as the combination of work and personal support ensured I got through this time. I did have some rattly days, but with support, I did get through that time.

I was grateful for that experience because I knew what level of support I had to put in place to support my officers who had to give evidence at a district court trial against one of their own. None of them wanted to be there, but the actions of their supervisor off-duty put them all there. They ran the risk to themselves and their reputations if they gave incomplete, evasive or untrue evidence.

I had attempted several times to provide support for the supervisor, including offering to go for walks with them, but they viewed me as responsible for their situation and had a large degree of animosity towards me.

At the time, I had offered this personal level of support to the supervisor in question, I was providing a similar level of support to several other officers going through mental health challenges and other challenges away from the workplace.

This support took the form of long two- to three-hour walks where it was easy for someone to talk, as they are not looking directly at you but they are still with you.

Another officer seemed broken during this time, but I found that if I trained in the gym with them, the person I knew came back for a couple of hours. I used to love those training sessions and seeing a glimpse of the person who existed before mental illness had halted their career.

On another occasion, this same officer had been awarded an important long service medal, but due to their mental illness was not able to attend a public medal presentation. I went to their house and presented the medal, with his wife and young baby present. A special day for me, and a day of dignity and respect for the officer concerned.

When the district court trial commenced against the supervisor, I ensured that our command had a senior member of staff there each day to sit in court and provide face-to-face support for our staff.

I enlisted the same senior police psychologist who assisted me during the Lindt Café Siege to help our people. She willingly attended and assisted our people for the duration of the trial. She gave our people the same support she provided me. The three crucial witnesses who had the main evidence to provide were also supported by the Internal Witness Support Unit.

This went on for two weeks. One of the main witnesses was also expecting a baby at the time so support was crucial. The support didn't end with the evidence. Once the trial was over, a guilty verdict was handed down by the jury. This meant that it would soon be public information that the supervisor of this team of young police had been found guilty of Perverting the Course of Justice by a jury of twelve people. This would be distressing news for the team of police involved. I had to ring the witnesses involved and advise them via phone before they read the outcome on social media or other media sources.

I again offered the services of the same police psychologist. This matter was still not over, the matter returned to the district court judge for sentencing several days later. The judge imposed a custodial sentence of 12 months' imprisonment. I again had to ring the members of the team who gave evidence to advise them of this outcome, as the severity of the sentence would potentially cause more impact on their wellbeing.

All those officers got through that time. They had each other, but they also had the support of the workplace. Three of the officers were later awarded commendations for their courage and integrity to come forward when the incident first occurred. I was there to watch them receive their awards with their families and friends. I was proud to see they were also proud of their actions and resilience during a very difficult time.

What these three officers did by coming forward was a very courageous thing to do. One was a probationary constable, the other a long-time member of our command but still relatively junior, and the other was an acting sergeant relieving in that role on the night in question when the offence first occurred.

The second officer I refer to here is a good example of the emotional cost this matter had from the moment it became known to this officer.

Once they learnt at the hotel what their off-duty supervisor had done to the probationary constable, they knew something was wrong and that wrongdoing had to be reported.

This officer set off the sequence of events for the matter to be officially reported and via that action, investigated.

This officer was in the witness box for two whole days being cross-examined at length by the supervisor's defence counsel.

This officer told the court that after they had reported the actions of their off-duty supervisor, they went to the locker room to get changed and then went home.

This officer was so dismayed at what had happened and the actions they were forced to set in motion that they headbutted their metal locker, leaving a large dent in the door. The jury heard this evidence and so did everyone else in the courtroom.

Reflections

I truly believe that with the right level of support, we can achieve anything and endure the hardest of challenges. At this stage of my career, and I had been around for awhile, I understood at what times people needed support and what that support could look like.

I had experienced the worst of times when I had no support and barely survived. I had experienced the most challenging of times where I had support from the most unexpected sources and ultimately thrived by making courageous and sound decisions.

It is crucial to let people know they are not alone, and that they have the support of those around them. In the context of police work, that support includes their work team, their supervisors, their managers, their boss and whatever employee assistance support that operate within the organisation.

In the case of the matter where constables were giving evidence against their own supervisor in a district court, I reached for the same level of support that got me through the Lindt Café Inquest. That support ensured no one was left behind.

19

Challenges Are Opportunities Dressed in Work Clothes (2017)

In April 2017, I received a call that my father's leukemia had become active and that he needed medical assistance. Leukemia is known as the "waiting disease". Its markers can lay dormant for several years and then suddenly, when it does become active, the patient is sick. One of the most common treatments is a blood transfusion. My father had his first blood transfusion from late 2016 to early 2017 and his health remarkably improved.

After a mix-up with a local chemist, my father did not receive the level of medication he was supposed to. Shortly after, he collapsed in the street whilst with his brother-in-law in Bundaberg. He was then admitted to hospital.

Something about this news was off, so after discussion and persuasion from my wife, I decided to travel to Bundaberg from Sydney to check on my father and how my mother was coping. I met with the medical team looking after Dad in emergency. They indicated his situation was not ideal, but they were confident that with the right regime of drugs, his condition would turn around. Sadly, this did not eventuate. My father's heart could not cope with the level of drugs given to him on that first night and he died in late April 2017.

We did the normal things, the funeral, the grieving and helping my mother with the loss of her partner to whom she had been married for 63 years.

Dad's death was a bit of a surprise in that my mother had been sicker than him for years, with regular visits to the vascular ward of the Royal Brisbane Women's Hospital for repeated blood clots to her legs with some of her toes having to be amputated.

Mum did not suffer from type-2 Diabetes nor was she overweight, she just had regular blood clots related to an irregular heartbeat and a pacemaker. My father was her rock for years, as many old people get so fearful of hospitals, they suffer from delirium and become totally irrational and hard to handle. Dad always sat by Mum's side during these episodes, supporting her through her fears.

Six weeks after Dad died, my wife had bi-pulmonary multiple blood clots in her lungs and, according to the respiratory specialist, she was fortunate to survive. This medical issue was completely out of left field and rocked our world. My wife had had several medical issues over the previous several years, which we thought were stress-related due to work pressures, but we never thought she might die. It was a very scary and distressing time.

Not long after my wife's medical emergency, my mother, on the advice of her local doctor in Bundaberg, drove herself to the hospital where her husband had died six weeks earlier. My mother was admitted due to the severity of the blood clots in her right leg. Shortly after that diagnosis and admission to the hospital, I had to fight with the medical system in Queensland to get her taken by air ambulance to Brisbane as her condition was quickly deteriorating.

Upon my mother's admission to a hospital in Brisbane, I received the diagnosis that my mother's right leg would have to be amputated below the knee, and then a long rehabilitation recovery would be required. I knew this was the right outcome, but the timing could not be worse. My mother had no family support in Queensland after the recent death of her husband. There was only me in Sydney.

I used the skills I had learnt over the last decade as a police commander and started asking questions. I asked the vascular surgeon in Brisbane if he had a counterpart in Westmead Hospital in Sydney, and if we could get my mother to that hospital who was prepared to do the surgery. The only impediment was the Queensland and NSW Health services would not agree to transport my mother to Westmead within their system, even though my mother would become a permanent resident in NSW after the amputation.

To overcome this obstacle, I had to sign my mother out of the Brisbane hospital, with direct medical advice not to remove her from the hospital due to the risk to her health. My mother was told several times by medical staff not to go with me to NSW as she might die in the process. I would have to put her on a Qantas flight to Sydney, and then drive her myself to Westmead Hospital.

We did do this. My mother was in agony as her right foot had gone gangrenous. Her right foot was almost black with parts of her toes going white. My mother vomited on the plane trip to Sydney, so the flight was not a pleasant one. I remember a kind soul sitting next to us gave Mum a few breath mints after she vomited so her mouth would not feel so awful.

It was a scary trip as I was continually wondering whether I had done the right thing in making this decision. I caught a taxi with my mother from the domestic arrivals terminal to the long-term car park behind the airport. I then drove my mother to Westmead Hospital in my own car, wheeled her into the emergency ward and told the triage nurse our story. True to their word, the vascular surgical team came out and admitted my mother for surgery the next day.

What flows from here is where resilience, support of work colleagues, mental health professionals and family comes into play.

I had my wife to look after and now my mother on top of a police command. My mother needed long-term rehabilitation after the amputation if she was ever going to walk again. It soon became obvious that my mother would never return to Queensland to live, and that due to her level of independence would not be able to live with relatives. She would need aged-care support.

This was a very challenging time for all involved. It was my awakening to the stages in life. Life wasn't only about birth, raising children, going to work, retiring and dying. There is another potential chapter in our lives, of deteriorating health and the prospect of long-term aged care, with all the minefields of government support and costs involved.

I did not handle this time well and needed my own professional mental health support to handle the circumstances more productively and supportively.

I was fortunate to have the support of a good workplace and senior officers who allowed me to take extended leave to get things under control. I had so many phone calls and visits of support during this period that went on for several months.

Just to make things interesting during this period of personal life challenges, the NSW Police had a new Commissioner appointed, shortly around the time my father died. In November 2017, my police command was going to be merged with the neighbouring command, and both commanders had to be interviewed to win the one position of commander of the new amalgamated command. This occurred across 12 other Sydney Commands. All the interviews were on the same day.

When the announcement about this process was made, I was still off on extended leave caring for my wife and my mother, who had by this time become a resident of an aged-care home near Westmead Hospital, which allowed her free community bus transport for ongoing amputee rehabilitation sessions.

I was still a bit shaky around this time and asked my wife, my son and my daughter if I should just bow out of the new commander process and not bother applying. All three of them, particularly my daughter, said, "Dad, it's up to you, but you don't want to be known as 'poor Allan'. If you have it in you, and I think you do, go for the job, give it your best and see what happens."

I did decide to go for the job. I sourced people who had gone through this process before to learn what to do, just like I did for my boxing adventure.

I went and spoke to four other commanders who had been the first commanders chosen to do a similar process about three years earlier. I asked them to highlight what they did, what worked and what didn't work, and how they managed those challenges. I took it one step further and interviewed staff who reported to those commanders to see what their understanding of the process was, and how they thought it could be improved.

I used John Kotter's "8-step Model for Leading Change" as I found it helpful in my circumstances. I created two one-page documents titled "What would you do?" and "How would you do it?" printed as one double-sided document, in effect a two-page plan.

My intent was to produce this two-page plan for every staff member of the new command if I was successful in achieving the nomination, so our staff had a clear picture of what our new command would look like. I intended to engage everyone right from day one.

I gained the confidence that I had a good plan and that I would be competitive in the upcoming interviews.

About two weeks before the interviews, I received a phone call from an influential senior officer who had the support of the Police Commissioner. The phone call was an acknowledgement of the challenging year that I had been through, with an offer that I did not have to put myself through the interview process as I would be offered another opportunity at another command which could do with my skillset.

I asked for 48 hours to consider my response to this offer.

When I thought about the offer, I decided I could not accept it. A lot of my staff were expecting me to apply for the position as they wanted me to lead the new command. Equally, a lot of the community partners I had worked with for several years were also expecting me to remain and continue the good outcomes we were achieving together. I could not let these people down by taking the easy way out. They did not want to have to restart this relationship with someone new if they didn't have to.

At a personal level, I had long held a goal that I wanted to be a commander of one of what I called the "Big 4" – the City, Kings Cross, Redfern or Surry Hills due to the challenges all these locations had. This new command could be an addition to the Big 4 expanding it to the "Big 5". The main transport access points into the Sydney CBD were through this new command by road, rail and sea. With the right preparation and training, and well-prepared staff, the new command could ensure that access to the city of Sydney would remain open no matter the challenge if the staff worked well together to meet this responsibility.

I respectfully declined the offer 48 hours later, thanking them for offering their support. My preparation for my interview was not ideal. My interview was on a Monday, and I spent the previous Friday, Saturday and Sunday in Queensland at my parents' old home, putting their car on a transport truck to Sydney so I could sell it for my mother's ongoing care fees, and packing all of their belongings to transport to Sydney.

Before I went to Queensland for this process, I had taken my wife's advice and practiced for my interview using the video function on my iPhone. I knew the interview was going to be 20 minutes long and I knew what the two main questions were going to be. It was soon evident on the video what worked and what didn't in my presentation. I made enhancements to my answers till it was clear in my own head what I would present.

When you spend three days on your own, packing at your parents' home, you are in your own head a lot. I practiced and practiced out loud what I would say at the interview, till the neighbours must have thought I had gone crazy. I remember sitting in the car having two more run-throughs till I was satisfied before the interview on Monday. For good luck, I wore my dad's old Citizen gold watch which I had picked up that weekend when I was packing.

At the interview, we were under strict instructions not to provide any handouts. However, as I went through "What would you do?"

and "How would you do it?", the panel could clearly see I had a two-page plan that seemed to set it all out very plainly.

They requested that I give them a copy each before I walked out the door. I had three copies ready for them as I thought this request might be made.

A couple of days later, I was advised that I had won the job as the commander of the new bigger command. I was over the moon. When I got the call, I was doing active armed offender training, which was a long, demanding and exhausting day where I did several real-time drills.

Even though I was exhausted, I stuck to my plan of visiting the new command. If I won the job, I would immediately go to the other command where I had not been the commander and introduce myself to the outgoing dayshift and incoming nightshift, with a copy of the two-page plan so they each had an inkling of what the road ahead looked like. I went in and spoke to this large gathering of police. I gave them time to ask questions and then started the plan for how to make this new command a success. It was an icebreaker and the connections I made that afternoon were enduring ones.

Successful change is not achieved by one big gesture, it is achieved by several small steps, connecting with as many people as you can so they are part of the change occurring. I learnt that I had excelled at that interview, coming first out of 12 other superintendents interviewed that day. My two-page plan was to be used as a template for this type of change management.

Once I was advised that I had been selected to be the police commander for the new larger, there was a very short timeframe to form the leadership team. I had command to select seven inspectors out of 12 people eligible for the roles, six inspectors from my old command and six inspectors from the new command.

The advice from my superiors was for our leadership team to be made up of 50% of my old staff and 50% of the new command. From all the research I had done on previous amalgamations, there was always an underlying tone of "us and them".

I was committed to forming the best leadership team possible. To do that I had to select team members based on merit, with transparency, and not past relationships. I also had to make the selection process as fair as possible. I invited the outgoing commander to be on the interview panel. The outgoing commander and I enjoyed a good relationship and respected each other. We also included an independent member on our interview panel.

At the end of the process, we selected a new leadership team that had five officers from the new command and two officers from my old command.

After it was all over, I had a moment of concern that I had not selected more from my old command out of loyalty, but the process had to be fair and open to give the new command the greatest chance of success.

When you select your own leadership team, one of the downsides is that you must advise the unsuccessful applicants. Some of my peers have the view that the applicants who are not successful are going to be upset with you anyway, so get someone else to tell them the bad news.

This concept does not sit well with me, so I rang the five people who were unsuccessful. I owed them the dignity and respect to tell them myself that they were not successful. I had to have the courage to give bad news. There was silence, there was anger, there was disappointment.

We have all dealt with disappointment. Some more than others. This process of people competing for their own jobs is very personal and had not occurred that often in the NSW Police before. I learnt that everyone deals with this process in their own way, in their own time. Part of my role is to let those people who were unsuccessful deal with their disappointment in their own time, to provide them that dignity.

We all write our own stories when we are faced with bad news and challenges. Some of these people never spoke to me again and blame me to this day for ruining their careers. That is their choice to act that way and I cannot do anything about that. Once I accepted that, the discomfort of their actions was not so intense and I have learnt to deal with it.

Once we had the leadership team formed, I had already booked two days away from the command at a naval base overlooking Sydney Harbour to set the direction of the new leadership team. The two days were about forming relationships with each other and setting the direction of how we were going to lead the new command through the change process.

As we were at a naval base, the base commander invited us to dinner on the first night. Part of police and naval tradition is to have dinner in the officer's mess. This is essentially a very posh dining room, which in this case also had the best view of Sydney Harbour.

Both the navy and police have officer's mess uniforms to wear to such important functions. Some say they look like penguin suits. With all the ceremony and tradition, it is an eventful night to be part of and something to remember. Both navy and police have reputations for being able to celebrate well, and this night was no different. One of our leadership team brought along this green moonshine-type rocket fuel for us to drink. We had a great night, and the base commander made an error in inviting us all back to his private rooms before we all called it a night.

The two days away did the job. We had formed relationships, we knew what we wanted to achieve together, and we returned to our new command and started the process of leading and influencing, all with the same message.

We learnt that all of us had things in common, things that were challenging, things that were personal, and things that made us a stronger team as we supported each other through these issues because we trusted each other.

Part of the change process was implementing a smooth and effective change management plan.

The Change Management Team needed 10 people, including five from my old command and five from the other merged command. I relied on the former commander of the newly merged command to nominate the five staff they would recommend. I had done my homework and the five people nominated were outstanding.

I won't go into every step of how the Change Management Plan was achieved but I will provide a couple of examples of good people achieving good outcomes.

I discovered one of the junior constables was a former employee of a national banking organisation who was responsible for national-level change management projects. It was natural to select this person as part of our Change Management Team despite them being relatively junior to the NSW Police.

This person created the charts of which tasks had to be carried out and in what order, updating the charts each week up to the date the two commands were to start as a new entity. A simple thing this person did was provide a time clock in days. I remember at our first change management team meeting, we had 88 days to go. At the end of every week, I would provide an email summary to all staff of what had been achieved that week, and what we were aiming to achieve the following week.

Some of the simple things we did were to use the 88 days to implement the change incrementally rather than have 255 people wait 88 days to implement the change. For example, on Day 60, Section A started working together in their new location, and on Day 40, Section B started.

The quote at the start of Part III highlights good leaders show that they care for their people, and everyone should be supported.

There was a good example of this in our newly formed command. There are unforeseen impacts on people who are part of the change. Our new command had a main station where all the first-response general duties police worked but there were two substations that required three constables to work at these locations every 12 hours.

These substations are at least 30 minutes by car away from the main station, and sometimes could be up to an hour away due to traffic which adds a lot of extra time onto an already long 12-hour shift.

A lot of our staff lived on the Central Coast some one to two hours away, each way. The cost of renting or purchasing a home in the Northern Suburbs of Sydney is cost-prohibitive on a police officer's wage, so many chose to live in locations more affordable but some distance away from where they work.

Under a normal business model in the NSW Police at that time, the constables working at these substations would first have to go to the main station to pick up their gun so they could wear this gun whilst on duty at the substations. These constables are already working a 12-hour shift, so to expect them to travel up to an extra hour each way at the beginning and end of the shift, was going to be a morale killer and potentially a real killer through fatigue.

Our project team had already anticipated this, and we were taking steps to address this. The only problem was what we wanted to do had never been done before. Every police officer in NSW is issued their own gun. They have and carry this gun every day they are an officer. They do not lend that gun to anyone else. It is not like what is seen on the British television series *Line of Duty* where each officer signs out a gun each day from the armoury. Despite this, guns are generally stored at the main station and not at the substation or taken home.

We came up with the concept of a station gun at the substations. This was a drawn-out approval process, but we identified this issue right at the start of our change management plan so we had over 80 days to influence and persuade the right people, and ultimately deliver a positive outcome. Initially, the concept was only authorised as a trial, but over time it just became the norm.

This meant that police working at the substations could go straight from their homes without the need to call in to the main station to get their guns. This was a simple process that sent a signal to first-response frontline police that we were doing everything possible to make their lives easier. We were showing that we cared for their wellbeing at an everyday level.

Nearly 12 months after the amalgamations had occurred, the NSW Police conducted culture surveys on all commands in the state. These surveys dealt with everything but focused on the leadership teams' capabilities and communication skills.

Culture surveys can be a challenging process as the responses are anonymous and people who have an issue with their leaders will take the opportunity to cause mayhem. When the results came in, some commands had poor results. Some commanders were moved because of those results. For us, it was a different story. Our outcomes were some of the best recorded and an indication to all 255 staff who made up the new command that we were doing something right.

We wanted to foster a culture of wellbeing, kindness and inclusive support. Some of the jobs our staff goes to are confronting, scary and upsetting. If our staff went to these types of jobs, we highlighted their good work and ensured they had the right level of support, so the confronting jobs could be shared around and not allocated to the same person or crew each time. These small things made a difference and built a good culture.

There are a lot of things that can indicate whether people feel safe, supported and included, or not.

At a personal level as a boss, it is not a popularity contest, but you do get an indication of how you make people feel when you walk into a room.

If people turn and avoid you, or they leave the room as you enter, I normally get the feeling that perhaps I am not connecting with people in a positive way.

On the other hand, if when I enter a room, things remain relatively the same and people are happy to engage in a chat about how things are going for them at a personal level, then I get the feeling that things are on the right side of ok.

A couple of things did encourage me that we were on the right track as we built this newly joined command.

The first one was the Christmas Party.

In the bigger commands, it is always challenging to get all the different sections to come together as a whole and celebrate together. How everyone gets on together, and how they support and understand each other is a good litmus test at a Christmas Party. I have seen small numbers attend at some other command locations, but then at this last command, I was blown away by the turnout and the representation of different units who wanted to come together and celebrate.

There was a genuine feeling that people who had only just come together in the last 12 months wanted to celebrate together and enjoy each other's company. Nearly every person had a happy story to tell about how they enjoyed coming to work and being part of a supportive team.

Whilst the Christmas Party is never an official guide to how well a place gets on, at an unofficial level I was over the moon at how everyone had come together and worked towards a supportive and inclusive workplace. Whilst my job was not over, I felt satisfied that we were on the right track.

The second thing that gave me hope that we were doing the right things as a leadership team was our Awards Ceremony. Each year a police command is required to host a ceremony for their staff to present long service medals and bravery medals, and to recognise outstanding work.

Police are traditionally shy when it comes to their personal awards and do not want to make a fuss. But the ceremony is really for the family and friends of the police to recognise the person for all they have done and see that person recognised in an official and dignified way.

As we approached our first awards ceremony for our newly joined command, I repeatedly highlighted at command briefings the importance of family and friends sharing the recognition they deserved. The Awards Ceremony was like the Christmas Party. It had the largest attendance of police officers and their loved ones that I had ever seen. Close to 200 people were in that room.

We were committed to building a workplace where we empowered others to lead and build a supportive and inclusive workplace. The signs were there that we were making it happen together.

Reflections

At a personal level, I had gone through a tough time, with the unexpected death of my father, the near-death experience of my wife, the amputation of my mother's leg, moving her to Sydney and vacating her home, and at the same time competing for my own job in a new process where the loser would have to leave their police command.

The outcomes show even though we doubt ourselves at times, we are stronger and more capable than we think we are.

We just need to give ourselves the opportunity to show ourselves that we a strong and capable. The only way this can occur is to commit to are course of action and have the courage to act. After you act and you have done your best, accept the outcome.

I remember after the interview for my own job. I knew I could not have done any better. If the interview panel did not want what I had to offer, I was ok with that. I would still be a superintendent, and I would look for the next opportunity.

I had failed as a leader and a commander in the past. And in the past, other commanders and their leadership teams had not done so well in merging commands. I had the chance to learn from the past and select a strong leadership team through transparent, open and merit-based practices.

Then with that formidable leadership team, we created something special because we trusted one another and I had empowered them to lead. This was without a doubt the most satisfying and amazing group of people I had ever worked with and we achieved some amazing things together.

20

Building a Supportive and Inclusive Workplace (2016–2020)

For police officers, that final farewell on their last day can be dignified and signify a close to one chapter of their life. This farewell can include an honour board, full of the officers' medals, rank insignia and other memorabilia. A Certificate of Service can also be framed and presented to the officer, either privately or at an official awards ceremony. It is a simple thing to do and honours the officer's contribution to policing at the end of their career.

Unfortunately, some work in environments where an officer's last day is not honoured, and they face their final day without any acknowledgement of their service in any way. The fact that an officer was discharged due to medical reasons should not have any impact on the level of dignity and support we provide them. And unfortunately, it is too common for officers to be medically discharged without any contact from their command or support.

Thankfully, due to the networks I had over a long career, I could step in at times to ensure their final days were treated with dignity and respect. Sometimes, officers cannot deal with an official farewell but they can accept messages of support in the form of phone calls, text messages or emails. Sometimes, a visit by a close peer to say farewell is all that is needed.

Whilst I was able to rectify the careless actions of some workplaces, I was not able to do this for everybody. Many staff either in the police or other organisations work for leaders who do not care at all how their staff exits their jobs. No recognition, no care, and no dignity.

I have heard it said that a formal farewell, or a dignified farewell in whatever format, is not only for the person leaving, but it also sends a signal to all staff that their contribution is and will be valued.

What this series of events highlighted to me was that we as leaders need to do better. We all lead differently and all of us can improve how we lead. I have been guilty of this myself in my early years as a leader, but over time I learnt how to ensure people feel valued. It is so simple to support people and treat them with dignity, but equally some leaders demonstrate anything but those compassionate characteristics. They do not possess the courage to show compassion.

A close friend of mine has a very apt saying: "Leadership is fifty percent courage and fifty percent compassion; sometimes you need courage to show compassion, and other times you need compassion to show courage."

A little bit of focus on the wellbeing of others goes a long way.

I found that after I started focusing on the wellbeing of others, in my team and to other commands when they were in need, I started to see the same gestures by other police commanders towards their peers. I also found that once I started to look at different ways to support our own staff, it was relatively simple to implement strategies that supported our people in their day-to-day activities and at the end of their careers.

For one of our people, a series of personal and challenging work circumstances saw them diagnosed with PTSD requiring them to exit the police force relatively quickly for their own wellbeing. I found I could support this person beyond what was the norm for a police officer.

I stayed in contact with their spouse, and assisted with a companion dog application that was granted. This companion dog was intended to help this officer recover and live in his new circumstances at his own pace.

At a day-to-day level, due to my experiences in the Mosman Collar Bomb, the Lindt Café Siege and my own personal life experiences, I could see an opportunity to train our leaders to be more aware of how they prepare themselves and their staff to take on the next challenges they may face as a police officer. This preparation for their own wellbeing was a crucial first step and would allow them to look after the wellbeing of those they led.

I planned and facilitated a two-day high-risk job workshop for all our inspectors and sergeants in our command. Other commanders external to our command learnt of this workshop and requested that some of their inspectors be allowed to participate. This accounted for nearly 50 staff members, across all sections of our new command.

The workshops saw presentations from the police commanders who led the response to the Bourke Street One and Two incidents in the CBD of Melbourne when civilians lost their lives.

Other commanders who had significant roles at Lindt Café also gave presentations. All these commanders highlighted the preparations they gave themselves before these jobs occurred, and what impact those jobs had on them and their families afterward.

An additional speaker we had at those two-day workshops was an ex-police officer, Alan Sparkes, CV, OAM, VA, FRSN, himself a victim of PTSD and the recipient of two National Bravery Awards. He is the author of *The Cost of Bravery*.

As an ex-police officer, Sparkes could talk from experience on what happened to him regarding PTSD and the support he sought after the diagnosis. Now he spends his civilian life presenting to organisations and communities in and out of the country on mental health in the workplace and what we can do to monitor our own and each other's wellbeing.

Sparkes was one of the best speakers we had. He uses a Canadian model called the Mental Health Continuum. There are many variations of this but essentially it has four columns. If you are in Column 1 or 2, then you are doing ok. If you are in Column 3 or 4, then you probably need help. The beauty about the model is once you know it, it doesn't have to be you to identify you need help, quite often we are the last to admit we need support.

The "Are you ok?" can come from a peer or a colleague because of some trait or behaviour you are exhibiting from Column 3 or 4. An interesting aside when discussing PTSD in the Canadian model is that they change the D to an I, making the acronym PTSI with the "I" representing "injury". The diagnosis of PTSI is not that someone is too soft or failed because they could not cope. The patient has an injury to their brain and nervous system that they will live with forever. They need help to manage this injury for the rest of their lives. It never leaves them.

After we heard Alan Sparkes speak that day, we created multiple copies of the Mental Health Continuum and a one-page sheet on daily tasks we can do to maximise our wellbeing. We created over 300 laminated notebook cards with these details on them for each officer in the command to place in their official police notebook as a personal aid.

We also displayed the same information on a laminated A4-sized document behind every toilet door in the command and on every noticeboard. Supervisors led the discussion and things started to happen. Several people were identified as needing support and were provided with employee assistance initiatives.

The early warning signs are always there: an employee who is always sick or is gaining weight suddenly or has psoriasis or similar outbreaks on their skin, or injures their back every time they move. It is our job as leaders to help guide our people through these times. It is not hard to see.

Normally, three or four people show this trend in a workplace at any one time. Arrange for their supervisors or managers to talk to them, and ask them if they are ok. Suggest some strategies, like having some "me time" every day; a walk, some Yoga, a training session, meditation, whatever that person needs since everyone needs a little personal time each day. When people take long absences from the workplace due to illness, it is often said that they always put their own wellbeing last.

Anecdotally, this trend is often shown by women, but not always. By default, women are the primary caregivers in the home. After a full day in the workplace, they go home, cook the meals, help with the children's homework and sport, and all the other domestic tasks before returning the work the next day, often with no care for their own wellbeing.

Reflections

As a police officer and as a police commander, I have regularly sought the services of psychologists when I knew I was struggling. Quite often these mental health tune-ups only took a maximum of six or so visits, just to change my thinking. And once I had a mental health tune-up, I was good to go again. I used both police psychologists and external psychologists depending on what the issues were. I was always open about these times of seeking mental health support and I was never demoted or sidelined from my operational duties.

It is ok to continue working when you see a psychologist unless the psychologist recommends otherwise. It is ok when we check on the welfare of our people if we think they would benefit from a mental health tune-up, to suggest they visit their doctor and have a mental health assessment. There is no shame in doing this, we service our cars and our coffee machines, and have our pets checked regularly, so it is ok to do a mental health service on ourselves.

It is commonsense to do so, and dumb not to.

It is important for leaders to lead the conversation that it is ok to see mental health professionals for our own wellbeing.

One of the best examples I saw of a leader leading the way for mental health support was in the Christchurch Mosque Shootings. At a presentation I attended, speakers from the New Zealand Police described the horrific scene they attended. It was shocking to those who were present.

Mental health professionals were brought in to help the investigation team. The normal reluctance existed, with many investigators saying, "I'm fine. I don't need help."

What happened next was a true example of leadership.

The lead senior investigator from New Zealand was the first to seek the services of mental health professionals. He sought mental health assistance in front of his whole team. He cried to the mental health professionals just how horrific the crime scene was. His example opened the door for the rest of the team to use those services.

21

Building Connections
(2016–2020)

Since I had learnt the lesson not to do other people's tasks but rather empower others to lead, I found I had a lot more time to connect with people. I no longer spent hours reviewing performance and chasing up why particular tasks were not done; I empowered and trusted our leaders to do all those tasks. It was possible for anyone in our command to press a button on a computer, using a data collection program such as Microsoft Power BI, to assess their own performance, their team's and the command's, and how we all fared against other commands.

I did not require team leaders or managers to waste time doing performance reports as we all knew where we were at, with most teams performing to a high level. It was obvious if one team was struggling, and that normally involved a short conversation with a direct report with someone on the leadership team to coach, advise or guide improved outcomes, all the while ensuring wellbeing was addressed.

Part of my daily tasks was the morning meeting. The purpose was to meet with all section leaders to review the last 24 hours. This review includes identifying jobs well done, and any other issues that posed a risk for victims, our staff or our command. This meeting took no longer than 20 minutes and set the tone for the day regarding what needed to be prioritised.

Once we had sorted this out, my favourite daily ritual was to walk from the ground floor of the command to the second floor where my office was. I never went straight to my office, sometimes it would take me up to two hours to get there.

I would start on the ground floor and speak to whoever was present there: front counter staff, car crews waiting to go out on patrol, supervisors, custody managers, inspectors or duty officers. As I made my way to the first floor, I would speak to the education officers and the investigators. Sometimes, there may be up to 20 investigators present working on their cases.

It became normal for me to know everyone's story, just by those daily walks from the ground floor to the second floor.

It was and still is important for me to know our people. Just like us leaders, they have lives, dreams and aspirations, and just like us, they have challenges. They live with those challenges and successes every day and bring those issues with them into the workplace. I used to learn so much on those daily wanderings from the ground floor to the second floor.

It is surprising when you genuinely get to know your staff because you want to. The list of things that were shared with me is endless but it included the following:

» a child suffering from diabetes who had a microchip inserted under their skin that send to their parents' smartphones an alert when sugar levels reached the wrong levels

» babies with brain tumours

» a partner's job who had been retrenched leaving the officer working longer hours to try to make ends meet

» a "Thank You" card in the desk drawer from a father saying thanks for our officer's work that led to the conviction of the person who murdered his daughter

» parents with dementia

» parents in aged-care

» parents needing palliative care

» engagements and marriages

» buying their first home

» buying their first investment home

» adopting their dead siblings' children

» recovering from a significant injury

» having trouble sleeping at night

» trying to get a transfer closer to home because they had to travel two hours to and from work for the last 10 years

» sending their daughter to a dance school in the US.

Everyone has a story.

Part of connecting with your people is knowing their stories.

When you connect with people this way, you can tell when they are having an off day, sometimes in a 30-second ride in the elevator. A simple question like, "Are you ok today; something feels a bit off?" can be a small step to addressing a bigger issue.

Offer support when needed, celebrate their wins and offer advice when they are struggling with a lengthy and challenging investigation process.

One day, I was in the detectives' office and one investigator was looking a bit down and seemed over it. When I asked if they were ok and what was going on, they told me the following story.

About four months earlier, there was a robbery of a jewellery shop where one balaclava-clad offender had used a sledgehammer to break the windows and jewellery display cases whilst the business was open. It was a terrifying experience for all involved. The offender had run to a nearby black Suzuki 4WD car with their haul of jewellery.

The black Suzuki 4WD was a rare vehicle. There were less than fifty of them in NSW, and can be narrowed down when looking at just Sydney. Over the past few weeks, this young investigator had been chasing down the whereabouts of every black Suzuki 4WD in Sydney on the day of the jewellery robbery. These enquiries had not brought any joy and the identity of the offender was still unknown.

I shared with this young investigator some of the challenges and breakthroughs we achieved in the investigation of the Allum Street executions (chapter 5). Our team slogged away for six months going through phone records and other leads, trying to get a breakthrough into the identity of the seven offenders responsible for executing two men when one day we uncovered the evidence trail that told us the whole story, just because we did not give up.

To my surprise, within the next two days, the young investigator found the vehicle used in the robbery. It had been a hire car. Hire car records did the rest and that jewellery robbery offender is now in custody serving a lengthy gaol sentence.

Part of the joy of this connection with people is a two-way street. I learnt new skills and interests because of these conversations. I have accessed so many new podcasts and audio books through these connections, and I am all the richer for it.

I wasn't entering into other people's tasks by engaging in these conversations. I was getting to know people at another level, letting them know that they are more than just a number. If anything came up that needed a different level of support, I would speak to the supervisor or manager of the person involved to ensure they had support.

Some leaders miss this opportunity to connect, becoming so busy in the minutiae of their leadership position that they rarely speak to anyone. They never get to know their staff, and often sneak in and out of the building using the back door or elevator. Quite often, their staff do not even know if they are in the building or not.

Connections can still be made when you do not know someone at all because they are linked to one of our staff.

One of the most challenging things I had to do as a police commander was deal with the death of a staff member. He was off-duty, riding his motorcycle with his mate, also an off-duty police officer when he had a fatal accident. This officer was very popular. One of the priorities when this type of horror occurs is to do all we can to alert the family, close work colleagues and team members that the worst thing that we can imagine has happened.

In today's world of social media and mobile phones, it is challenging to alert those who should be advised before they learn the horrific news from other sources, but I made the commitment to meet with the parents of our officer as soon as we could get there. I have had to do this a few times now and it never gets any easier. I won't go into what was said. Suffice to say the main message was one of support and connection: their child is forever a part of the police family, and they have our support.

I also learnt that the other motorcycle rider, a young police officer who was with our officer when the accident occurred, was doing it tough and not coping. I had learnt that their workplace had done nothing to provide support, and this officer was feeling isolated and alone.

I arranged to meet with this officer at their home, off-duty, and brought another compassionate officer with me, one of our best. We spent several hours with this young officer, who we had never met before, offering our support and condolences, reminiscing over all the funny stories and mischief we knew about our departed officer. It is a decent and kind thing to do to form a connection with people when they need it most, even if you don't know them.

I was the police commander for countless major events, including New Year's Eve, Vivid Sydney, Sydney Marathon, City2Surf and a multitude of events at the Sydney Cricket Ground and precincts. Most of these events were with staff who I had never met before.

Traditionally, the police commander comes into an operational briefing before an event starts, after all the police are in the briefing room. I did not favour this way of doing an operational briefing. If you came into a room like this, there was a sea of faces, sometimes up to 200 people and it was impossible to have any type of connection if you just relied on this method.

I always wanted to connect with staff, even those I did not know, especially if they were about to go out in the field and do a police operation that may last 12 hours. If I could connect in some way, they may understand the importance of them giving their best effort for the next 12 hours rather than looking at it as just another job.

What I did instead was greet people at the sign-in roster table, or as more and more people turned up for their duties for the day, I would meet them as they came in groups.

By adopting this approach, I usually found some commonalities. I had either worked at their station at some point, knew their boss, or knew their workmates.

This common point helped form a level of connection. None of those major events over a 15-year career ever had anything go wrong. In fact, a lot of them were recognised as best practice, as people did try that little bit harder and arrested offenders who may have been intending to cause disruption or worse.

One of the regular supervisors for those events shared with me towards the end of my career that when he first met me at these major event operations, he thought I was a little bit weird. Police are a suspicious bunch, so he thought I was up to something as I was different from other commanders, trying to connect and be nice to my colleagues. Once he knew what I was on about, he enjoyed working with me when I oversaw these large events and accepted my weirdness was well-intended.

I often get feedback from other agencies about how different all the police commanders are. I hear from my own peers that they don't waste their time getting to know who they are working with, and they keep detailed notes of their decisions to cover themselves in case other agencies get it wrong.

I shake my head when I hear these approaches as it shows, firstly, that the leader does not care and, secondly, they have no trust in who they are working with. In the 15 years that I led major events and worked with other agencies, I never once considered taking notes to justify my conduct over the conduct of other agencies. I just worked together with the other agencies to get a successful outcome.

We had some hairy moments but by working together we did achieve some amazing things. I recall in the early years of Vivid Sydney, our team always volunteered for the peak nights as they posed the greatest challenges. One night, the biggest challenge was that the Vivid Sydney Event was too popular, and crowds were streaming into Circular Quay and it was beyond capacity. We faced the possibility of crowd crush, with families and young children being the likely victims.

We had 30 minutes to an hour to turn this situation around, to relieve the pressure on the Circular Quay precinct. I assigned one of our police inspectors to work with Transport New South Wales, Sydney Trains, Sydney Ferries and Sydney Buses to come up with a solution. Working together, they redirected all ferries and buses away from Circular Quay and dropped their passengers into the Darling Harbour Precinct. The trains did not drop off passengers at Circular Quay. This was all we needed at that time.

I have referred to large events in which I was the police commander, including New Year's Eve from 2011 to 2020, the Sydney Marathon for seven years, Vivid Sydney for several years, The City to Surf and Mardi Gras. When I went to these events, I had a core group of people who were the reason these events were successful. They were our Logistics and Operations Team. Sergeant Cindy Larsson was our Logistics Commander for every job. There was no one I have ever worked with like Cindy.

New Year's Eve at North Sydney Forward Command had over 550 police rostered every year. The majority of the other events had 200 police or more. Equipping and feeding this many police takes serious skill and Cindy and her team did it with ease. Senior Constable Paul Waite supported Cindy in most of these events when he was not fulfilling at support commander role. Sergeant Chris Patrech was our operations officer in nearly every big job. Chris would look after the minutiae of the radio and telephone calls for most of these events and would only involve me when a significant command decision was needed. This allowed me to focus on the strategies needed during these big jobs to ensure the event could be a success.

One of the things we did in this group that didn't happen in many other events was that we introduced the Refreshment Bag, which contained as many lollies and chocolate bars as we could fit with a bottle of water and some fruit. Cindy would go out to Costco days before a big event and buy big on lollies and everything else. Then Cindy's team, which sometimes included our large contingent of

Police Volunteers, bagged up all lollies into individual goodies bags, much like a children's birthday party.

We would deploy the bags about halfway to two-thirds through a 12-hour event. We wanted to send a message to our staff, that we did care, and we wanted to acknowledge their efforts and reward them. It is a simple gesture but one we repeated at every event. I remember one night during a late-finishing Vivid Sydney, we had too many leftover lollies in the Command Centre and we were all very sick from eating too many Mars Bars.

I also wanted to acknowledge and reward Cindy's continued efforts in how she led the logistic teams for our big jobs. I sent her to a Logistics Commanders Course, thinking it would be a nice reward for her. Cindy rang me a few days later admonishing me. I had sent her to a Logistic Commanders Course for Superintendents and above. Cindy was the only sergeant there. Each day, commanders were sent home who were not good enough to finish the course. Cindy finished the course without issue, but it wasn't an easy few days. She eventually forgave me for my error.

In the leadership workshops, we had a new group of participants every year. They were going to spend one day per month for six months, culminating in a group assignment showcasing their capabilities. It was important that these participants formed a connection as quickly as possible with each other and with me as the facilitator.

I learnt from former colleague Mike Homden and the Police Leadership College at Manly, a couple of ways to connect, even with people you don't know. The opening session of the leadership workshop would entail every participant, including myself, answering the following three questions.

1. Why are you here doing this leadership workshop?

2. What is your first experience in leadership?

3. Tell us something about you that no one knows.

My answers to these three questions are:

1. I am here to provide an environment for all of you to learn what is possible to become a leader who focuses on and empowers others to lead. You will be exposed to authentic leaders over the next six months who will highlight their successes and failures, and how those experiences formed the leaders they are today.

2. My first true experience in leadership was at the Mosman Collar Bomb. I was the police commander of that job. When my boss, Mark Murdoch, came to the job he didn't take over but let me continue to run it. But what he did do, which I will be forever grateful for, was he did all the media conferences. All the media wanted to know what we were doing. How Mark Murdoch addressed the media that night was the best I have ever seen.

3. Something about me that not many people know is I am the world's worst boxer. I'm a lover, not a fighter, but somehow, I agreed to take part in the charity fundraising for Police Legacy by getting in the boxing ring with another police officer and raising money for the privilege. I had two fights. I won the first year on points, just, and the second year I got absolutely flogged with the fight ending in 90 seconds when the referee stopped the fight.

As I led with such an honest approach, what flowed from the rest of the group was nothing short of amazing. We had people who captained rugby union sides in Japan because they could speak Japanese, we had very young people who had done their PhDs on Russian outlaw motorcycle gangs, we had someone who judged the grade of wheat at the Royal Easter Show every year, and we had musicians and singers – we had such a depth of talent that unless this question was asked we would have never known, as most police and people are generally reluctant to talk up their skills.

Another way to connect with our staff was when I learnt that something good or challenging had happened to them. If I didn't have the officer's mobile phone number, I would ask their supervisor to give it to me and let the officer know that I was going to call them. There is a funny story behind letting officers know that the boss will be calling them. There have been several well-known stories where officers received a phone call from the Commissioner of Police, and as the officer thought it was one of their mates playing a prank on them, they not-so-politely told the Commissioner of Police to go away in colourful language.

I recall the first day I relieved at Sydney City Police Area Command for a three-month period when two of the officers on the night shift had gotten into a really confronting physical altercation with a large offender, who caused them a lot of grief and concern until backup arrived.

Both officers were shaken over the experience, and they had done well to endure the altercation with only minor injuries. I rang their supervisor, got their phone numbers and then rang the two officers. This small gesture showed these officers, and their peers, that their relieving commander did care.

Connections can occur at all levels, but the strongest connections occur when we play and have fun together.

I had learnt from my mentor and other peers that when we train and exercise together regularly, lifelong bonds are formed, with our physical and mental health wellbeing enhanced, making us all more resilient due to the relationships formed and increased fitness levels.

For several years, a group of us trained at our local Police Citizens Youth Club in North Sydney before work, every morning. Some of these sessions were legendary, and the mix of staff who attended made it a lot of fun.

When we formed our new command, we were in a five-level building if you included the basement and the roof. Every Tuesday and Thursday morning, a group of us – again, a mix of all types at our workplace – did boxing fitness on the roof of our building, even on the coldest and hottest of days. Part of these sessions included the opportunity to hit the boss as hard as you could, in one of the boxing fitness drills. This was a popular segment of the training. Some of the fun of training together is making fun of how poorly the old guy (your boss) might be going against the fitter young ones. The group that trained on the roof on those mornings became known as "No Rank on the Roof".

Some of my best days in the NSW Police were "No Rank on the Roof", having fun with staff and looking after my own physical and mental wellbeing.

Most leadership roles require good connections outside of the workplace. As a police commander, those connections required good productive relationships with other government agencies such as ambulance, fire and rescue, transport as well as the myriad of non-governmental organisations that operate within communities, where leaders either work collaboratively together or divisively against each other because they haven't taken the time to know how intrinsic their commonalities are.

I have made a career of identifying who I must connect with in order to get the best outcome.

This started at a detective level when I needed a good healthy relationship with the Director of Public Prosecutions Prosecutor who would be presenting our hard-earned investigation to the courts. I learnt that it was imperative we were on the same page working together to achieve a conviction in the challenging arena of our justice system. If we were against each other in a court matter, we were only doing the defence's job for them.

Most of the time, I formed a good relationship with our partners, but sometimes that relationship was challenging. If it was challenging, the reason we weren't getting on was likely that we hadn't taken the time to get to know each other. When this occurred, I had to take ownership of my own culpability as I hadn't invested the time to get to know my partner.

I found the best way to get over this issue was to invite the person for a coffee or lunch at my expense. I never had anyone stand me up when I made the invitation as a police commander offering to pay for lunch. This type of invite doesn't happen every day.

What flowed from those meetings, in an informal setting, was that we got to know each other. We got to know how we could help each other and identify the issues that were making it challenging to work together. Normally, the solution was reaching an understanding of how we could help each other. It was that simple.

The next chapter of this book will detail how my counterparts in ambulance and fire and rescue formed connections with each other that enhanced the capabilities of our staff, and our partners, whilst providing a better capability for us to collectively serve our community when a challenging job occurred.

We realised that we had similar challenges and similar skills to help each other. We made the commitment to meet up for coffee amongst our busy work schedules, we became friends and mates. We called ourselves the "Three Amigos" and we looked amusing in our respective uniforms when we had a group photo.

From these organised get-togethers, we hatched an idea to conduct all-agencies exercises to build the skills of our staff and our government partners, so we had a level of readiness for the next big job like the Lindt Café Siege. These exercises had up to 200 people in an auditorium, but they involved everyone in the process. There was nowhere to hide and the process built trust, relationships, and an understanding of what we could do for each other in a challenging situation.

The last bit of advice I have about making connections with the people we lead came about by accident.

At our new command, I asked if I could have a locker in the men's locker room, relatively close to the showers so I could train in the mornings, and not waste time running between the showers on level 1 and my office on level 2 to get changed. What started as a purely practical and logistical exercise morphed into one of the best ways I have ever found to connect with staff.

The Men's Locker Room at our new command had lockers for over 100 staff. If you were in the locker room during the change of a shift, there would be many officers starting or finishing their shifts. You would hear the jokes, the highs, and the lows of what had happened in the last few shifts. When people are getting ready to start or finish work, they talk into their open lockers to one of their peers on the other side of the locker room. The content can be colourful and loud. A lot of the time they had no idea I was in the locker room.

A lot of the time I would be in the locker room on my own. At these times you could hear a pin drop. I would hear an officer come into the locker room, not knowing that someone else was in there. I would hear them go to their locker, open it, and then I would hear a massive sigh.

The sigh was not a happy, exhausted sigh. It was a distressed sigh. I heard this several times. Each time, I would make my way around to where the officer was and ask a simple question. "Everything ok?" It was either a personal or work issue that the officer was struggling with. Once, it was an officer who had just separated from their partner. They had children together and our officer was truly struggling with how to navigate this challenging situation. We talked, I provided support, made sure they had an external support network so they were not on their own, and gave them my number to ring me 24/7 if they needed to do so.

Other times I would be getting changed as a very junior officer would come in at the end of their shift, elated at their first arrest or some other significant incident on shift. I had already been briefed on whatever incident it was, but to hear the same story told through the eyes of a junior police officer was invigorating to see the world through eyes so young.

The absolute beauty about conversations held in the locker room is there is no filter. It was the same principle as "No Rank on the Roof".

One of the most amusing things about the men's locker room at the start of a shift is that there is only one ironing board. So, sometimes you might have five or more officers lining up with the boss to iron their shirts to start their shift. It was so normal to be with everyone talking about anything, waiting to iron your shirt.

I have worked at other places where the boss has their own shower. Whilst this may seem at first a very useful luxury, that luxury robs you of the chance to connect with your staff at the most natural of levels.

Reflections

I truly believe this is the most important chapter in the book.

Without connections as a leader and as a human being, life is solitary, and we travel through it on our own. Whilst we might enjoy and even prefer being on our own, we never experience the joy of working together with a committed group of people to achieve something amazing.

With connections, we share the highs and the lows of being human, and through those connections, we influence people's lives for the better because they know they are not on their own. If we genuinely make it our purpose to empower others and through support include them, we create an environment where people can do their absolute best.

22

Preparation Meets Opportunity

Since I had learnt to build a formidable leadership team that collectively empowered other leaders to lead, I had the time to think and act at a strategic level. This gave me time to build strategic relationships that would benefit our partners and our community by doing things at a different level. I was no longer stuck in the role of merely managing business, as I could influence creativity in how we operated now and in the future.

With my counterparts in ambulance and fire rescue, we planned several training exercises involving up to 200 participants from emergency services, transport, hospitals, schools, major shopping centres and councils to hone our responses and how we worked together in the next major incident.

Humans learn best when they play together.

We held training exercises in large auditoriums with a stage.

The concept was to build a training environment with several smaller incidents building up to a major incident. These large exercises were an opportunity to play together, simulating real jobs, but with the luxury that it was a training exercise. It didn't really matter if we got it wrong in training as long as we learnt from it. We were there to learn how we could help each other and build trust in each other's capabilities.

As each incident occurred, the agencies that needed to work together would go down onto the stage to the table that represented their incident and sort out in real-time what they had to do to resolve it. There was a microphone and an appointed leader at each table who would have to brief the whole auditorium on what they came up with as their priorities in the first 10 minutes and then at 30-minute intervals.

An example, the first incident was a murder in the emergency ward at a major Sydney hospital, that serviced all of northern Sydney. A patient was killed, and two ambulance officers received knife wounds from the offender on his way out of the ward. The offender was a wardsman at the hospital.

All the agencies in one room with the ability to talk to each other in real-time had never been contemplated before. Suddenly, the pressures of the hospital team, the ambulance team, the investigation team, and the incident management team that was overseeing the whole job had a vested interest in working together to get the best outcome.

At the hospital, if a murder happens in the emergency ward, they contemplate certain actions, actions that impact other hospitals, the entire ambulance service and every person who uses that hospital, as the main triage point of entry into a hospital is the emergency ward. Each action by one agency impacts another agency, so we had to work together.

My counterparts from ambulance and fire and I would have microphones and speak to the participants as they approached the stage. We would interview people at their tables about what they were thinking at that moment and the challenges they were facing.

We had all layers of response in the auditorium. The police car crew responded to the job as the first responder crew, the police supervisor attended to back them up and the police inspector conducted oversight and coordinated the high-level job.

I asked them what they were thinking, who did they need to help them, and how were they going to get that help. As their response evolved, a leader from the group around the table briefed the whole auditorium on what strategies they had come up with. What flowed from that initial briefing was other groups then provided advice about how they could assist the evolving situation.

When you put seven tables on a stage, with evolving incidents impacting each other and requiring inter-agency coordination, the environment becomes very noisy, very real and very tiring.

For our training exercise, because we were emergency services, we selected major incidents that would stretch our capabilities.

Any business has a worst-case scenario that would challenge them on any day that would require elements of the business, their stakeholders and their customers to work together to overcome those challenges.

To face that scenario in a training exercise allows everyone to build relationships and trust as well as identify holes in the way normal business is conducted.

As the offender left the hospital, he was involved in a fatal accident on a major arterial road that impacted the road network that serviced the Sydney CBD, and from there he met up with family members in a major shopping centre such as Westfield. There, he murdered two people, and then tried to ram his truck carrying gas bottles into the front entrance of Westfield very close to a major transport interchange that involved trains, buses and metro trains, and a large business district.

The incident was a domestic violence incident gone horribly wrong and the mayhem it caused made the exercise feel like the real thing. But the advantage is that the exercise in a training environment is designed to build resilience, learn each other's capabilities, and build relationships and trust.

I replicated this exercise several times over two years at varying levels of scale. One scenario had the offender going to a school instead of a shopping centre. I put 20 school principals into that exercise, asking them two major questions:

1. How would they respond if the police had information that they needed to lock down their school in 15 minutes?

2. How would they respond if they learnt their major traffic interchange was no longer accessible for over 2,000 students at the end of the day? What would they do?

I have facilitated several of these large training exercises and continue to do them today.

The skills needed are transferable to any incident that goes beyond the norm within a business or community. The end goals of these training exercises are better relationships, better preparedness and better resilience of all involved.

The exercises always involve representatives of all levels of the organisation, so that frontline staff, supervisors, managers and the CEO or equivalent are all in the same room responding to whatever the situation is and at the same time gaining an understanding of the motivations each level within an organisation must answer to.

There is normally a variant introduced that the CEO or equivalent is away at some important business meeting and cannot respond to the situation for several hours, so the next level of leadership must step up and lead.

When this happens, that tends to have a cascading effect, as each level must step up to the next level, beyond their normal day-to-day duties.

Each level then has a better understanding of what the pressures and demands of that next level are. Invariably, the relieving CEO or equivalent is required to address the media about the crisis. Everyone is challenged, everyone learns, and our team now has a greater depth of talent.

I have used the exercises to prepare response agencies for the following situations:

» a prison riot and siege

» a resident at a youth hostel under strict bail conditions escapes, then goes to a party and commits a murder

» a bus on fire outside of a major traffic hub and shopping centre which demands a multi-agency response within the Sydney CBD.

The prison exercise demonstrated that both frontline staff and administrative staff in the prison head office must work together and support each other. It soon became apparent what the strengths of the operational and head office staff were, and how they could work together. What the exercise achieved was to identify the depth of skills possessed by staff.

Once that knowledge was known, you could feel the level of trust, acceptance and respect enter the room. The participants had just experienced a collective challenge and formed a relationship because of that challenge, all in a training environment.

If we have trained together and have an awareness of what we may need to do to help ourselves or our partners, then we already have an image in our brains about what we may do and how to achieve it before a real incident occurs.

If we have not done any such training, our responses can sometimes be paralysed because we have no clue. We sometimes rely on policies that do not address the enormity of the incident, and we are not sufficiently prepared for the challenge in front of us.

There were several examples of successful training initiatives that were relatively simple which involved colleagues and partners working together in a training environment.

When the London Bombing occurred with the buses and underground trains being the target, the police leadership resources were away at a training workshop practicing how they would respond to the next major terrorist incident. Because the people who were required to respond to the real incident were already training together when they responded to the real thing, the analysis of their response was a very glowing one.

Likewise, when an armed offender started shooting automatic weapons at a large music festival crowd causing multiple fatalities in the centre of Las Vegas, law enforcement and emergency service were commended for their response. I have listened to a live-audio of this horrific incident, with continuous automatic gunfire from the gunman, the cries of anguish of the surviving victims, and the professionalism of law enforcement in bringing the incident to a resolution.

The local FBI leader in the Las Vegas job had been in the area for less than 12 months but had insisted that all law enforcement and emergency services conduct training sessions and exercises together. So they knew how to work together, even when the worst of the worst was occurring because they had trained for it.

A good personal and local example of where preparation meets opportunity is in early January 2019 in Westfield at Chatswood.

On this day, five Middle-Eastern youths were seen carrying into the large shopping centre five pistols that looked like Glock automatics and made no attempt to conceal them from other shoppers. Reports of this occurrence soon reached our police.

The police on duty comprised of several sergeants and a duty inspector with several car crews consisting of constables. One of the sergeants and the duty officer had recently gone to one of our large training exercises which Westfield security representatives also attended.

Since the police and Westfield's security had trained together, they knew how they could help each other. Our sergeant deployed a car crew to work with security and directed our police crews into the location where the five youths were, still in possession of their firearms.

What ensued was a professional, armed offender arrest, well-led by our sergeants and duty inspector. This meant that the five offenders were lying on their stomachs, all handcuffed behind their backs with the five guns laid out a safe distance away from them, and no longer a threat to the public or police. This occurred without injury to any offender, civilian or police.

All five weapons were secured and later found to be replicas. The five youths had intended to play a joke on other shoppers. They were fortunate the policing response was considerate and professional, with no one being hurt in a highly charged environment where police may have chosen a more lethal option.

Our police were later complimented by a new educational unit in the NSW Police called the Best Practice Unit. What had occurred was a great example of identifying risk, training for it with all persons involved, and having the real thing, or close to the real thing occurring on your watch. What I loved about this occurrence was that I was on holidays. I didn't have to be there in the workplace for good things to occur. Our people did what they had trained to do and excelled.

From the experiences of the Lindt Café Siege and Mosman Collar Bomb, I wanted to prepare our police in a more specific manner.

With the help of the leadership team, I planned a two-day Resilience Workshop for all our supervisors and inspectors at the Navy Base on the Harbour. The purpose of the two days was two-fold.

Firstly, I wanted to acknowledge the outstanding roles our supervisors and inspectors had played in leading our command to being a great place to work, that looked after the wellbeing of others, and achieved good productive professional outcomes.

Our command had recently been highlighted in a state-wide leadership survey of every command, as having one of the highest staff satisfaction levels of any command. Other commands had not fared so well, seeing commanders removed from these commands and given a chance to reflect on their leadership styles. The outcomes our command had achieved were directly down to how these supervisors and inspectors had led and influenced our people to achieve the outcomes we had.

Secondly, I wanted to provide our leaders with the best platform I could achieve in preparing them for the next big job like the Lindt Café Siege.

It was foreseeable there was going to be another major event in which our people were required to lead. How they led in that next major event could be maximised. I did everything I could to prepare them mentally and operationally to respond to their next major challenge.

The workshop was a chance for all of us to get together, outside of the normal work environment, and learn from other experts how we could improve what we were doing.

This two-day Resilience Workshop had guest speakers who had led major events in Australia, including the two commanders who were responsible for the Lindt Café Siege when armed police ended the siege. A lot of our sergeants never had the chance to hear speakers of this calibre tell their stories. Their story is about what it was like to lead policing and emergency resources in the worst of times when casualties were likely.

My friend and colleague who was the police forward commander when the siege came to an end gave their presentation with all the emotions and angst that will probably be with them forever. In a room of over 50 police supervisors and inspectors, you could have heard a pin drop given the awe and respect they gave this presenter.

Each was left wondering what and how they would have responded had they been in the shoes of this forward police commander when the order was given to end the Lindt Café Siege. This order came after the offender had killed a hostage and was believed to be wearing an active bomb.

Each wondered how they dealt with the aftermath: two hostages dead, one from the offender, and one likely from a police officer's gun; another two hostages suffered bullet wound injuries; and a police officer had been shot in the face by a ricochet.

Each police supervisor and inspector had a newfound awareness of the accountability required to lead police and other emergency services into an incident of that level.

This same police forward commander shared that when the Lindt Café Siege happened, he and his spouse were on holidays. He volunteered to come back for the night shift during a critical period of the siege. At the time, he would have been one of the most experienced, highly trained and prepared police forward commanders in Australia. He was a Nationally Accredited Counter-Terrorism Commander who trained and accredited other budding officers all over Australia in this challenging area of law enforcement.

This police forward commander was publicly ridiculed by every armchair expert and media commentator who wanted to have an opinion about what occurred at Lindt Café. He was removed from any duties related to counter-terrorism and transferred from a job he loved to a job he did not want.

It was believed by some this was to influence his resignation from the NSW Police. Only one senior officer supported this police forward commander after the siege was over.

After the Lindt Café, I was given the opportunity to become a counter-terrorism-trained police forward commander. I went to several National Counter-Terrorism Training Exercises as an observer, and attended National Accredited Police Forward Commander training courses with other police from all over Australia.

Our same forward police commander who had led our response to end the Lindt Café Siege, and was now removed from all counter-terrorism-related duties in NSW, was the primary lecturer of choice by all other national policing agencies. He was revered by all other policing jurisdictions in Australia as a subject matter expert and someone with experience.

This officer shared the pain and learnings of what that job does to the person who leads the response to such a major terrorist incident.

When you train to become a police forward commander in the counter-terrorism environment, you learn an incredible amount of intelligence on current threats and methodology. I am not inclined to share what that is, and nor should I. One realisation when you train to respond to an event such as the Lindt Café Siege is that the casualty outcome, no matter what you do, may be high. There will likely be civilian casualties and causalities of emergency services personnel.

What this means for police officers who volunteer to take on this mantel to lead an emergency response to end a terrorist siege is the ultimate accountability and responsibility.

It is almost certain that the actions of the police commander will be publicly scrutinised at a public inquest. It is almost certain that the scrutiny from the legal profession will not only come from the families of civilians who were killed, but also from the families of any police officers killed. These are high stakes and not everyone is prepared to take on this level of responsibility.

I was selected as the NSW Police representative to be a participant in the Queensland Police Leadership Command Course to upskill all their superintendents and assistant commissioners because of the findings of the Lindt Café Siege.

Due to my experiences with the Mosman Collar Bomb and the Lindt Café Siege, I was not only a participant in the Queensland Police Command Course but also a presenter. I was present when their former Queensland Police Commissioner briefed the cohort of Queensland police commanders. I will never forget the reality of what he said that day. He told all the budding Queensland police commanders who wanted to lead a response to a terrorist incident a very direct message.

He said, "You are going to have to make decisions where people may die. You are going to be accountable for those decisions. If you think you are unable to make those decisions, I want you to leave this training program now, you do not belong here."

No one left the training program at that time, but there were sober looks shared across the table that day. The reality of what we were training to do was made very clear.

The leaders who command defence service personnel know that there is a likelihood they will send some of their people to their deaths if war occurs. Police leaders, up until the last few years, have never had to face that reality, but the world has changed.

Police are now expected to enter and resolve active armed offender confrontations. They are trained to do so, but the reality is police can die. The police leaders who order their staff to enter the stronghold and resolve the conflict will be held accountable for the outcome, good or bad.

These police leaders are normal people with families and responsibilities. Most of us become police officers to make a difference in people's lives. That does not include sending our staff into highly hazardous situations, where they may die.

Another guest speaker at that two-day Resilience Workshop was another police commander who was responsible for coordinating all the Tactical Police Resources used at the Lindt Café Siege, including the Tactical Operations Unit police, the negotiators and the bomb squad. This same officer was also the link with all counter-terrorism police and investigators, so they played a crucial role in what went down during the whole incident.

This officer just left the crowd in awe. They shared their operational plans and considerations, and how each phase progressed during the Lindt Café Siege. Again, each police supervisor and inspector had a newfound awareness of the accountability required, to lead police and other emergency services into an incident of that level.

This same guest speaker was also able to speak to our audience about another recent media story about a team of homegrown terrorists who attempted to carry a bomb onto an international flight at Sydney Airport, designed to explode after take-off. Thankfully, the bomb was not carried onto the flight.

A subsequent time-pressured investigation occurred to arrest all offenders involved in that plot. The pressures involved in this investigation were beyond any seen in a television series. It was the real thing and the leader who was involved in doing this job was there talking about what it is like to lead a job like that. It was a sobering story to hear, and one that anyone in our two-day workshop could be enlisted into assisting the arrest phase of the terrorists involved within the suburbs of Sydney.

Another guest speaker was the Melbourne police commander responsible for the two Bourke Street incidents that occurred in the heart of Melbourne.

In the first incident, an offender used a car to kill several innocent people running over mothers, fathers and children. In the second incident, an offender used a knife to kill, and a car with gas bottles in it to attempt to kill other innocent people and cause mayhem. He also threatened two very junior police at knifepoint, who reluctantly shot this offender, after giving him every chance to stop his threatening behaviour.

This commander's presentation highlighted how we are all ordinary people, and on any given day, we can be selected at random by fate to be the extraordinary commander of two of the biggest incidents in the history of the Victorian Police Force.

I also presented my experiences as the police commander of the Mosman Collar Bomb and the forward police commander of the Lindt Café Siege.

What became clear across all presentations of these high-risk jobs was that each job was led by leaders who had given themselves as many opportunities as possible to lead when the circumstances were beyond normal. Each leader had a team of people who were skilled at working together, without ego, and who had a proven track record of resolving challenging situations.

What also became clear was each story highlighted exceptional skills in working with other organisations. The leaders who led the final stages of the Lindt Café were working with many other agencies, including international agencies, and our own Armed Services.

The Melbourne commander was thrown into two of the worst and most public killings we had ever seen. Whilst he was on the ground where the killings had occurred, he had the capability and the relationship skills to coordinate a myriad of governmental agencies including, health, transport and other support agencies to bring the city back to normal, whilst addressing all the evidentiary checklists such a level of killing require.

Reflections

Leadership will always exist. Good and bad.

There will always be situations where leaders need to step up and create the environment to help people to do their best to resolve whatever challenge they are faced with. Some leaders will relish this challenge, some will not meet the standard, some will be found wanting, and some will go missing in action and not lead at all.

There will always be new leaders, experienced leaders, lazy leaders, and selfish leaders.

There will also be leaders who empower others to do their absolute best because they have done and continue to do everything thing in their power to make themselves and their people operate in supportive and inclusive workplaces.

There will always be the question asked, "Have you done enough for yourself and your people as a Leader to face the next challenge?"

Only you can answer that question.

23

The Courage to
Create New Beginnings

In 2020, I sat back and looked at what our new command was achieving. We had created a culture where people felt safe, secure and included. We were doing everything we could to provide them with the skills they would need to lead when the next major incident occurred.

I knew deep down that this was the best team and the best group of people I had ever worked with, and that I could do no better in leading them. I realised I had been in this moment several times in my career.

Early on in my career, I loved being in the rescue squad, but when the opportunity came to do investigative work as a detective, it was time to say farewell to the rescue squad. After completing the investigation regarding the executions in Allum Street, I came to the same realisation that I could do no better as an investigator and that it was time to pursue something new.

When I was unsuccessful in holding my inspector's job at appeal, I had the opportunity to stay at the audit group as a sergeant. But I chose to do something new and decided to become a team leader, a sergeant leading general duties crews as they responded to first-response tasks.

After a relatively short time as an inspector, I had the opportunity to apply for and receive a nomination for a police commander's job as a superintendent.

Each time I did something new, it was a challenging space to be in. I had to learn new skills and enhance old ones. I was sometimes more adept at making the change than others. The key skill I knew to my success or failure was to adapt. Leaders who learn and adapt get better at leading and are better resources for those they lead. Leaders who refuse to adapt become useless.

I sought to write my own story by seeking support and creating strong relationships.

Through those relationships, I learnt to build formidable leadership teams that focused on creating a supportive culture that nurtured the wellbeing of others.

It was in this environment as I approached the anniversary of my 40th year in policing that I made the decision to retire.

I had never worked in such a positive supportive command with such a good group of people. It was a positive thing to do, to retire on a high at the top of my game, rather than retire past my use-by date.

I had seen several senior police work harder in their later years, only to see their marriages end, or worse, see their partners die unexpectedly. This was such a sad occurrence. After a spouse had supported them through their long careers, they died. They had arrived on the day that they had been looking forward to but they were on their own. Others had become so unhealthy that they could not enjoy a fruitful retirement with their loved ones and friends.

I did not want that story for me. I wanted a different story.

At the age of 58, I retired from the NSW Police to spend time with my wife, two children and, at the time, one grandchild with another three on the way. My mother was still quite spritely but did need regular medical and wellbeing support.

I sought out a leader who I respected outside of the NSW Police Force and met with them over a coffee. I asked their advice on what the best way to retire was. They told me a story about one of their old bosses who let everyone know about 12 months in advance that they were going to retire. This sent a strong signal that the boss was leaving and that for the next 12 months, anything goes. My colleague provided sound advice that it was best to have a short retirement notice. That way, you were still effective as a leader, and the experience was a better outcome for all involved.

I then let my immediate superior know that I was leaving on 24 March 2020, in about six weeks. This was 40 years exactly to the date I joined the police on 24 March 1980. I was still fit and healthy, both physically and mentally. I was the exact weight that I joined 40 years earlier. I was fitter at 58 than I had been at 18.

Retiring was and still is amazing. I am no longer ruled by the 24/7 cycle of being on-call. I spend an amazing amount of time with my wife and really enjoy it, and the kicker is she enjoys having me around as well. I constantly thank my lucky stars that I have my wife alive and well despite nearly losing her five years ago with multiple blood clots in her lungs.

It is a gift that I get to spend days looking after our grandchildren and that they know me because of how often I see them. I am not some stranger who is too busy going to work.

Some people view being a babysitter of your grandchildren as being slave labour. I can safely say that being available to see your grandchildren take their first step, say their first word, give you that look and then burst out laughing ... there is no better gift in life than to have a place in your grandchildren's life. What no one tells you is how tiring it is, no matter how fit you are. After a couple of days of looking after our grandchildren, we both need grandpa and grandma naps to catch up.

I had a few goals going into retirement. I wanted to never stop learning and looked for new challenges.

I became a beekeeper and everything that comes with that, like the inevitable bee stings as they always get you when you get too confident with them. What started as one hive is now three. Every spring, a hive will choose to swarm. This is natural as it is how they grow their numbers when a new queen goes looking for somewhere else to live. I caught two of those swarms and started a new hive because the swarm was close to the ground where I could catch it. The last swarm was about 30 metres up a tree, so I could see it but no way I could get it. The satisfaction you get when you research what to do with a swarm and then catch one is amazing.

The other satisfying thing about beekeeping with a flow hive system is you harvest your own honey with a system that has a tap. Every flow frame can have a different flavour, depending on where the bees get their nectar and pollen. There is no other taste like it. Bought honey is just a poor second.

I also started dallying with playing the guitar, baked sourdough bread and took up Yoga. I wish I had known about Yoga during my working life. The flexibility and inner peace that come with Yoga are astounding.

I even did private investigations for a well-known firm but that environment was not healthy for me. I had made a career challenging and looking to do things differently despite the police protocols. Although not bounded by those same protocols, the private investigative world, ironically, clings to a set formula and does not look for anything outside of that, so after a time, they let me go without sending any more work my way.

One of my main goals in retirement was to start writing this memoir, my first book. Like anything new, it takes awhile to identify methods to go about it. My first draft of the book met with a lot of feedback that it was not hitting the mark. The responses to the first edit were a resounding, "You need someone to help you." And I did get that help.

The beauty of writing a book is that it takes awhile to complete, in my case three years. This timeframe allows me to talk about what it is like to be retired and focus on the things I want to focus on away from the responsibilities of work.

Whilst I was a police officer, I developed a love for developing other leaders, something I continued once I became a commander.

My passion was and still is developing other leaders, to empower others to create supportive and inclusive workplaces, environments or communities where people can do their absolute best. I spent each of the last 15 years of my career conducting 6-month leadership development workshops, influencing at least 240 people to look at leadership differently.

In my retirement I created a consultancy business called RRR Consulting, the three *R*s representing Relationships, Resilience and Reputation. If a leader lacked abilities in any one of these three areas, it would be difficult, if not impossible, to achieve anything since the leadership road was full of distractions.

In the world of private enterprise, there was already a wealth of individuals and companies that offer this type of service that were already doing good things, so I had to find my niche. I tried different things, learning new skills along the way. I created my own website and regularly updated the content as I learnt new skills. Some of the strategies I came up with did not really hit the mark, but I was continually learning.

I found whilst I was writing this memoir that I could be doing something else to shine a light on other leaders who have the skills I wanted to highlight. Part of writing a book for publishing also involves raising the profile of the book and the author so people will be interested in purchasing it and reading it when it is available.

The idea came to me that I could start my own similarly named podcast, "The Courage to Lead Interview Series", and interview leaders who possessed the skills which my memoir highlighted.

I had to learn how to record a podcast, upload it on a podcast link called the RSS feed and then make that link work on my website. At the same time, I also learnt how to place the podcast on Apple,

Spotify and Google Podcasts. I can tell you this was not without its challenges, as any new endeavour always delivers challenges whether you want them or not. I can assure you there were lots of error messages on my computer during that time.

When I first started the podcast in August 2022, I used the free version of Zoom which stops after 40 minutes. But I didn't know that until it happened during my first interview for the podcast series. So my first interviewee, Erin Longbottom, had to wait whilst I sent her another connection to continue the interview about 10 minutes later.

I soon learnt the capabilities of Microsoft Teams and have used that medium ever since I upgraded it to a business level. In those early days before the upgrade, I used to record the interviews on my iPad, sitting it next to the laptop speakers. The quality of the recordings in the early days was not good and detracted from some great conversations, especially the interview with Mick Willing.

The problem with Microsoft Teams at a personal level is it does not offer the record meeting function, that only applies to the business version. I only learnt that after several days of scrolling the internet to find out why I could not find a record button. Once I upgraded my systems to that capability, the recordings improved.

Then my daughter, who is very tech-savvy, would give me feedback about the quality of my podcasts. She told me as only a daughter could to a parent, "You need to improve what you are doing, Dad. You can't keep putting those interviews out."

She suggested I should include an introduction to each interview about what the series is all about. Then the next suggestion was I needed to provide a summary and introduction of each guest before the actual interview started so that I did not keep them waiting at the start of the podcast twiddling their thumbs whilst I talked about their bio.

The next suggestion was both introductions should have a musical overlay. Then at the end of the interview, I needed to provide a summary of what the guest had just covered, with another musical overlay.

Well, to say I had no clue how to do this would be an understatement but that is the beauty of YouTube and our connected world in the 21st century. You can find out how to do anything on YouTube. So, I did. I learnt what programs to do the music overlays, introductions and editing required to make this work. For me, this was GarageBand on Apple, but I am sure there are other programs that are similar.

I also learnt that if I use music, I would likely have to pay royalties. I learnt a way around this, as there are communities on the internet that produce music that is free to use as long as I credited the artist.

I found a great track called "Legacy" by Savik. I love the track and its name. Most leaders seek to leave a legacy in their workplace, that legacy being to leave the workplace in a better condition than when they first started. I know this is the mantra that all All Blacks rugby union players have when they have the honour of donning the All Blacks Jersey. Leave the jersey in a better condition at a reputation level than when you first put it on.

I have been tempted to go back and provide this level of strategies to the earlier interviews, but I think it is healthy to show how the quality and content of the podcast process have grown. That is essentially what leadership is, trying a strategy, learning what worked and what didn't and continually improving. The podcasts definitely show that trend.

I also had to acquire a mixing deck so I could connect a microphone and headphones to enhance the quality of the podcasts. This is still a work in progress, but it is improving and learning is a very satisfying activity.

One thing I had to learn quickly when I had my eighth guest on the show was that my old website could only accommodate seven podcast episodes. I couldn't accept that limitation, so I quickly researched what I had to do. So I made a new website using WordPress and linked my original website to the new website that could accommodate all my podcasts.

That process took me two weeks to learn. There were some frantic moments during those two weeks as I started from scratch. I knew nothing about building a website, but I did get there. Countless companies out there will build the website for you, for a cost, but I was really keen to learn the skills myself. The website is pretty basic, but it does the job. Like anything else, the more knowledge you learn, the more tweaks you make, incrementally improving with each tweak.

What I did learn that I was totally unaware of, was listeners would often prefer to go directly to the website and listen to the podcast from there, rather than going through something like Spotify or Apple podcasts. Everyone is different but the analytics support that notion.

To date, I have interviewed over 17 guests, publishing an episode every fortnight.

I am not well-known, so the show only goes to my own network and normally to the guest via social media. This has recently started to change after the interview of NSW State Emergency Services (SES) Commissioner, Carlene York. She is a well-regarded, supportive and inclusive leader who leads an organisation that includes 10,500 volunteers all over the state. Each of those volunteers has their own circle of friends. The SES volunteers, quite deservedly, are very proud of their leader as she truly does provide a community where people can do their absolute best.

Since the interview with Carlene York was posted, listeners have started binging all the other episodes of "The Courage to Lead Interview Series" on the website and the RSS feed website on SoundCloud. At the time of writing this book, the podcast series has reached over 7,400 listens from all over the world but predominantly in Australia. There are over 200 listens in New York every week. Who would have thought the show would have that reach?

What I have found is that I absolutely love interviewing these amazing leaders and sharing the wisdom and humility they possess with a wider audience. It replicates the satisfaction I used to get from conducting leadership workshops in the NSW Police. I have found a medium, where if people want to, they can listen to some amazing leaders who emulate the skills of empowerment.

To date, these guests include:

» Erin Longbottom, Unit Manager of the St Vincent's Hospital Homelessness Outreach Team

» Wayne Larden, CEO of Pont3, the company behind the Sydney Marathon which will soon be a world-recognised marathon at the same level as the New York Marathon and others

» Peter Scott, former Commodore of the Australian Submarine Fleet and author of *Running Deep*

» Michael Willing, former Deputy Commissioner of the NSW Police

» Steven Van Zwieten, General Manager of Exact Security and a presenter at the leadership workshop every year they were conducted

» Daniel Strickland, a former police officer and current Manager for Mission Australia, Councillor for Goulburn City Council and Funeral Director

» Uncle Len Sicard, who just turned 100 years old, still does 30 pushups a day and was a rear gunner in bombers for the Allies during World War II

» Trina Jones, CEO of Homelessness NSW

» David Knoff, Australian Antarctic Station Leader when COVID-19 hit the world, stranding him and his team there for 537 days, and author of *537 Days of Winter*

» Rebecca Pinkstone, CEO of Bridge Housing, a community housing provider that helps people avoid homelessness, winner of Best Workplace Award 5 years running

» Aiden Grimes, an expedition leader for the Kokoda Track in Papua New Guinea who has conducted over 125 expeditions with a 100% completion rate

» Alex Greenwich, MP, independent member for Sydney who was the driving force behind the Same-Sex Marriage Act being passed and the legalisation of abortion in NSW, amongst other things

» Mark Berridge, author of *A Fraction Stronger*, a story of incredible strength and resilience after a pushbike accident that left him with broken vertebrae

» Emma Doyle and Natalie Ashdown, world-renowned coaches of business, and in Emma's case of tennis at an international level and the authors of *What Makes a Great Coach?*

» Carlene York, Commissioner of NSW State Emergency Services (SES)

» Matt Elliott, an elite Super League and Rugby League coach, and owner of "The Change Room" program helping with the wellbeing of employees suffering from mental trauma and PTSD, and author of a book with the same name

» Paul Watkins, a self-confessed nerd who used to run pharmacies in rural Victoria and then changed his life completely, ending up competing two years in a row in an ultra-marathon of over 600 kilometres within seven days in the Arctic

» Nick Jonsson, General Manager and Co-founder of the Executive Support Group foundation in Singapore and Asia, offering confidential welfare support to CEOs who have no one else to talk to, and also the author of *Executive Loneliness*

» Jan Willett, Director of Events for NSW from 2004 to 2021, one of the humblest and most effective leaders you will ever meet.

Interviewing these amazing leaders every fortnight is invigorating. I explore how these leaders created the skills they possess to empower others to create supportive and inclusive places where people can do their absolute best. Each story is different, engaging, inspiring and a lot of fun. The medium of the podcast allows me to share these amazing stories with just about anyone who has an internet connection.

In my business of 3R Consulting, I offer help to address the perennial problems facing workplaces. A workplace cannot experience the joys of being a supportive and inclusive place where people can do their absolute best unless courageous leadership exists.

The skills and services I offer include coaching leaders at an individual level and helping leaders form a formidable leadership team. Once these two foundations are in place, help form the direction of the whole team by involving the whole team. I help organisations with each of these steps and mesh it all together.

There is a new era in workplace wellbeing evolving and in fact, is already here. Some organisations are only now becoming aware of it. This goes by a number of titles but the phrase "psychosocial safety legislation" best describes what the concept is and outlines how workplaces will change.

In its simplest explanation, a leader has to build a supportive and inclusive culture where people can do their absolute best.

Psychosocial refers to how people are treated within a workplace, and what the workplace has done to make that workplace a safe and supportive place to be. The current data indicates that over $900m in workers' compensation was paid for Australian workers with work-related mental health conditions in 2019 and 2020.

I believe that the current reach of the podcast is growing with the common messages of the exceptional leaders who are guests on the podcast will be shared more widely. These leaders are already demonstrating what traits leaders should have, but their messages may inspire examples of best practice to avoid psychosocial legislative penalties and create workplaces of choice.

Leaders who empower others to create supportive and inclusive workplaces where people can do their absolute best can be described as relentless leaders.

They have not always had success as leaders, but they have been relentless in creating a workplace where people can thrive because they are valued and treated well. These leaders spend their time creating other leaders in the same fashion so that the culture of the workplace changes for the better. We need more of these types of leaders. These leaders are courageous, resilient and compassionate and they replicate leaders and cultures who foster the ideals making their organisations employers of choice.

In organisations that have relentless leaders, they have a learning culture. People have the autonomy to make decisions and if they make an error, they are not crucified or punished but rather trained, coached, mentored or developed to make better decisions in the future.

Organisations that have ruthless leaders should be concerned.

A ruthless leader is someone who is best described by a mountain climbing analogy. A ruthless leader will push other climbers off without care or thought, just as long as no one impedes their climb up the corporate mountain.

When a ruthless leader reaches the top of their mountain, that leader will still push off other climbers (leaders) since, in their mind, there can only be one leader. Anyone else who has better skills can't be allowed to be seen or exist.

Ruthless leaders do not care for their staff, they just care about their position in leadership. Ruthless leaders only select people who comply with how they do business and will not entertain any person who threatens their position. We have all seen examples of what the outcome of this type of ruthless leadership looks like in the media, with such leaders promoting their mates for the best and most lucrative jobs.

The sad thing about organisations that allow ruthless leaders to flourish is that those around them replicate those patterns of behaviour. This breeds a culture where everyone is expendable and there is no trust or support because everyone is looking for the next promotion or is too busy trying to protect themselves.

Instead of the "learning culture" of the relentless leader, the ruthless leader creates a disciplinary culture where if a mistake or error is made, then there has to be a demonstration made that errors will not be tolerated. I have heard some horror stories about what some leaders say in these types of disciplinary cultures. "Better to kill one and scare 2,000" has been recounted by one organisation as an acceptable thing to say.

I was recently speaking to a very respected leader within my network, someone who is regarded as exceptional. They work within a disciplinary culture and said, "Everything is good while I am making good decisions but if I make a mistake, I am afraid no one will have my back."

A symptom of this toxic culture usually includes problems with recruitment and retention, and an ever-rising level of mental health conditions, especially in those absent or exiting from the workplace. These types of ruthless leaders can be quite elusive in how they present themselves. They may create wonderfully well-worded welfare and inclusion policies that say they care but their actions, the negative culture they allow to metastasise and the data say otherwise.

What is quite remarkable about this type of ruthless leader phenomenon is that the data or evidence is there for everyone to see.

The health insurance companies, the workers' compensation payouts and the myriad of mental health professionals that step up to address the fallout of such regimes, would be able to readily identify which organisations have the highest mental health injury claims, and through those claims, which leaders are commonly attributed as having played a part.

There would be an identifiable evidence-based trail, especially if the behaviour of some ruthless leaders has continued unaddressed for several years. If you meshed the data sets together using a program like Microsoft BI or a company like MuleSoft, a simple sort function would identify which organisations and which leaders are responsible for the most psychosocial harm.

The future I hope to see is that organisations that know they have ruthless leaders in them and do nothing about it will be subject to review and potentially a legislative penalty. As most leaders at this level are normally on a contract, answerable to shareholders or the community that voted them into government, their existence at a leadership level may be very short. We recently saw the shortest term of the UK Prime Minister in late 2022. Whether accountability and liability remain at an organisational level or personal level or both remains to be seen.

This is not just my view. In preparing to write this memoir, I have read countless non-fiction books, sometimes two per week. Through

Expert Author Academy, I have become friends with several authors who write about the outcomes of people who have worked for organisations that did not value their people.

I found two books particularly helpful: Fleur Heazlewood's award-winning *Resilience Recipes – Making Space for Wellbeing that Works* and Cassandra Goodman's *Being True – How to be Yourself at Work* are full of useful strategies on how we can improve the wellbeing of our people within a workplace.

If we were getting leadership right, there would not be any need for books such as these, but $900m in workers' compensation for mental health injury claims in 2019 and 2020 indicates we have a long way to go.

All of us want to work for an organisation that values them, supports them, and genuinely cares for their wellbeing. All of us want to work for an employer of choice.

Look up websites called *Voice Project* (now under the Xref banner) and *Sonder*, organisations that create an active care culture where their people are empowered to take control of their wellbeing. There are organisations that are making significant progress in creating workplaces that empower others to create supportive and inclusive cultures where people can do their absolute best. These are not fanciful ideas, they are actually happening now.

As for the next crop of leaders, they will need the courage to lead because things won't change without leaders saying something as simple as "You can't do that" and then doing something about whatever "that" is.

Those challenges for future leaders will:

» focus on wellbeing, safety, support and inclusion so that no one gets left behind because of their social status, sex, gender, religion, politics or race

» create workplaces where women are equally valued and paid, including receiving sufficient maternity leave and superannuation to provide for their retirement

» help men who advocate and demonstrate that is it not ok to be violent towards women in any way, either physically, emotionally or financially

» help men who are equal partners at home and in the raising of the family at both a cognitive and physical level

» put their own health and that of their staff as a priority, including what we eat, how we exercise, how we nourish our minds, and how we socialise and work together

» work with a group of committed people to end homelessness, so that no one is left behind

» empower leaders to create supportive and inclusive workplaces, environments and communities so that people can do their absolute best where creativity is nurtured and not punished.

I will do my part in the simplest way I know how.

* * *

I will shine a light on leaders who emulate these empowering qualities in "The Courage to Lead Interview Series" and in my business 3R Consulting where I focus on Relationships, Resilience and Reputation.

If you have any empowering and courageous leaders you would like to shine a light on, please email me at allan@allansicard.com.

If you wish to engage me in discussion, consultation or any support for your organisation or at a personal level, you can find me on my website https://allansicard.com. All my contact options are available on that website.

Acknowledgements

The Leadership Workshops mentioned in this book would not have been successful without the commitment and enthusiasm of the following presenters:

- » Commissioners Ken Moroney, Andrew Scipione, Mick Fuller and Carlene York
- » Deputy Commissioners Mick Willing, Dave Hudson, Dave Madden, Jeff Loy and Paul Pisanos
- » Assistant Commissioners Mark Jones, Anthony Crandell, Alan Clarke, Mark Murdoch, Mark Walton, Leanne McCusker, Gelina Talbot and Stacey Maloney
- » Superintendents Dave Donohue, Paul Carrett, Deb Wallace, Donna Adney, Mark Hutchens, Greg Rolph, Beth Stirton, Craig Sheridan and Karen McCarthy and Luke Fruedenstien
- » Inspectors Caroline O'Hare, Kirsty Hales, Jane Prior
- » Alex Greenwich, MP
- » Denis Shelley
- » John Trevallion
- » Steve Pearce
- » Steve Van Zwieten
- » Trina Jones
- » Rukhsana Zeb
- » Wayne Larden
- » Michael Homden
- » Jaryn Baigent
- » Isaiah Dawes
- » Shane Phillips.

This book would not have been possible without the support and guidance of the following people:

- » Kelly Irving and The Expert Author Academy
- » David Brewster
- » Debbie Lee
- » Peter Scott
- » Mark Berridge
- » Anna Glynn.

My life and the enriching chapters of my life would not be at all possible without my family:

- » Kerrie, my wife
- » Kirk and Maddie, our children
- » Brooke, Kirk's wonderful wife and their children, Liam, 13 years old, and twin boys Luca and Noah, 2 years old
- » Sylvia, Maddie's daughter and our granddaughter, 2 years old, and, of course, my parents Marie and Terry, where it all started.

Photo 1 Mum and Dad with me at my Passing Out Parade, Redfern Police Academy 24 March 1980

Photo 2 My mum watching my Marching Off Parade in Chatswood in 2020, 40 + years later. Not everyone gets to have their parents there at the start and finish of their career, especially with 40 years in between.

Photo 3 Police Rescue Squad training glued to the side of a cliff

Photo 4 That woman I fell in love with in 1984 walking across the pedestrian crossing in Goulburn, when I said to my mate, "Who's that?"

Photo 5 In 1984 I ended up in a lifelong relationship with this amazing person, my best friend. This is the start of us together, a local news photographer took a picture of us together buying lunch at a local café.

Photo 6. My final day as an Operational Command in 2020, my best friend is still with me, we did it together.

Photo 7 Madeleine Pulver, Karen Lowden and the rest of the brave officers who risked their lives to save Madeleine in August 2011, receiving their National Bravery Awards at Government House. A very proud moment.

Photo 8: This is a special photo for me. A few years after the Mosman Collar Bomb incident I was awarded a Commissioner Unit Citation for my role in that job. The most important things about Police Award Ceremonies are for our families to be present and share the recognition together, as in a Police Family they all live the challenges of these demanding jobs. This our son, Kirk, my wife Kerrie, and our daughter Madeleine, all on stage together taking a family moment.

Photo 9: The end of the Kokoda Track at the Port Moresby end, early on the 24 April 2014. My son Kirk still had the energy to pick me up sideways just to celebrate.

Photo 10: One of the river crossings at the Kokoda Track. Notice the safety handrails and safety ropes in place should you fall in. Terrifying.

Photo 11: Anzac Day Dawn Service at Bomana War Cemetery, Port Moresby. To be able to share this with my son Kirk, after doing the Kokoda Track together was a life changing experience that I will cherish forever.

Photo 12: September 2014. The final decision in my Police Legacy Boxing match against Peter "Silver" Mcerlain. Allan "Buttercup" Sicard was declared the winner on a split decision. I was as surprised as "Silvers" corner team, have a look at their faces in the background.

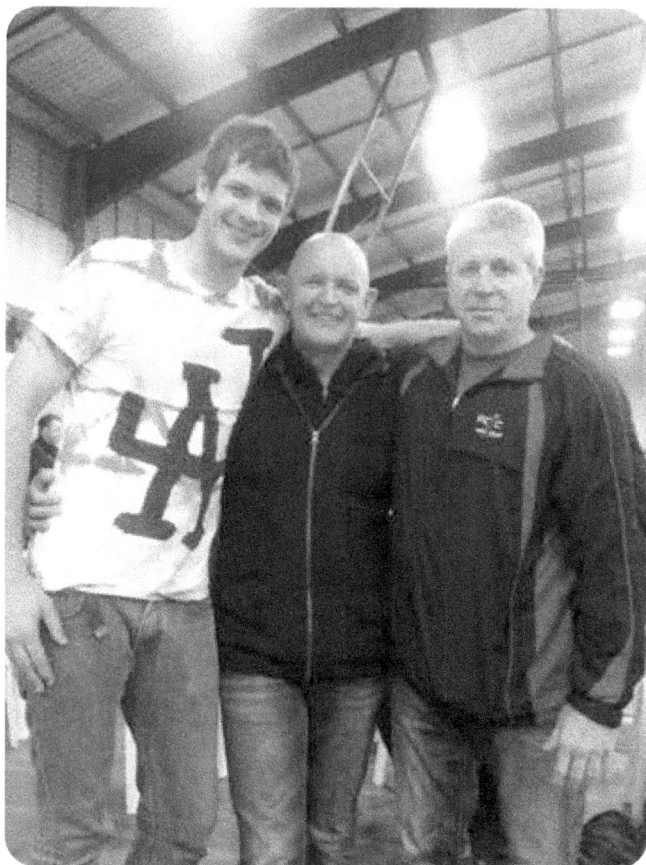

Photo 13: My Police Legacy Boxing Corner team for my fight against "Silver". My son Kirk and very experienced and kind boxing trainer, Mark Pitts.

Photo 14: After the Police Legacy Boxing Match against "Silver" we took the opportunity to have a photo with my trainer, Mark Pitts and my mentor and ring partner for several months, Assistant Commissioner Alan Clarke. The boxing ring behind us is very small as it is in one the old police cells under Surry Hills Police Station in Goulburn Street, Sydney.

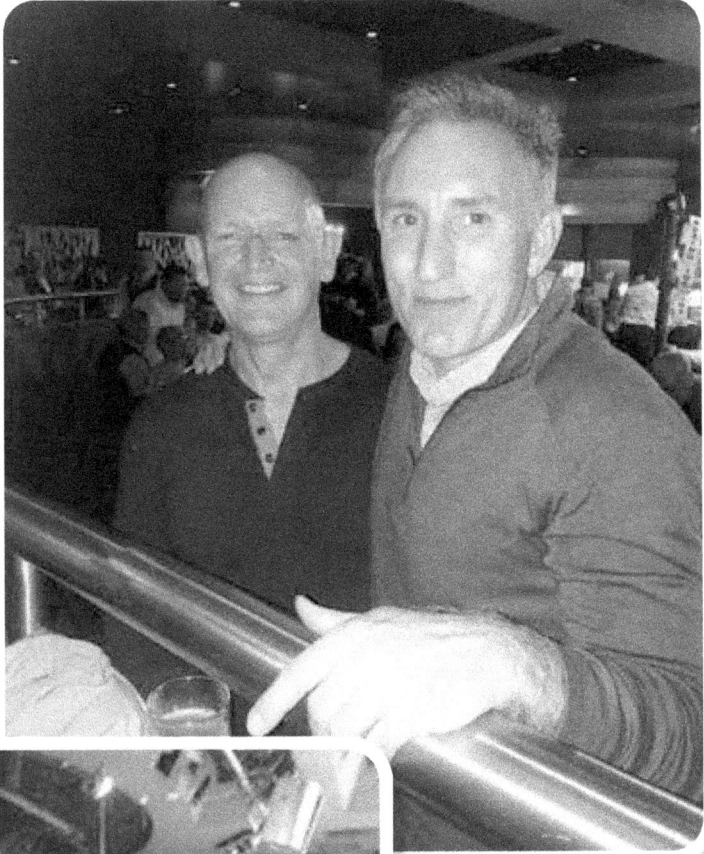

Photo 15: My next Police Legacy boxing match in 2015. I got flogged in 90 seconds by this beast, Marcus "the Destroyer" Drago. Yes, that's his real name. Look at the size of his hands, and I never saw any of his punches coming.

Photo 16: The only time ever I will be on the Fight Card in front of Champion Boxer, Danny Green. I had to get a photo after my fight with the champion.

Photo 17: The morning after getting flogged in 90 seconds by Marcus "The Destroyer" Drago I was back at work promoting Wear it Purple Day at Taldamundie Youth Refuge in Neutral Bay, Sydney. Wear it Purple was founded in 2010 in response to global stories of real teenagers, real heartache and their very real responses in 2010. Several rainbow young people took their own lives following bullying and harassment resulting from the lack of acceptance of their sexuality or gender identity.

Photos 18: The NSW Police Homelessness Week Boot Drive collection for those vulnerable people in our community. I arranged for the NSW Police to partner with Mission Australia to distribute second hand police boots after they had been donated by officers all over the state. This occurred for several years in a row from 2013 onwards.

Photo 19: A very happy recipient of donated Police Boots in Belmore Park opposite Central Railway Station.

Photo 20: One of the groups I crossed the Sydney Harbour Bridge 24 hour relay, we did for several years, raising awareness of Homelessness, during Homelessness Week.

Photo 21: Getting ready
to abseil off a 40 storey
building in Market Street,
Sydney to raise awareness
for Youth Homelessness.

Photo 22: Yes that's me
with 40 floors to go before
I am back on the ground,
raising awareness for
Youth Homelessness.

Photo 23: One of my most favourite photos ever. As Forward Police Commander of the Hyde Park precinct at the start of the Mardi Gras Parade in Sydney I was asked to be the Decency Inspector for all the participants. I did this with one of the crew from the Mardi Gras Organisers. In the middle of this inspection, I was questioned as to my credentials by these young police officers.

Photo 24: Building and enriching a Formidable Leadership Team. Best team I ever worked with. Back at HMAS Penguin in Mosman after 1 year together, celebrating our wins and building on the future.

Photo 25: The same formidable leadership team. We have just spent several hours walking the ground for all our precincts for New Year Eve the next day, North Sydney Forward Command from Greenwich Point to Taronga Zoo and everything in between. We finished for a late lunch and a bit of bonding before the long shift the next day.

Photo 26: Having fun at work. This is the Pink Test at the Sydney Cricket Ground for the Breast Cancer Charity Day for the Jane McGrath Foundation. All of us who worked that day donated our 12 hour wages to charity and worked for free.

Photo 27: Having fun at work.

Photo 28: Having fun at work. Some of the No Rank on The Roof gang. Note the time.

Photo 29: "The Three Amigos" Superintendents Allan Sicard (NSW Police), Damian Hughes (NSW Ambulance) the mascot, and Kel McNamara (Fire and Rescue NSW). Together we were mates, colleagues and we formulated some amazing joint exercises together to build our capabilities and trust.

Photo 30: Having fun at work. I only ever had one photo in my career receiving an award from the Commissioner of Police. So, my ever-supportive leadership team, photoshopped my picture, and made me Gollum from The Lord of the Rings, with a "My precious" caption. I treasured this photo, and it had centre place on my bookshelf behind my desk for the last 5 years of my career.

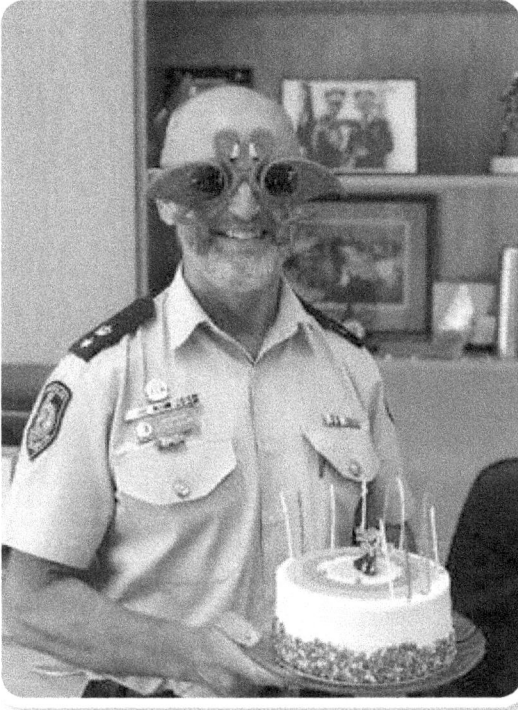

Photo 31: Having fun at work. Celebrating my birthday at work. The "Gollum" photo is pride and place behind me.

Photo 32: Having fun at work. I came in for my birthday and found some mischievous staff had wrapped everything in my office in birthday paper. My chair, my police hat, my computer keyboard and my computer screen. I must admit I couldn't take the smile off my face all day, and the photo brings back all the fun of that workplace.

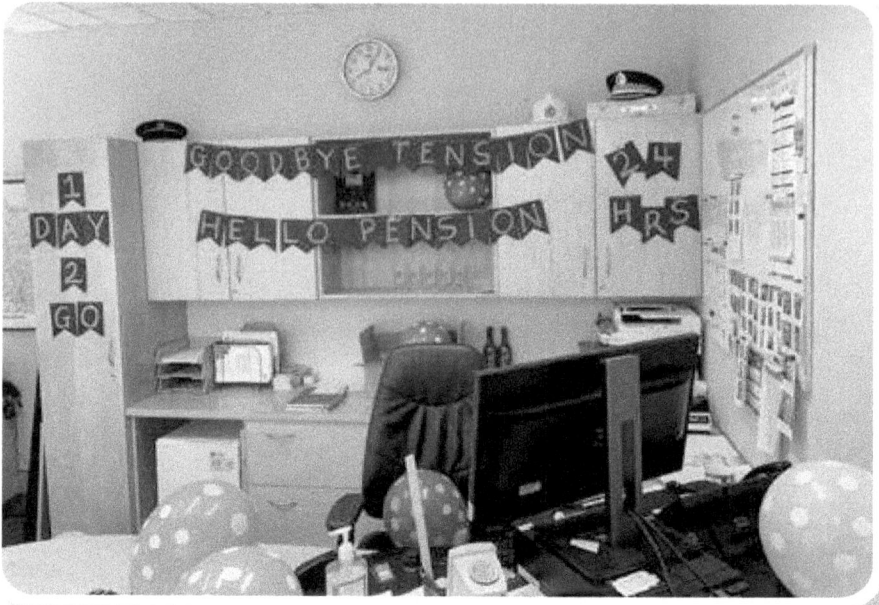

Photo 33: Having fun on the final day at work. That same group of mischievous staff had done it again.

Photo 34: Having fun on my final day at work. I switched between having Gollum jokes made about me or sometimes Yoda jokes – something to do with my bald head and big ears. I had figurines of Yoda and Gollum on my desk in my office. One of my gifts given to me on my final day was a full-size Yoda Mask that I was required to wear for part of the farewell. Yoda looks pretty good with a silver beard underneath.

Photo 35: The final Leadership Development Cohort. This is the final day of the 6-month program where Commissioner of Police Mick Fuller was a guest speaker. The Commissioner is like a rockstar, everyone wants a formal picture with them.

Photo 36: Fun is back again. Whilst I was walking Commissioner Fuller to his car, I left my phone on the desk with this responsible Leadership group. I found I had an unexpected photo on my phone later in the day. Initiative and taking opportunities are something you want to develop in future leaders.

Photo 37: The final day of a police officer is a special day and regardless of how they finish their career, if they can have a formal farewell, we should offer it to them. This wonderful man is Sergeant Mick Martin. 40+ year veteran, with injuries and illness challenges that kept him restricted duties for the later part of his career 2 or 3 days a week, but he loved coming to work and helping the public and his fellow police officers. We arranged his last day marching down the streets of Mosman, with his family and work colleagues saying farewell. A young officer said to me after this farewell, that it was wonderful to do something so formal for someone alive rather than a police funeral.

Photo 38: Our family treasures this photo as it almost did not happen. This is my wife, Kerrie Sicard's final Award and Medal presentation, with her mum and our daughter, Madeleine. Shortly after Kerrie was to be Medically Discharged, not willingly, with PTSD, (Post Traumatic Stress Disorder). Kerrie's Commander and their team had set up obstacles to make this day challenging to achieve. I went to my boss, Assistant Commissioner Mark Jones, and the then boss of Human Resources, Assistant Commissioner Leanne McCusker to see if they could grant my wife the dignity of having her medals presented to her whilst she was still a serving police officer. They did so in a heartbeat, and to top it off made me the Acting Assistant Commissioner to preside over my wife's award ceremony with the Northern Beaches Local Area Command. This is the only photo my wife has with her mum receiving a Police Award, and a couple of years later, Kerrie's mum died of cancer.

Photo 39: My final day, with a guard of honour to make sure I did leave.

Photo 40: This photo has pride and place in our home. Kerrie and I, our last official photo in uniform together all made possible by Assistant Commissioner Mark Jones and Assistant Commissioner Leanne McCusker. Thank you for your compassion for letting this happen. We did it together.

www.ingramcontent.com/pod-product-compliance
Lightning Source LLC
Chambersburg PA
CBHW052110030426
42335CB00025B/2920